teacher's edition

EXPLORING MUSIC 4

Eunice Boardman • Beth Landis

Consultants:

*Milton Babbitt • Bjornar Bergethon •
Robert W. Buggert • Chou Wen-chung •
Harry Coopersmith • Lucrecia R. Kasilag •
Egon Kraus • Alan Lomax •
Kurt Miller • Juan Orrego-Salas •
Virginia Stroh Red • Henrietta Yurchenco*

HOLT, RINEHART AND WINSTON, INC., New York

CONTENTS

ACKNOWLEDGMENTS

Grateful acknowledgment is given to the following authors and publishers:

Alfred A. Knopf for "Velvet Shoes" by Elinor Wylie. Copyright, 1921 by Alfred A. Knopf, Inc. Renewed, 1949 by William Rose Benet. Reprinted by permission of the publisher from *Collected Poems of Elinor Wylie*.
American Ethical Union for "Brethren in Peace Together" from *We Sing of Life*. Copyright by American Ethical Union. Used by permission.
American Ethical Union for "We Sing of Golden Mornings," adaptation of the text by Vincent Silliman from *We Sing of Life*. Copyright by American Ethical Union. Used by permission.
Mrs. Dorothy M. W. Bean for the words to "All Beautiful the March of Days." Used by permission of Mrs. Dorothy M. W. Bean.
Broadman Press for "Psalm 100" by Jane M. Marshall. © Copyright 1960, Broadman Press. All rights reserved. International copyright secured. Used by permission.
Cooperative Recreation Service, Inc., for "The Happy Plowman." Copyright 1953 by the Cooperative Recreation Service, Inc., Delaware, Ohio. Used by permission.
Crown Publishers, Inc. for the English words to "Mister Urian," translation by Ronald Duncan, and "The Butterfly" translation by Iris Rogers from *Classical Songs for Children* by the Countess of Harewood and Ronald Duncan, and copyrighted in 1965 by the authors. Used by permission of Clarkson N. Potter, Inc.
J. Curwen & Sons Limited for "O Give Me a Cot," English words by Florence Hoare from the *Oxford School Music Series*. Used by permission of J. Curwen & Sons Limited, 29 Maiden Lane, London, W. C. 2, England.
Danish American Young People's League for "Hiking, Laughing, Singing," "Snug 'neath the Fir Trees," "Cherries So Ripe." Used by permission.
Grace Guiney for "Out in the Fields" by Louise Imogen Guiney. Used by permission.
Gulf Music Company for "America for Me," "Windy Nights," and the words to "Pretty Little Pony." Copyright 1966 by Gulf Music Company. Used by permission.
H. W. Gray Company for "The Yodlers' Carol" by Mary E. Caldwell. Copyright by H. W. Gray. Used by permission.
H. T. FitzSimmons Company for "Gustaf's Skoal" from the collection *Folk Games of Denmark and Sweden* by Neva L. Boyd. Used by permission of the publishers, H. T. FitzSimmons Co., Inc., of Chicago.
Harcourt, Brace & World, Inc., for "in Just" by E. E. Cummings. Copyright 1923, 1951, by E. E. Cummings. Reprinted from his volume *Poems 1923-1954*, by permission of Harcourt, Brace & World, Inc.
Harcourt, Brace & World, Inc. for "Lines Written for Gene Kelly to Dance to" by Carl Sandberg. © 1960 by Carl Sandberg. Reprinted from his volume *Wind Song* by permission of Harcourt, Brace & World, Inc.
The Macmillan Company for "Sea Fever" from *Collected Poems* by John Masefield. Copyright 1912 The Macmillan Company, renewed 1940 by John Masefield. Used by permission.
Oxford University Press for "Banana Boat Loader's Song" from *Folk Songs of Jamaica*. Copyright 1952 by Oxford University Press. Used by permission.
Oxford University Press for "Forest Green" adapted and arranged by Ralph Vaughan Williams, 1872-1958. Music copyright. Reprinted from *The English Hymnal* by permission of Oxford University Press.
Norman Holmes Pearson for "Storm" by Hilda D. Aldington from *Collected Poems of Hilda D. Aldington*. Published by Liveright Publishing Corporation, copyright © 1925, 1953 by Norman Holmes Pearson.
G. Schirmer, Inc. for "Jesus the Christ Is Born" by John Jacob Niles. Copyright 1935 by G. Schirmer, Inc. Used by permission.
G. Schirmer, Inc. for "Marching to Pretoria" from *Songs from the Veld* by Josef Marais, copyright 1942 by G. Schirmer, Inc., New York, New York. Used by permission.
Summy-Birchard Company for "Stodola Pumpa" from *Birchard Music Series, Book Seven*, © 1959 by Summy-Birchard Company, Evanston, Illinois. Used by permission.
Summy-Birchard Company for "Weggis Dance" from *Birchard Music Series, Book Four*, © 1962 by Summy-Birchard Company, Evanston, Illinois. Used by permission.
Theodore Presser Company for the musical quotations from the *Hary Janos Suite* by Zoltan Kodaly. © 1927 by Universal Edition, © assigned 1952 to Universal Edition (London) Ltd., London, © renewed 1955. Used by permission of Theodore Presser, agents for Universal Edition.
Janet Tobitt for "De Bezem" from *The Ditty Bag*. Used by permission.
United States Committee for UNICEF for "Once" from *Book 2* of the *Hi Neighbor Series*, published by the United States Committee for UNICEF, United Nations. Used by permission.

EXPLORING MUSIC: A CHALLENGE TO THE TEACHER

TO HELP THE CHILD DISCOVER THAT

music is part of his heritage

The history of man can be found in his music. Woven into the musical fabric of the centuries is the tale of man's striving toward a richer life. As children in the classroom learn the simple, direct songs of the people and the music of the artist, they will become aware of the place of music in the past and present life of man.

music is a vital part of life

Many of the significant events of life have an accompanying musical expression. As the child explores music, he will realize that music has been an important part of rituals of primitive and sophisticated cultures. As he learns music from many countries and periods in history, he will discover that music reflects the culture from which it springs. The child will come to know and value the musical life of his own society. Through involvement in a variety of musical activities, he will find ways to participate in that life.

music is a means of personal expression

Music provides an avenue for personal expression in a way that language does not. Music is not bound, as words are, by specific meanings. Through music, each individual can communicate his own musical ideas or reflect the ideas of others. The child will discover his own potential for musical expression as he is given the opportunity to explore many different areas of musical performance and response.

TO HELP THE CHILD DEVELOP

a knowledge of the literature of music

As children discover their musical heritage, they should have an opportunity to explore many kinds of literature: folk songs and dances, music composed for solo voices or instruments, choruses, orchestras, or other instrumental ensembles. As children study music literature, they will become aware of the infinite variety of musical expression and of the many different media through which it may be communicated. The teacher will help children realize that the exploration of music can be a lifetime pursuit.

understanding of the structure of music

Although anyone may enjoy music on a limited level without knowledge of its structure, musical independence is contingent upon an understanding of musical organization. The teacher will move beyond the obvious and help children become aware of the principles which govern rhythm, melody, and harmony. He will guide them in the comprehension of musical form, style, and expression. Such understanding results in musical maturity, deeper musical enjoyment, and more complete participation.

skills of musical performance and response

Every child should have the opportunity to explore the activities through which music can be an expressive medium for him: singing, playing, listening, dancing, creating. Each skill contributes in a different way to the total musical development of the child. The child should also learn to perceive musical ideas visually through the written symbol. As the child develops skills of performance and response, he will find greater satisfaction in expressing his feelings and ideas through music.

REVIEW OF MUSIC THEORY: RHYTHM

Rhythmic notation. The following chart gives the names of the various notes and rests. It also indicates the relative duration of each. All basic note values are based on a 2–1 relationship.

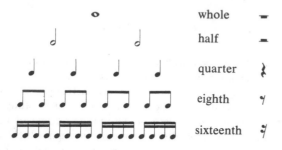

whole	
half	
quarter	
eighth	
sixteenth	

Note values based on the 3–1 relationships are shown by triplets or by dotted notes.

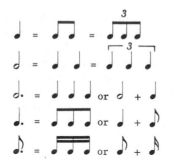

Meter and rhythm.

Beat: The underlying pulse of the music.

Meter: The systematic grouping of beats resulting from the **accenting** of certain beats.

Bar Line: Vertical lines across the staff which indicate metric groupings.

Measure: A single metric grouping marked off by two bar lines.

Meter Signature: The symbol which indicates the meter of the composition and the note which will be the beat note. The meter signatures found in this book follow:

$\frac{4}{4}$ The song moves in fours and the quarter note is the beat note.

$\frac{2}{4}$ The song moves in twos and the quarter note is the beat note.

$\frac{3}{4}$ The song moves in threes and the quarter note is the beat note.

$\frac{2}{2}$ The song moves in twos and the half note is the beat note.

$\frac{3}{8}$ The song moves in threes and the eighth note is the beat note.

$\frac{6}{8}$ There are six beats in the measure with accents on beats 1 and 4. The eighth note is the beat note. In quick tempo the song seems to move in twos, and the dotted quarter acts as the beat note.

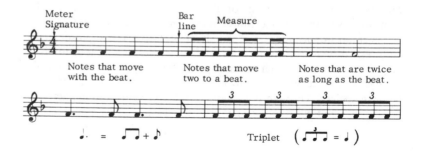

REVIEW OF MUSIC THEORY: MELODY

Pitch notation. Pitches are indicated by **notes** on a **grand staff**. The grand staff consists of two staves, treble and bass. Each staff consists of five lines and four spaces. Ledger lines may be added above or below each staff for additional pitches. The treble staff is indicated by the G clef establishing the second line of this staff as G. The bass staff is indicated by the F clef establishing the fourth line of this staff as F.

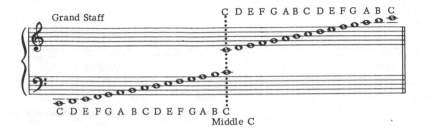

Grand Staff

Middle C

Scales. A scale is a group of tones arranged in a particular sequence of whole or half steps or a combination of both. Scale steps may be named by letters, indicating their pitch; by numbers, indicating their position in the scale; or by syllables. (Numbers and letters are used in the pupil's book. For those teachers who wish to use syllables, the syllable names are included here for the major and minor scales.)

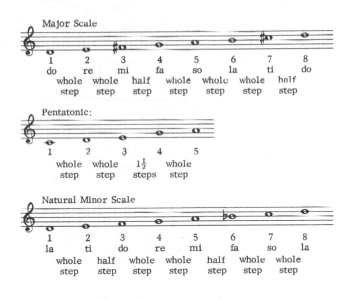

Major Scale

1	2	3	4	5	6	7	8
do	re	mi	fa	so	la	ti	do
whole step	whole step	half step	whole step	whole step	whole step	half step	

Pentatonic:

1	2	3	4	5
whole step	whole step	1½ steps	whole step	

Natural Minor Scale

1	2	3	4	5	6	7	8
la	ti	do	re	mi	fa	so	la
whole step	half step	whole step	whole step	half step	whole step	whole step	

The lowered third is characteristic of all minor scales. The harmonic minor scale is the same as the natural minor scale except that the seventh step is raised, which creates a step and a half between the sixth and seventh steps.

In the melodic minor scale the sixth and seventh steps are raised a half step when ascending and are unaltered when descending.

Keys. The key of a composition, which indicates the scale on which the composition is based, is symbolized by the key signature, which appears at the beginning of the first staff of a song. The key signatures found in this book are listed following the discussion of chords.

Chords. A chord is the simultaneous sounding of several tones. The most common chords are called triads, made up of three tones each a third apart. Occasionally, a fourth tone is added to a chord; these chords are called seventh chords because the fourth tone is seven tones above the first tone of the chord. The most common chords are those based on the first, fourth, and fifth steps of the scale. Following are the I, IV, and V7 chords for the keys found in this book. The largest note is the home tone of the key.

Key of C — I IV V7 / C F G7
Key of G — I IV V7 / G C D7
Key of D — I IV V7 / D G A7
Key of A — I IV V7 / A D E7

Key of E — I IV V7 / E A B7
Key of F — I IV V7 / F B♭ C7
Key of B♭ — I IV V7 / B♭ E♭ F7
Key of E♭ — I IV V7 / E♭ A♭ B♭7

Key of A♭ — I IV V7 / A♭ D♭ E♭7
Key of G♭ — I IV V7 / G♭ C♭ D♭7
Key of C♭ — I IV V7 / C♭ F♭ G♭7

Key of A minor — I IV V7 / A D E7
Key of D minor — I IV V7 / D G A7
Key of G minor — I IV V7 / G C D7
Key of F minor — I IV V7 / F B♭ C7

Musical Growth in the Fourth Grade

	LISTENING	SINGING	PLAYING
SKILL	Is increasing in ability to listen with perception and discrimination.	Sings accurately and independently within range from B flat to F: [musical notation] Is developing control of tone and diction.	Is improving in ability to play a variety of percussion instruments accurately. Is expanding skill in chording on the autoharp and the piano. Is developing skill in playing a recorder-type instrument.
LITERATURE	Is familiar with two- and three-part song forms, simple rondo forms, themes and variations. Is adding examples of tone poems, suites, and incidental music to his repertoire of descriptive music. Can identify many compositions by title, form, composer, or time.	Is expanding his repertoire of songs to include folk, composed, unison, and part.	Is developing a repertoire of songs which he can play on melody instruments or accompany with percussion instruments.
CONCEPTS Melody	Perceives major, minor, and pentatonic tonalities. Identifies melodic patterns based on scale or chord-line patterns. Recognizes tonal sequences within a melody line.	Sings scale and chord-line patterns accurately, using numbers, letters, or neutral syllables. Demonstrates awareness of the relationship between melodic contour and musical expression.	Plays simple melodies on bells, piano, or recorder-type instruments from notation as well as by ear. Reveals understanding of scale structure by playing major, minor, and pentatonic scales on piano or bells. Establishes tonality for songs by playing appropriate scale or chord patterns on bells, piano, or autoharp.
Rhythm	Distinguishes meter, beat, accent, and rhythmic patterns. Recognizes common note relationships within rhythm patterns based on 2-1 or 3-1 relationships: [musical notation]	Reproduces rhythm patterns accurately as he sings. Demonstrates awareness of accent and beat through his singing style.	Is developing finer precision as he plays rhythmic accompaniments on original percussion compositions. Demonstrates awareness of meter and of rhythmic patterns, including syncopation, based on 2-1 or 3-1 relationships.
Harmony	Is sensitive to the existence of independent melody lines and supporting harmonies in a composition. Recognizes the need for chord changes in accompaniments. Identifies common harmonic intervals (thirds and sixths). Distinguishes I, IV, and V7 chords in major keys.	Demonstrates sensitivity to contributions of accompaniment as he sings. Exhibits increasing ability to perform independently in singing chants, rounds, descants, and simple two-part songs.	Reveals awareness of combined tones as he plays simple accompaniments. Demonstrates increasing awareness of chord qualities and of consonance/dissonance as he plays autoharp accompaniments.
Form	Recognizes repetition and contrast of phrases or sections. Perceives the structure of two- and three-part song forms, simple rondo forms, and themes and variations.	Demonstrates awareness of form by singing a phrase as a single musical thought.	Indicates his awareness of design and of repetition/contrast when planning accompaniments. Demonstrates understanding of the relationship of introduction and coda to a composition as he plans accompaniment.
Expression	Is aware of the wide variety of expression possible in music. Feels the expressive contributions of melodic contour, rhythmic pattern, meter, tonality, and harmonic sequence. Senses musical climax and is conscious of how tone color, tempo, and dynamics contribute to it.	Reveals his sensitivity to musical expressiveness by singing with appropriate tempo, dynamics, and tone quality. Indicates awareness of musical climax by supporting such points with appropriate singing style.	Selects instruments and plans accompaniments which show sensitivity to the expressive possibilities of various instrumental combinations. Demonstrates his awareness of tone color and variations in tempo and dynamics when playing instrumental compositions.
Style	Identifies general stylistic qualities of music as characteristic of a specific time and place.		Shows consideration for country, background, and origin when selecting instruments and planning accompaniments for representative songs.

MOVING	CREATING	READING
Is developing a vocabulary of dance movements with which to interpret music. Is gaining an inventory of traditional dance steps.	Improvises his own melodies using common melody instruments and voice. Develops accompaniments for class songs using percussion instruments, autoharp, and piano. Works with others to develop instrumental compositions.	Is expanding his ability to associate symbols of musical notation with musical concepts. Uses notation increasingly as an aid when listening, performing, and improvising.
Is acquiring a repertoire of folk dances and singing games. Is expanding his repertoire of music suitable for dance interpretation.	Is building a repertoire of original compositions which members of the class have developed and notated.	
Shows awareness of melodic contour in his dance interpretations.	Demonstrates his knowledge and understanding of scale-line and chord-line patterns and applies his understanding of melodic sequence in his original composition and improvisation. Explores major, minor, and pentatonic tonalities in creating original melodies.	Reproduces scale and chord-line patterns accurately when singing and playing melody instruments. Uses numbers and/or letters in singing, playing, and improvising melodies. Interprets key signatures to determine tonality. Uses knowledge of sequence as an aid in music reading.
Shows his understanding of meter and rhythm pattern by clapping appropriately. Reveals sensitivity to rhythmic nuance through dance interpretations. Exhibits awareness of differences in rhythmic structure when executing folk dances.	Applies his knowledge of meter and rhythmic relationships when improvising accompaniments or percussion compositions. Works with others to create rhythmic compositions using several different patterns simultaneously.	Reproduces accurately common rhythm patterns made up of common 2-1 and 3-1 relationships. Interprets meter signature to establish meter and determine relationships of various notes.
Indicates sensitivity to cadence in dance interpretation. Plans dance movements which reveal recognition of independent melody lines.	Reveals his awareness of consonance/dissonance by improvising accompaniments to pentatonic songs. Uses his knowledge of I, IV, V7 chords to accompany original melodies on the autoharp.	Follows chord symbols (Roman numerals or letters) to play accompaniments on the autoharp. Interprets notation when singing and playing simple two-part harmonizations.
Plans dance movements which show understanding of two- and three-part forms, rondos, themes and variations. Indicates increasing awareness of repetition and contrast in his dance interpretations.	Reveals understanding of two- and three-part forms, rondos, themes and variations by developing compositions based on these designs.	Uses knowledge of repetition/contrast as an aid in interpreting notation. Identifies two- and three-part forms from notation. Indicates design of composition by appropriate letters (A A B A, A B A B, etc.).
Displays sensitivity to the expressive component of the music and to variations in tempo, dynamics, and tone color in his dance movements.	Displays sensitivity to expressive qualities of different instrumental combinations when selecting instruments for accompaniments or original compositions. Reveals awareness of expressive contributions of tempo and dynamics when improvising melodies, accompaniments, and dances.	Is aware of meaning of common expression markings found on the song pages.

EXPLORING MUSIC: PROCEDURES

EXPLORING MUSIC THROUGH SINGING

Teaching children to sing expressively

The extent to which classroom singing fulfills human and musical needs depends upon the quality of the singing. A song which is intended to inspire noble feelings cannot do so if it is sung in an inappropriate tempo or out of tune. A song meant to be sung for recreation cannot be effective unless it is sung with enthusiasm and with an appropriate tempo, mood, and tone quality. Singing, as an important activity in the study of music, will lead to musical understandings only when the singing itself is musical and when the teacher is aware of the possibilities inherent in the music. Playing accompaniments, descants, rhythm or melody patterns, adding original stanzas, and understanding the scale on which a song is based are all part of a good singing program.

. . . The children should hear a song for the first time with books closed and thus concentrate on the aural experience. Then they should study the words of the song. The words are an important key to interpretation and expression.

. . . Help children discover that the words of a song often suggest the tempo. When children have examined the meaning and purpose of a song, they will learn to express these through appropriate tempo.

. . . Help children match their tone quality to the mood, meaning, and purpose of a song. Whether the class sings in full voice, lightly and crisply, or in one of the many variations of either should be determined by the song and its content.

. . . Help children produce beautiful tones through attention to diction. Children enjoy learning to use lips, teeth, and tongue so that their words are carefully spoken or sung. Pure vowel sounds often will greatly improve the tone quality. Beginning and closing consonants should be clearly enunciated.

. . . Make sure that children's singing is never "halfhearted." Enthusiasm for expressing the song is important on all occasions. For this reason, it is suggested that a variety of songs be sung for "opening exercises" and during the Christmas season as well as on other occasions. Remember that repeating the same songs too frequently may result in singing without thought or emotional stimulus.

. . . Help children sing in tune with proper phrasing, correct pitch, and rhythm. To assist children to sing in tune, establish a strong feeling for tonality by singing 1-3-5, by playing on an instrument, or by listening to the introduction on the recording. Learning the song carefully will usually assure that it will be sung correctly through the year, but corrections should be made whenever necessary.

Teaching a song through listening

Learning a song by listening as others sing is a time-honored method. All through history man has passed on much of his musical heritage in this fashion. As one learns a new song through listening, he is absorbing many things in addition to the words and melody. He is becoming sensitive to the expressive qualities of the music, to the performing style of the singer, to the contributions of the accompaniment, and to nuances of shading and phrasing which constitute a musical performance. For these reasons, all the songs in the fourth-grade book have been recorded.

When teaching a song through listening, the following steps are suggested as a basic sequence from which each teacher may develop his own plan.

. . . Enjoy listening to the complete song with books closed. Draw from the children their observations about the overall mood of the song, as well as comments regarding the words, the melody, the accompaniment, or anything in the performance which they find of particular interest.

. . . Replay or sing again the complete composition so that all children may enjoy those things which some children had noticed on the first hearing.

. . . With books open, focus attention on the words. Discuss the word content with the children until they have grasped the expressive intent and understand the meaning of unfamiliar words.

. . . Discuss the musical content. Ask the children to listen for distinctive characteristics of the song such as the phrase pattern, characteristic tonal and rhythmic patterns, and unusual accompaniments. Focus attention on particular features each time the song is replayed.

. . . Encourage the children to sing as much of the song as possible without assistance from the teacher or the recording. If the song is long or the melody complex, invite them first to sing softly with the record on the refrain and easier sections. After they have heard the stanzas and the more difficult sections a number of times, ask the children to sing the complete song.

. . . After the children have sung the song without assistance, help them identify any inaccuracies in melody or rhythm which may have occurred. Guide them to correct their own errors by listening to the recording once again.

. . . Children will enjoy singing some songs with autoharp or piano accompaniment; other songs may be sung entirely unaccompanied. Still other songs will be enjoyed as the children sing with the record.

. . . Draw attention to the recorded performance of the singer and discuss such things as phrasing, tone quality, and dynamics which will add to the children's own expressive singing.

. . . Continue to enjoy the song and listen for interesting accompaniments on the recording. Experiment with instrumental accompaniments, physical movements, or descants and chants.

Teaching a song through reading

One may learn a great many songs by listening to others sing. However, such a method limits one to a life of musical dependence. The ability to interpret the musical score allows one to expand his musical repertoire more quickly and to gain satisfaction from his own independent performance. When children can feel that their study of notation has actually helped them learn a new song independently, they will see the skill of reading music as being meaningful and desirable.

Essential to the ability to read music notation is an understanding of the musical concepts for which the notational symbols stand. Aural experiences with these concepts must be firmly established before children can be expected to reproduce any pattern from notation. Children should be asked to listen carefully to patterns of melody and rhythm as they learn new songs through listening. Help children realize that musical sound can be pictured in symbols which they can understand and interpret.

Fourth-graders study the following notational symbols and terms:
>   **meter signatures**
>   **rhythm patterns** including **half, quarter, eighth, sixteenth, dotted quarter, dotted eighth,** and **dotted half notes**
>   **melody patterns** which move by **steps** or **skips** of the scale, identified by scale letters and numbers
>   **key signatures**
>   **marks of expression**

Development of music reading skills will occur only if the teacher indicates regularly to the child that he is expected to follow the score. The teacher should allow the child to be as independent as possible in his attempts to reproduce melodic and rhythmic patterns from notation. The following steps are suggested as a basic procedure for learning a new song by reading.

. . . Scan the notation of the song after an introductory study in which the meaning of the text and the general characteristics of the song have been discussed.

. . . Locate the symbols and musical patterns already familiar to the children. Locate new symbols. Discuss their meaning and function.

. . . Establish the rhythmic movement. After meter signatures have been introduced, children may establish the rhythmic movement themselves. Ask them to clap or tap the beat with proper accent.

. . . Establish tonality. After key signatures have been introduced, children may establish tonality for themselves, determining the home tone from the key signature and play 1-3-5 on the bells or the piano.

. . . Study the design. Notice phrases that are the same or different.

. . . Sing the song with numbers in the correct rhythm. Sing the songs with words.

EXPLORING MUSIC THROUGH LISTENING

School music, to be effective in our present-day society, should reflect the artistic life of that society and lead to a richer musical culture. This is no longer a country in which the folk song and the dance of the play-party are the only musical experiences. Recordings are bought by the tens of thousands, and people are hearing the most sophisticated music of the ages. Concerts bring music of every type to people of all economic and educational levels. Learning simple folk songs is not enough for full participation in such musical life. Children must also learn to understand music in its varied and larger forms if they are to make music an important enrichment of daily living.

Contrary to the belief of some inexperienced persons, listening to music with the greatest satisfaction does require musical study. Lilla Belle Pitts, a great teacher, once said, "Listening to music is an extremely difficult skill. It requires a background of appreciation which takes a lifetime to develop." Listening to music must be more than hearing. It must also be more than feeling. The deepest experiences in listening come with the ability to think as we hear. We must be able to analyze the ways in which melodies, harmonies, and rhythms are used and to observe the composer's style. When music is known in this way, it becomes something more than a background of sound which arouses only superficial feelings; and we are able to understand the messages of the great musical poets.

Listening lessons are included in this book for the purpose of studying music which children cannot perform. The recorded music is especially prepared to accompany the series because it is believed that the convenience of having the compositions available and at hand is important to the teacher. Representative compositions are presented. The teacher may wish to add others which she especially likes or which have a particular purpose in her classroom. Some general suggestions follow.

. . . Occasionally begin with the question, WHAT DO WE THINK ABOUT WHEN WE LISTEN TO MUSIC? Through the search for answers to such a question, the true nature of music can be revealed to children. They can be guided away from answering, "We try to make up a story or imagine a scene," as they learn to observe the musical elements of the composition—its melody, rhythm, harmony, form—and to recognize that its greatest charm may lie in one or more of these elements.

. . . After the children have listened to a composition, help them verbalize their reactions. In order to avoid too much lecturing about the music, use discussion and question methods that will draw from the children many of the observations and ideas needed in the study. Assist children to expand their vocabulary so that they can express ideas about music with more and more precision.

. . . Help children realize that design in music is the order in which things happen. The study depends upon recognition of repeated melodies or sections of the composition. Children can learn to raise their hands when the melody begins again or when the new melody begins. They can understand the use of letters to indicate melodies or sections of compositions.

. . . Whenever possible, help children to study music through genuine participation: class discussion, interpretation through movement, playing themes on melody instruments, or playing the rhythm of themes on percussion instruments.

. . . When a composition is too long to study in one lesson, use the principle of presenting "the whole-the part-the whole." In the first lesson hear the whole composition or enough of it to grasp the general character of the piece. In subsequent lessons study sections of the composition in detail. Make any digressions which are pertinent, such as the study of a specific instrument. Finally, replay the entire piece.

. . . Give opportunities for children to hear and rehear the compositions so that more of the beautiful details will be observed. Completion of the initial study should be considered as preparation for enjoyment of the music on many occasions.

. . . In order that children hear the music as perfectly as possible, pay attention to the tone quality and volume of the record player. The volume should be set to make the reproduction as much as possible like a real performance. Even small record players usually have tone controls which will improve sound when properly adjusted.

EXPLORING MUSIC THROUGH DANCE

An excellent way for children to comprehend music is for them to interpret it through free movement. Expression in movement can be derived from the rhythm of music, from melodic line and phrasing, design, instrumentation, or from program notes of the composer. Much of the music will be revealed to children when they are permitted to be "in" it—to express the music as it passes through their minds and feelings into their feet and bodies. This is a way of listening intently and of participating joyfully. In addition to the musical values, free movement has very rewarding human values. Remarkable personality development and behavior changes are sometimes noted as a result of the activity. It allows every child to succeed. It provides an outlet for true expression and originality. It provides physical freedom which is genuine, yet acceptable in the classroom. The limits of the activity are determined by the music itself. An opportunity is provided for the finest kind of self-discipline and cooperation as "ensemble feeling" develops in the interest of making the dance express the music. The following teaching techniques may be of help.

. . . Adequate space is essential since hampered movement is neither expressive nor satisfying.

. . . Provide periods of time for "warm up" dancing in which the children listen and dance freely to various pieces of music with little or no structuring or preliminary study. This gives an opportunity for the children to find new ways to move and to concentrate fully on the music as they hear it.

. . . Help individual children and the various groups to develop favorite dancing pieces which fit their personalities and natural style of movement.

. . . Divide the class into groups so that not too many children are on the floor at once. Involve the seated groups by asking them to WATCH FOR MOVEMENT WHICH LOOKS LIKE THE MUSIC.

. . . Simplify class procedure and avoid crowding by assigning a starting place on the floor to each member of a group. The simple instruction, GROUP ONE, TAKE YOUR DANCING PLACES, will save time and make the activity more effective.

. . . Let the movement be as natural and untaught as possible. Improve movement by pointing out the work of children who achieve freedom and originality in their movements.

. . . Remind children often that DANCING WILL BE MORE FUN IF YOU THINK OF THE MUSIC THE WHOLE TIME AND NOT OF YOURSELVES. Use descriptive phrases to encourage them to improve: I CAN SEE THE RHYTHM PATTERNS OF THE MUSIC IN "JOHN'S" FOOT PATTERN. SEE HOW "MARY" WEAVES THAT LONG MELODY INTO HER DANCE.

. . . When a composition has been learned through dance interpretation over a period of time, add an "identification of success" culmination in the form of a TEST TO SEE WHETHER WE REALLY KNOW THE MUSIC. DANCING HAS HELPED US TO KNOW THE MUSIC AND REMEMBER IT. WE DO NOT DANCE OUT MUSIC WHEN WE HEAR IT AT A CONCERT. TODAY WE WILL NOT DANCE THE GAVOTTE FROM BACH'S "SUITE NO. 3." LET US PRETEND WE ARE AT A CONCERT. IF WE HAVE LEARNED THE MUSIC WELL, WE WILL BE ABLE TO CONCENTRATE ON IT ALL THE WAY THROUGH AND HEAR THE DESIGN, THE INSTRUMENTS, AND ALL THAT WE HAVE LEARNED.

. . . Children move more freely and devise more complex movements if they dance in bare feet. The slippery soles and the weight of the shoes inhibit movement considerably.

. . . It is not necessary and usually not desirable to costume for this classroom activity. However, a ribbon, a sash, or a comfortable mask may help to free an inhibited child. On special occasions when dances are presented in their finished form, simple costuming can be effective.

Singing games and folk dances have musical value as well as social value. A number of songs and other compositions in the text are developed through dancing in folk style. When some dances are learned through specific instructions, the figures can be used by children in their own way as they improvise original folk dances and singing games.

. . . Make sure that children hear the beat and the accent of the music since folk dances are based on these.

. . . See that the dancers dance with "style" and vitality of movement that are characteristic of this kind of dance.

EXPLORING MUSIC THROUGH PLAYING PERCUSSION INSTRUMENTS

Selection of instruments

Playing percussion instruments should be an important part of the music class at this grade level. Many musical concepts will be more readily learned through this activity. If the experience is to be valuable, however, the instruments must produce a musical sound. In selecting instruments, tone quality should be a major consideration. Although it is impossible to describe accurately the quality of percussion sounds, instruments which might be called "thuddy" drums, "toneless" sticks, "clangy" triangles, and "clonky" cymbals should be avoided. A few instruments of good quality are preferable to many inferior ones which are little more than toy noise makers. Better instruments are more durable, more satisfactory musically, and more conducive to musical learning.

The basic percussion instruments fall into four classifications: membrane sounds, wood sounds, metal sounds, and rattle and abrasive sounds.

Membrane	Metal	Wood	Rattle/Abrasive
snare drum	sleigh bells	rhythm sticks	tambourine
bass drum	triangle	wood blocks	rattles
tom-toms	cymbals	tone blocks	sandpaper blocks
tambourine	cowbells	temple blocks	sleigh bells
all other	tambourine	coconut shells	jingle clogs
drums	jingle clogs	castanets	maracas

Explore the effect of various striking devices on the sound of different percussion instruments. All the following types of mallets are available in numerous sizes, weights, and textures: snare drum and bass drum beaters, timpani sticks, yarn, rubber or plastic mallets. In addition to the standard mallets, experiment with other items such as nails, pencils, and so on.

Playing techniques

tom-toms and other drums

1. Hold stick with forefinger and thumb under the hand, palm down.
2. Use different types and sizes of sticks or tap with the fingers.
3. Strike in various spots on the rim.

tambourine

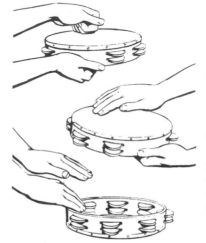

1. Hold by rim with one hand, head of tambourine on top.
2. Strike with knuckles in center.
3. Tap with tips of fingers: in the center, at the edge, between center and edge.
4. Press heel of hand in center and tap with fingers.
5. Play with various mallets.
6. Turn over and tap rim.
7. Place on a cushion and tap rim.
8. Shake for a sustained tone.

sleigh bells

1. Shake to produce a jingle sound.
2. Strike against hand or leg.
3. Tap strap or stick with hand.

triangle

1. Suspend by string or gut holder.
2. Strike with metal beater; experiment with other types of beaters.
3. Strike on part of triangle parallel to the floor.
4. Use different sizes of triangles for variations of sound and volume.

cymbals

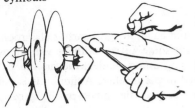

1. Strike pair together or suspend a single cymbal and strike with different sticks and mallets.
2. Use different sizes of cymbals for tone and volume variation.

temple blocks

1. Use five blocks to produce resonant sounds of various pitches.
2. Strike with soft rubber or yarn-wound mallets in the center of the top of the block.

coconut shells

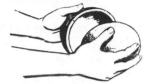

1. Strike together or use one and strike a flat surface.
2. Strike different surfaces of the shell with a mallet for variations in tone.

rattles

1. Play by shaking in circular motion.
2. Tap lightly with fingers.
3. Use different sizes; experiment with different textures of sound.

castanets

1. Use castanets which are attached to a handle.
2. Strike in the air with a whip-like action.
3. Strike against palm of hand or leg.
4. Hold stick in one hand; tap handle with fingers.

sandpaper blocks

1. Rub together.
2. Produce variation in sound by using different pressures and different speeds.
3. Use different sizes of block and different grades of paper for variation in sound.

jingle clogs

1. Shake in the air.
2. Strike against palm of hand or leg.
3. Strike handle with tips of fingers.

claves

1. Cup one hand to form a resonating chamber; hold one clave in this hand.
2. Strike it with the other clave.

Experimenting with sounds of familiar objects

One of the reasons percussion performance is so interesting is that there are so many possibilities for variations in sound. Encourage children to explore these endless possibilities by experimenting with different playing techniques and by exploring the sounds of familiar objects. Experimentation will reveal that many interesting sounds may be derived from sources other than the basic percussion instruments. Following are a few suggestions.

. . . Flick the edge of a glass or goblet with one finger.

. . . Find a frying pan which has a gong-like sound when struck with a yarn-wound mallet.

. . . Find an automobile brake drum which has a pleasant sound when struck with a yarn-wound mallet.

. . . Make the sound of an alarm clock fit into some particular composition.

. . . Strum the bottom of a plastic glass with finger nails.

. . . Occasionally, experiment with tin cans which have plastic tops as drums. Tap with the fingers or eraser ends of pencils. The lower end may be closed or open. Use them for special effects.

Constantly encourage children to be sensitive to qualities of sound in objects around them and to explore any object for its possibilities as a percussive instrument.

EXPLORING MUSIC THROUGH PLAYING MELODY AND HARMONY INSTRUMENTS

Children in the intermediate grades should be given many opportunities to play melodic and harmonic instruments. Understanding the relationship between musical sound and the printed page will be developed more quickly if the child has an opportunity to play an instrument. Each child should be encouraged to develop proficiency on at least one classroom instrument, such as bells, autoharp, piano, recorder, or song flute. Provide time for the child to practice by himself. Children may wish to purchase one or more of these instruments for use at home.

Playing the resonator bells

Resonator bells will be invaluable in helping children relate the symbols on the staff to pitched sounds as they learn to play descants and melodies in their book. The bells will also help children develop their own musical ideas through improvisation and composition. Here are several other suggestions for using resonator bells:

. . . Use bells to teach letter names of notes.

. . . Help children learn scale structure as they play the bells. Guide them to choose bells for a specific scale (major or minor) by ear. Then help them determine the sequence of whole and half steps within the scale.

. . . Ask individual children to play the bells to establish tonality and starting pitch of a song. When a song has a definite key center, the tonality may be established by playing the complete scale or the tones of the I chord (1-3-5).

. . . Teach children to play chordal accompaniments on the bells by arranging the bells in groups, one group for each chord (I, IV, V7). Strike the bells lightly and rapidly to produce sustained tones. Bell accompaniments sound best with songs where each chord is sustained for several beats (as in "Lovely Evening" and "Old Texas.").

Playing the piano

The piano, if one is available, should be an integral part of classroom music activities. The teacher with some piano training will enjoy accompanying the class as they sing and dance. However, the use of the piano should not be limited to the teacher. Although it is not expected that children will learn to play the piano in the general music classroom, they should be encouraged to explore the keyboard as an additional means of expanding their musical understanding and enjoyment.

. . . Discover that the black keys occur in groups of twos and threes.

. . . Locate specific pitches by letter names. First locate C to the left of two black keys; then locate other pitches in relation to C.

. . . Play the bell descants on the piano by ear as well as from notation.

. . . Establish the tonality for songs by finding the home tone, 1-3-5-3-1, and the starting pitch on the keyboard.

. . . Add a simple accompaniment to familiar songs. The autoharp chords are indicated above some songs in the pupil's text. These pitches may be played on the piano to create a simple one-note accompaniment. They will sound best if played in the octave below middle C.

. . . Discover major-scale structure by playing up eight tones from a given pitch. Decide, by listening, which black keys need to be played.

Playing the autoharp

Children will enjoy accompanying class songs on the autoharp. Give individuals time to practice by themselves before accompanying the class. Help children follow these directions.

. . . Place the autoharp on a flat surface with the long strings closest to the player.

. . . Press the chord buttons down firmly with the fingers of the left hand. Usually the index, middle, and third fingers are used.

. . . Strum the strings with the right hand. Use a pick or the finger tips. The strings may be strummed on either side of the bars, although a better tone is obtained by strumming them to the left of the fingerboard.

. . . Strum away from the body with a sweeping motion, moving from the lowest to the highest strings.

. . . Strumming picks for the instrument should not be too harsh and must be durable. A pick can be made from vinyl flooring by cutting an oval piece about 1½ inches long.

. . . Occasionally, for special effects, experiment with various picks such as erasers, pencils, and paper clips. Discuss the difference in quality of sound.

To add an accompaniment to a song, the following steps should be observed.

. . . Discover the chords which are to be used in the song. Practice moving the fingers of the left hand from one chord to another. Be sure the chord button is pressed down firmly.

. . . Establish tonality by playing the I chord (tonic); the starting pitch may also be plucked if the song is unfamiliar.

. . . Play the chords as the class sings. Determine the chord sequence by ear or by reading the chord names written above the song.

. . . Plan an introduction to a song; use the chords which are needed for the accompaniment. End the introduction on a I chord.

The autoharp can accompany only those songs written in the keys of G, C, and F major and in A, D, and G minor. Songs written in other keys may be transposed; that is, played in another key which is either higher or lower.

When you transpose songs, choose the autoharp key which is closest to the original key of the song: songs in B or D, play in C; songs in E flat or E, play in F; songs in A or G flat, play in G; songs in Bm, play in Am; songs in Cm or Em, play in Dm; songs in Fm, play in Gm.

For example, a song written in B flat would need to be accompanied with the following chords: B flat (I). F7 (V7), and E flat (IV). Not all of these chords are on the autoharp. Therefore, the song would need to be transposed to C and the following chords would be used: C (I), G7 (V), and F (IV).

In this book the chords for songs which must be transposed for the autoharp are written in the teacher's book. When the song must be transposed, the autoharp key to be used is listed with the general directions at the top of the teacher's page. The chords for the song will appear above the music on the reproduction of the pupil's page in the teacher's manual. No transposed chords appear in the pupil's book.

Playing orchestral instruments

Invite children who are studying orchestral and band instruments to share their abilities with the class.

Plan concert days when these children may perform for the class. Assign children who play orchestral instruments to learn the instrumental descants included in their book.

Provide opportunities for the children to work in small groups. Children who play piano or an orchestral instrument may join with others who are learning to play the bells or autoharp. The group may learn to play some of the songs in their book.

Invite the instrumental music teacher in your school to visit the class. Ask him to demonstrate various instruments and to explain the instrumental music program to the class. Cooperate with him in identifying children who would profit from such instruction. Ask him to assist members of the class as they prepare music for performance.

EXPLORING MUSIC THROUGH EXPERIMENTATION AND CHILDREN'S COMPOSITIONS

For some children, activities that develop their own musical expression will be the most satisfying and stimulating of all music activities. Their creative efforts may seem primitive, but they represent the children's own choices of music organization.

Suggestions for various creative activities are made throughout the pupil's text. Class experimentation need not be limited to these suggestions. The teacher will find many situations that lend themselves to creative activity. Such situations may arise in anticipation of a special occasion or in the sharing of a new idea or emotion.

The fourth-graders' experimentation with musical organization may take a variety of directions. Following are some general suggestions for guiding musical experimentation in the classroom.

Here are three ways children may plan percussion accompaniments.

. . . List words and short phrases which occur in the song. Notice the rhythm patterns. Select an appropriate percussion instrument and play one or more patterns as an accompaniment to the song.

. . . Find interesting rhythm patterns in the notation. Select two or three contrasting ones. Repeat them throughout the song. Choose different percussion instruments with tone qualities that fit the mood.

. . . Encourage one child to improvise a rhythm accompaniment as the class sings. Notice that the accompaniment is more interesting if it moves in patterns different from the melody rhythm.

Songs based on the pentatonic scale (a five-tone scale with no half steps between any two tones, which can be played on the piano's five black keys) are excellent for improvisation. This scale's structure allows any two tones sounded together to produce an acceptable harmonic sound. Here are ways children may add a pentatonic accompaniment.

. . . A child may improvise free accompaniments to familiar pentatonic songs, "Song of Itsuki," and "A Good Day in Japan,"

pages 58, and 60. Experiment with a two-tone accompaniment, then a three-tone, then the complete five-tone scale.

. . . Two children may improvise simultaneously on the piano's black keys. For best results, they should agree on rhythm patterns before beginning. One may move in quarter notes while the other moves in eighth notes.

Introductions and codas may be planned in a variety of ways.

. . . Discuss the mood of the song. Select instruments and rhythmic or melodic patterns that enhance the mood. Play them as an introduction.

. . . Sing an introduction by making a simple vocal call. For example, "All aboard!" could be an introduction to a train song.

. . . Select the bells which form the scale of the song and create a melody using any of these tones.

Compose an original song as a class project.

. . . Select a familiar poem or use one a class member has written. Discuss its expressive intent. Discuss ways the music may support the sense. Should the music move evenly or unevenly? Do the words suggest a specific melodic direction? Do the words suggest a rhythmic movement? Should the song move in twos or threes?

. . . Determine the tonality and the starting pitch. Children may do this or the teacher may make an arbitrary choice.

. . . With tempo, rhythmic movement, and starting pitch selected, individuals or the class may improvise a melody for the first phrase.

. . . Sing the entire first phrase together. Proceed directly to a second phrase which grows out of the first.

. . . Repeat these steps until all phrases are set to music. Sing the entire song. Discuss suggestions for further improvement.

Help children to understand music through experiences not related to their songs.

. . . Encourage children to play the resonator bells in original melodic patterns. In addition to exploring major scales, minor scales, and pentatonic scales, children should be encouraged to compose a "new scale" and select tones different from the usual scales.

EXPLORING MUSIC: PAGE BY PAGE

The section that follows contains specific and practical aids for the teacher. In it, each page of the pupil's book is reproduced, slightly smaller in size and in black and white only. Next to that page are aids for the teacher— essential information about the song, suggestions for handling the lesson, recording information, and occasional supplementary material. These notes carefully coordinate all parts of the program. They follow a regular pattern. The teacher's edition page, combining the reduced pupil's page and the teacher's aids, carries the same page number as the regular pupil's page. These features make this section particularly easy to use.

Song Information: At the very top of the teacher's edition page, the key and the starting tone are noted. In parentheses after the letter name of the starting tone is the number of the scale step for that one.

Next comes information about the autoharp accompaniments. Autoharp chords are given wherever appropriate to the song. When the autoharp accompaniment must be transposed from the key in which the song is written, the autoharp key and starting tone are given. You will also find a statement indicating that the autoharp chords are or are not in the pupil's book. In keeping with the playing ability of fourth graders, a number of songs in the pupil's book do have autoharp chords. Many more songs in the teacher's edition have autoharp chords. They have been added, in place, on the reproduced pupil's page.

Then the meter is indicated in two ways: (1) the meter signature as it appears in the song, and (2) in parentheses an interpretation of that signature. For example, if a song is in $\frac{3}{4}$ and should be felt three beats to a measure, the interpretation will be $\frac{3}{\downarrow}$. If the song is in $\frac{3}{4}$ and should be felt one beat to a measure, the interpretation will be $\frac{1}{\downarrow}$.

Finally, if a piano accompaniment for the song appears on a page in the back of this book, there is a statement to that effect. The piano accompaniment section, pages 189-289, is set off by the gray bands along the edge of each page. Songs in it are keyed to songs in the pupil's book by a number that appears in front of each song title. That number tells the page on which the song is found in the pupil's book. As a further convenience, a symbol above the staff of the piano accompaniments shows where each line of music begins in the pupil's book. For instance, $\overset{2}{\blacktriangledown}$ means that the second line of the song in the pupil's book begins at this point.

Teaching Suggestions: Most of the space on the teacher's edition page is devoted to specific suggestions. Often more are included than can be used during the initial lesson. In the basic study, use the suggestions from the pupil's page. Subsequently, select from the other ideas. Return to songs many times for new discoveries. The words printed in small capital letters may be addressed directly to the children.

Recordings: Under the reduced pupil's page is a reference to the recording made for the lesson. The record number, side, band, and information about the performance are given. All listening lessons and songs in the pupil's book are recorded. Use these recordings regularly. They can help the children learn new songs, study expressive performance, and become acquainted with various compositions, instruments, voices, ensembles, and accompaniments.

For teaching convenience, the recordings are banded. The songs are simply separated by locked grooves. The appreciation records, however, have three types of bands: (1) locked grooves to separate major compositions or complete listening lessons; (2) standard five-second bands to separate movements of a larger work or arias of an opera; and (3) bands of a continuous sound to isolate particular sections of a composition for concentrated study. These visible intermediate bands are marked in the teaching suggestions by the symbol ◉ . The recordings come in a boxed set of eleven 12-inch long playing records and are available from Holt, Rinehart and Winston, Inc., 383 Madison Avenue, New York, N. Y., 10017.

Supplementary Material: On a number of pages in the teacher's edition you will find special articles included as an aid to better teaching. Some treat the musical status, ability, and expected growth of children at each grade level. Others provide historical or musical background of composers and musical styles. Of significance, too, are the articles on the orchestra (pages 174a, 174b, 174c, and 174d). They discuss the history and make-up of the orchestra and all the major orchestral instruments and tell how the sound is produced, the range, the quality of timbre, and the relationship of instruments within a family. The articles are listed in the Classified Index of Musical Skills under "Supplementary Material."

Organization: This book is organized in five sections. The emphasis is on music from various periods and places. Each unit also contains a study of music and other arts. Material in the teacher's edition on unit-opener pages and on pages marked "Music and Other Arts" will help the teacher relate music to the other arts.

This book also emphasizes a study of musical instruments. The teacher's edition contains studies of orchestral instruments (pages 170-174 and 174a-d), of ancient instruments (pages 89a-d), and of the pipe organ (page 185).

Green Violinist

BY MARC CHAGALL
BORN 1877

This painting is the first of a selection of reproductions of works of art to be studied throughout this book in conjunction with the music. At the beginning of each of the five sections of the book, is a full page reproduction. These can be used as a starting point for discussions of the ideas on the unit-opening page. They can also be examined in terms of basic ideas about form and expression. In addition, there are discussions of the relationship of music to the other arts within each unit.

You may ask the class to leaf through their new books, looking at the rest of the art before you return to a discussion of this painting.

In the *Green Violinist,* the artist captures the feeling of a small Russian village. Marc Chagall was born in Russia in 1877, and this was the world he knew best. He organizes his painting in a dream-like manner; people float in the air, dogs are as large as houses, and the large central figure is sitting on nothing. But the painting is a real expression of this segment of the world because it is true to the spirit of the place and its people.

The artist not only captures the spirit of the place, he also expresses his ideas about it. He uses subdued colors for the town and its people and makes us feel that the village is part of the violinist by extending the background colors into the clothing of the central figure. The bright green of the violinist's face and hand and the purple of the coat make him stand out as a particular individual.

Chagall later moved to France and, except for a few years when he lived in the United States, he spent most of his life there. His work developed a more universal sense of place after he left his native land, and he experimented with new methods of expression.

In Russia, Marc Chagall had worked for a decorator doing art work for the Russian Ballet. Later in life, he was chosen to create works of art for the Paris Opera House and for the new Metropolitan Opera House at Lincoln Center in New York. You may be able to find clippings of these paintings in back issues of magazines.

xviii

THE SOLOMON R. GUGGENHEIM MUSEUM COLLECTION, Marc Chagall, *Green Violinist* (1918)

Let's Explore Music

As you explore music, you will find much that is familiar to you. You will find music which tells of interesting places and of exciting things to do. You will find music which expresses feelings that are often your own.

Music is an expression of the **people.** As you explore, you will find music of people at work, at play, and in worship. You will find music which expresses love of country, love of nature, and love of home.

Music is also an expression of the **composer.** As an artist the composer expresses his own musical ideas. He studies the materials of music and discovers ways of using them. He looks for new kinds of musical expression.

Music can suggest activities and feelings which we all share. We can enjoy playing and singing music, dancing and listening to the music of the people and the artists of different times and places.

As a part of the exciting first music lesson of the year, allow the children to look through the music book to enjoy and discuss the pages of art, songs, listening lessons, and so on. Ahead of time, choose a few songs you think the class will like and be prepared to play the recordings as examples of the music for the new school year. Conduct a discussion of what is already known by the class members—who has had music lessons apart from school, who will be studying piano or some other instrument this year, what music they have heard in concert, what records they have at home, what they remember about music from other school years.

After the preliminary exploration of the book, read and discuss this page with the class. Ask the children to find an example of each type of music mentioned on the page. Here are some possible examples of music of the people: at work—pages 3, 36, 129; at play—pages 6, 48, 154; in worship—pages 20, 110, 128; love of one's country—pages 2, 50, 184; love of nature—pages 14, 146, 158; love of home—pages 62, 64, 104.

Ask the children to notice the titles of the five sections of the book (see contents page, too) and to locate pages which express music of the people from the several categories, "Far Away," "Long Ago," "Here and Now." Ask them to locate lessons based on music of composers found in these categories. To help the children answer this question, point out the credit which appears under the title of each song, make sure they understand the difference between a credit such as "folk song" and one saying, "Words and Music by ———."

Refer to this page occasionally throughout the year as children learn musical examples. Emphasize the exploration approach which the authors of the book have outlined. Include the children as you make plans for the music lessons of the week. Discuss the main ideas to be learned. Assist children in choosing some of the songs they will learn. If possible, make plans to attend some concerts and take field trips related to musical experiences. Invite performers of music to sing or play for the children in their classroom several times throughout the year.

America

Key: F Starting Tone: F (1)
Meter: $\frac{3}{4}$ (♩)
Piano accompaniment on page 186

ABOUT THE SONG: This is possibly the best known and most frequently sung of our patriotic songs. The melody is from England and is used for the English anthem "God Save the King." The words for "America" were written in 1832 by the Reverend S. F. Smith.

* EXPRESSION: Discuss the meaning of the text. WHY DO YOU THINK REVEREND SMITH CHOSE THE EXPRESSIONS <u>MY</u> COUNTRY, <u>I</u> SING, <u>MY</u> FATHERS, AND SO ON INSTEAD OF <u>OUR</u> COUNTRY, <u>WE</u> SING, <u>OUR</u> FATHERS? (He wanted to express his personal feelings for his country.)

Read each stanza as choral poetry. Pay particular attention to word endings such as the "ng" in "sing" and "ring," the "d" in "pride" and "died." Sing the hymn with the dignity and pride that reflect the meaning of the text.

MELODY: Many hymn melodies are composed to lead toward the highest note. Notice the gentle rise in the melody that leads to the high note in measure thirteen. Notice also, the unifying rhythmic pattern that occurs throughout the melody. ♩ ♩ ♩ | ♩. ♪♪ |

SCORED FOR INSTRUMENTS: "America" and four other songs in this book are scored for instrumental accompaniment in the "Exploring Music Instrumental Supplement." This sign, 🎺 at the bottom of the teacher's edition page, will indicate the songs so scored.

America

Music Attributed to Henry Carey
Words by Samuel Francis Smith

We express our devotion to our country in this song. What other songs do you know that express love of country?

1. My coun - try, 'tis of thee, Sweet land of lib - er - ty,
2. My na - tive coun - try, thee, Land of the no - ble free,

Of thee I sing; Land where my fa - thers died,
Thy name I love; I love thy rocks and rills,

Land of the pil - grims' pride, From ev - ery __
Thy woods and tem - pled hills; My heart __ with __

moun - tain - side Let __ free - dom ring.
rap - ture thrills Like __ that a - bove.

3. Let music swell the breeze,
And ring from all the trees
Sweet freedom's song;
Let mortal tongues awake;
Let all that breathe partake;
Let rocks their silence break;
The sound prolong.

4. Our fathers' God, to thee,
Author of liberty,
To thee we sing;
Long may our land be bright
With freedom's holy light;
Protect us by thy might,
Great God, our King.

Record 1 Side A Band 1. VOICES: children's choir.
ACCOMPANIMENT: brass quartet.
FORM: Introduction, *4 meas.*; Vocal, *vv. 1-4.*

 Scored for instruments.
See "Exploring Music Instrumental Supplement."

2

The Shanty Boys in the Pine

Lumberjack Song

The music of people at work has various purposes. Sometimes people sing while they work. They find a rhythm for the song which makes the work easier. Sometimes people sing about their work. Discuss the purposes of the work songs on these pages. Talk about the people who sang them. Notice other work songs from far away, long ago, and here and now.

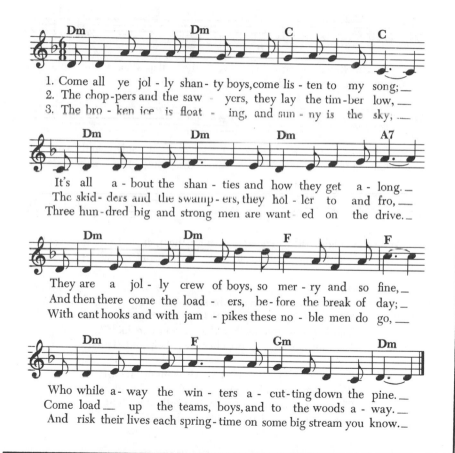

1. Come all ye jol-ly shan-ty boys, come lis-ten to my song; —
2. The chop-pers and the saw — yers, they lay the tim-ber low, —
3. The bro-ken ice is float — ing, and sun-ny is the sky, —

It's all a-bout the shan-ties and how they get a-long. —
The skid-ders and the swamp-ers, they hol-ler to and fro, —
Three hun-dred big and strong men are want-ed on the drive. —

They are a jol-ly crew of boys, so mer-ry and so fine, —
And then there come the load-ers, be-fore the break of day; —
With cant hooks and with jam — pikes these no-ble men do go, —

Who while a-way the win-ters a-cut-ting down the pine. —
Come load — up the teams, boys, and to the woods a-way. —
And risk their lives each spring-time on some big stream you know. —

Record 1   Side A   Band 2. VOICE: baritone.
ACCOMPANIMENT: percussion.
FORM: Introduction, *2 meas.*; Vocal, *vv. 1-3.*

Key: D minor   Starting Tone: D (1)   ## The Shanty Boys in the Pine
Autoharp chords in Pupil's Book
Meter: $\frac{6}{8}$ $\left(\frac{2}{\downarrow.}\right)$
No piano accompaniment

* **EXPRESSION:** Play the recording of the song and discuss with the children the kind of work described. Discuss the meaning of the words in all stanzas, the parts of the United States where lumbermen would be found, and the scenes described in the song. The word "shanty" originally meant a little house where the lumbermen lived to be near their work, but later the men themselves were referred to as "shanties."

Encourage the children to sing the song vigorously with a strong feeling of rhythm and without piano accompaniment.

* **RHYTHM:** Work songs are often written in $\frac{6}{8}$ meter with two strong accents to which workers move. Assist children to choose several kinds of movement to use in dramatization as they imitate the work of "choppers," "sawyers," "skidders," and so on. Playing the autoharp with two strokes to the measure will intensify the "work rhythm."

* **MELODY:** On first hearing the song, some children may be able to identify the melody as being in **minor.** Assist the class to discuss the quality of the minor sound in music in contrast with the **major** sound. Play minor and major chords on the autoharp or piano. Children may call the minor chords "dark," the major chords "bright." Point out the chief characteristic of the minor chord (the lowered third) as you play the D minor (D-F-A) and the D major (D-F♯-A) chords. Play the D minor scale on which the song is based and write the note names on the board (D E F G A B♭ C D). Ask children to discover which scale tones are used in the song and which one is not used (B♭).

HARMONY: The roots of the chords (see autoharp chords) can be played on bells with the accented beats, to give more emphasis to the "work rhythm" and to add harmony.

The Railroad Corral

Key: G Starting Tone: D (5)
Autoharp chords in Pupil's Book
Meter: $\frac{3}{4}$ $\left(\frac{3}{\downarrow}\right)$
Piano accompaniment on page 187

* EXPRESSION: After the class has heard the recording, discuss the kind of work reflected in this work song. Make sure that children know the meaning of words in the song and that they understand the work and life from which American cowboy songs were derived. IS THIS A WORK OF TODAY OR OF EARLIER TIMES? (Earlier times.) Discuss the changes that have taken place in our country, such as proximity of railroads to ranches and the practice of feeding cattle in pens near the place where they are to be slaughtered. All of these are evidence that the cowboy pictured in the early songs of the West no longer exists except in movies and television shows.

* RHYTHM: Ask some children to improvise, as an accompaniment, a rhythmic pattern on desks, wood block, or coconut shells to imitate a "riding" sound as others sing. Such patterns as these would be possibilities:

$\frac{3}{4}$ ♩   ♫ ♩ |

desk   left right clap
         knee knee

or

$\frac{3}{4}$ ♫ ♫ ♫ |

or

$\frac{3}{4}$ ♩ 𝄽 ♩ |

MELODY: Study the **major** sound of this melody in contrast with the **minor** sound of the song on the preceding page. Play the G major scale (G A B C D E F♯ G) and the G major chord (G-B-D). Discuss the quality of sound. Help the children discover that the tones of the G major chord recur frequently in the melody.

HARMONY: The autoharp chords appear in the pupil's book because this song requires only two chords. It is a good song for a "first experience" at learning to play the autoharp. Stress that the child needs to hold the bars down firmly while strumming the strings with his finger or a pick. He should stroke the strings on the first beat of each measure.

The Railroad Corral

What kind of work does this song tell about?

Cowboy Song

1. We're up in the morn - ing ere break - ing of day,
2. Come take up your cin - ches, come shake out your reins,

The chuck wag - on's bus - y, the flap - jack's in play.
Come wake your old bron - co and break for the plains;

The herd is a - stir o - ver hill - side and vale,
Come roust out your steers from the long chap - ar - ral,

With the night rid - ers crowd - ing them in - to the trail.
For the out - fit is off to the rail - road cor - ral.

3. The afternoon shadows are startin' to lean
   When the chuck wagon sticks in the marshy ravine;
   The herds scatter farther than vision can look,
   You can bet all true punchers will help out the cook.

4. The longest of days must reach evening at last,
   The mountains all climbed and the creeks all are past;
   The herd is a-drooping and fast falls the night,
   Let them droop if they will, for the railroad's in sight!

Record 1 Side A Band 3. VOICE: tenor.
ACCOMPANIMENT: harmonica, guitar, double bass.
FORM: Introduction, *6 meas.;* Vocal, *vv. 1-2.*

John seems to have some special work to do. See if you can tell what it is. Sing the song and play the melody on the bells. Later, sing the song as a round.

Where Is John?

Czechoslovakian Folk Song

Where is John?— The old red hen has left her pen.

Where is John?— The cows are in the corn a-gain.

Oh, John! _____

Yangtze Boatmen's Chantey

Chinese Chantey

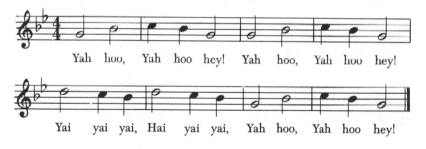

Yah hoo, Yah hoo hey! Yah hoo, Yah hoo hey!

Yai yai yai, Hai yai yai, Yah hoo, Yah hoo hey!

Some of the class may sing this chant while the rest sing the song above.

Yah hoo, Yah hey! Yah hoo, Yah hey! Yai yai yai, Hai yai yai, Yah hoo, Yah hey!

Record 1   Side A   Band 4. VOICES: children's choir.
ACCOMPANIMENT: piccolo, oboe, French horn.
FORM: Vocal (unison); Vocal (3-part round); Instrumental.

Record 1   Side A   Band 5. VOICES: children's choir.
ACCOMPANIMENT: bells.
FORM: Introduction (bells on chant); Vocal; Vocal.

Key: D   Starting Tone: D (1)
Meter: $\frac{6}{8}$ ($\frac{2}{\downarrow}$)
No piano accompaniment

Where Is John?

* MELODY: When children have listened to the song, ask them to discuss the commentary in their books. (John had the duty of closing the gate or of looking after the chickens and cows and, as all boys and girls sometimes do, he evidently forgot or neglected his duty.)

As children are learning to sing the song and play the melody on the bells, help them to discover that the first four measures include the first four tones of the D major scale. The next four-measure phrase is the same melody. However, it begins three tones higher (on F sharp instead of D). This is called a melodic **sequence.** Be sure that children can sing and play the melody well before they attempt to sing and play it as a round.

HARMONY: The tones of the first and second phrases sung or played together sound in **harmony.** The tones of the lower and higher notes are three steps apart when sounded together. The third phrase sung on step 1 of the scale an octave higher makes three-tone harmony that is even more interesting. Children can sing the three-part round, or one part of the round might be played on the bells.

MUSICAL SYMBOLS AND TERMS: Sequence, see pages 32, 161.

Key: G minor   Starting Tone: G (1)
Meter: $\frac{4}{4}$ ($\frac{4}{\downarrow}$)
No piano accompaniment

Yangtze Boatmen's Chantey

* EXPRESSION: Assist the children to study the song and sing it in a style and tempo that will suggest the men at work. Pulling boats against the river current has been an important work of Chinese men for generations. The songs these workers sing are a part of the country's music. In this song the workmen sing in a rhythm that makes their rhythm of work go more smoothly. Ask the class to locate other songs of people at work in their books.

HARMONY: Make sure that children know the song and can sing it expressively before singing the descant. As an intermediate step, they might play the chant on bells.

Hiking, Laughing, Singing

Key: C   Starting Tone: G (5)
Autoharp chords in Pupil's Book
Meter: $\frac{2}{4}\left(\frac{2}{\downarrow}\right)$
Piano accompaniment on page 188

* **EXPRESSION:** THE ESSENCE OF THIS SONG IS A JOYOUSNESS THAT REFLECTS OUR FEELINGS WHEN OUT OF DOORS ON A GRAND AUTUMN DAY WITHOUT A CARE IN THE WORLD. EXPRESS THIS SPIRIT IN YOUR SINGING. Hiking songs are often sung by men and boys in Sweden and other countries of Europe. The "Tra-la" syllables are pronounced differently in hiking songs than in songs of small children. Swedish boys sing "la" so that the "l" is somewhat lengthened by pronouncing it forward in the mouth with the tongue behind the upper front teeth. Practice this with the class to improve the tone quality and clarity.

For variety in singing the song, divide the class into groups and try different effects: boys may sing the words, girls the "Tra-la" refrains; girls sing the words, boys whistle the "Tra-la" refrains; trio or duet sings the words, class sings the refrains. Discuss with the class a way of singing the song to give the impression of hikers coming from a distance, passing in front, then going off into the distance.

RHYTHM: Explore and point up the rhythmic elements of the song through activities such as this: the boys may tap the 1-2 steady pulse with their feet, being sure to accent beat 1 with the left foot, while girls tap out the rhythm of the melody with pencils on their desks. Another idea would be to have one group begin to tap the rhythm of the melody. Then, on the last eighth note of the first full measure, have a second group begin tapping the rhythm of the melody. Make sure both groups know the rhythm well before combining them in a **Rhythmic Canon.**

MUSICAL SYMBOLS AND TERMS: |1. | |2. |
See page 46 for explanation.

Hiking, Laughing, Singing

Old Swedish Hiking Song

No one works all the time! This song and the dances on the following pages can be enjoyed by people at play.

1. Let us stride a - long to - geth - er In the sun - ny au - tumn weath - er, Tra - la - la - la - la - la - la - la - la - la - la - la, We are Tra - la - la - la - la - la - la - la - la - la - la - la - la. 2. We will throw a - way mis-giv - ing In the joy, the joy of liv - ing, As we breeze a - long the high - ways And ex - plore for - got - ten

hik - ing, laugh - ing, sing - ing To the tune with - in us ring - ing,

Record 1   Side A   Band 6. VOICES: children's choir.
ACCOMPANIMENT: accordion, guitar, double bass.
FORM: Introduction, *2 meas.;* Vocal, *vv. 1-3.*

by - ways. If the sun fails to keep shin - ing, We will

seek the sil - ver lin - ing. Tra - la - la - la -

la - la - la - la la la la la - la - la.

3. In the new-born au - tumn day we hike a - long the high - way

O'er the mead-ow and the lea we sing so mer - ri - ly.

Sing tra-la - la - la - la, tra - la, Sing tra-la - la - la - la, tra - la,

Sing tra-la - la - la - la. Tra - la - la - la - la - la - la.

In connection with the idea of "work," teach children this rhyme. They might memorize it and say it together expressively.

The Happy Farmer

Old English Rhyme

Let the mighty and the great
Roll in splendor and in state,
I envy them not, I declare it.
I eat my own lamb,
My own chicken and ham;
I shear my own sheep
   and I wear it.

I have lawns and green bowers,
Fresh fruits and fine flowers,
The lark is my bright
   morning charmer.
So God bless the plow
In the future as now—
A health and long life to the farmer.

Guide the children to determine the rhythm of the words. Help them to see that the first two lines will be said in $\frac{4}{4}$ meter.

Let the might - y and the great
Roll in splen - dor and in state

Then help them discover lines in the rhyme which can be said in $\frac{6}{8}$ meter. Beginning with the third line, the rest of the rhyme can be said in this rhythm. (The first word "I" is on a pick-up note preceding the accent.)

I en - vy them not, I de -clare it_____

I eat my own lamb, my own chick-en and ham

I shear my own sheep and I wear it_____

Since the first two lines of the rhyme are in a rhythm moving in groups of twos rather than in groups of threes, an interesting introduction might be composed in that rhythm. Children might be challenged to try to combine the "threes" with the "twos" by playing the rhythms on percussion instruments.

Dance Your Own Dance

On the day before teaching this lesson from the book, arrange for a large space for dancing and allow the class to dance to the Bach "Gavotte." Assign members of the class "dancing places" (see page xi, "Exploring Music through Dance"). Play the music; ask children to listen to it once before they dance. Play it again, ask the children to dance to the music. DANCE IN ANY WAY THE MUSIC MAKES YOU FEEL LIKE DANCING. BE CAREFUL NOT TO TOUCH ANOTHER PERSON OR INTERFERE WITH ANYONE ELSE'S DANCE. TRY TO THINK OF THE MUSIC THE WHOLE TIME AND NOT OF YOURSELF. LET YOURSELF MOVE FREELY WITH THE MUSIC.

After the children have danced to the composition, ask them to return to their "dancing places" and listen to your comments. Make comments about your observations of the work of the class as a whole and of individuals. I NOTICED THAT YOU DIDN'T USE ALL THE SPACE; SOMETIMES YOU COULD NOT DANCE FREELY BECAUSE YOU WERE TOO CLOSE TOGETHER IN THE CENTER OF THE ROOM. I NOTICED THAT SOME OF YOU SHOWED THE RHYTHM AND THE ACCENTS VERY WELL IN YOUR DANCING. IN JANE'S DANCE I COULD "SEE" THE PHRASES OF THE MELODY. I SAW DAVID DANCING WITH THE MUSIC OF ONE SPECIAL INSTRUMENT. I LIKED YOUR DANCES VERY MUCH. YOU WERE LISTENING CAREFULLY. YOUR DANCES LOOKED THE WAY THE MUSIC SOUNDS.

Play the music again as children dance to it. Since this may be the first dance experience of the year, participation by the entire class is desirable, if space permits.

On the next day, read the page with the children and conduct a discussion of their experience in dancing to the music. Help them decide whether anyone had danced with the "rhythm," the "phrases," or the "design" of the music. Let the discussion of the dance experience lead into a more detailed study of the music.

Suite No. 3 in D Major
Gavotte

BY JOHANN SEBASTIAN BACH
BORN 1685   DIED 1750

Read the lesson with the class and play the music. Discuss the strings, timpani, and harpsichord instruments (the music also uses

Dance Your Own Dance

Dancing while you listen can help you concentrate on music. Each person can be free to express what he hears in the music. Each one can dance with his own movements and develop new ideas. You can work together to compose dances that express musical composition.

You can dance to the rhythm of the music. You can dramatize the phrases of the melody. You can give your dance the design of the music. Your dance can have the style of the music you are hearing.

Suite No. 3 in D Major

Gavotte

by Johann Sebastian Bach

More than two hundred years ago at the time of Bach, the gavotte was a favorite dance. Bach and other composers of that time wrote concert music based on this dance rhythm.

Listen to the "Gavotte" and enjoy the merry rhythm with accents in twos. Listen for the sound of the string instruments

Record 8   Side A   Band 1.
Concertgebouw Orchestra of Amsterdam,
Eduard van Beinum, conductor.

and of the trumpet. There are two gavotte tunes in Bach's composition. The first gavotte begins with this melody.

The second gavotte begins with these measures.

Study the design of Bach's composition. Why do we say that he arranged the two gavotte melodies in the design A B A?

Bach did not write this music for dancing; but you can dance to it, making a picture in movement of all that you hear. Experiment until you have dance patterns which you like for each melody. Discuss how you will give your dance the same design as the music. Work together and compose a dance that expresses the musical composition.

oboes and trumpets), the melodies written in the book, and the design of the composition. ABA indicates that the composition is in three sections with the third section based on the same melodies as the first and the second section based on different melodies.

"Gavotte I" (Section A) begins with the notes in the book. All instruments play the first part of the theme; the trumpets and timpani drop out in the next part, giving the phrase a "question-answer" sound. The main melody is repeated. The second half of the gavotte begins with a melody which has an "upside down" sound. Compare the "Gavotte I" melody in the pupil's book with this melody.

Notice that the second and third notes move down-up in **inversion** of the up-down direction of the notes written in the book. Help children discover that the two melodies have the same rhythm but always move in the opposite direction from each other. The second melody is also repeated.

"Gavotte II" (Section B) begins with the notes in the book. These form the "question" part of the theme and the higher notes of the next measures, played only by the higher strings and oboes, are the "answer." After the measures notated in the book are heard the second time, there follows a different "answer" which is then repeated one tone lower (a musical **sequence**). This is all repeated. The second half of the gavotte begins in the key of A major and is also repeated.

"Gavotte I" (Section A) is the same as before except that neither of the two melodies is repeated.

As children become more familiar with the music through listening, discussion, and dance, they will be able to hear and "dance out" much of the musical content: the melodies with question-answer, sequences, and repetitions; the changes in dynamics and instrumentation; the over-all design. Half the class might work out the dance for the A section, the other half for the B section of the composition.

Another dance experience at this time might be based on a study of the "Fugue and Three Old-Fashioned Dances" of Hindemith, page 182. Compare the musical sounds of Bach, a composer of long ago, with those of Hindemith, a composer of our time. Interpret the Hindemith composition in "modern" dance.

The Crested Hen

A Melody

B Melody

In each set of three dancers there is a center dancer with a partner on each side. The dancers of each set join hands. The sets form a circle around the room. During the playing of the A melody, each set circles left in seven step-hop patterns, ending with a stamp. On the repetition of the A melody, the set circles to the right in the same way.

During the playing of the B melody, the center dancer and partner to the left raise joined hands in an arch, the left partner dances in place. The right partner dances through the arch with four step-hop patterns (four measures of music) and returns to place. The center partner follows him, unwinding by turning under the raised arm. With the repetition of the B melody, the same dance is repeated.

Variety can be given the dance by sometimes dancing with running steps rather than the step-hop pattern. Also, the center dancer can wear a peaked cap which the other dancers try to snatch as they pass through the arch.

The Crested Hen

Danish Folk Dance

This dance gets its name from the pointed caps which the Danish boys often wear while dancing. The cap resembles the crest of a hen. The girls have great fun trying to snatch the caps. "The Crested Hen" is called a **trio dance** because the children dance in groups of three.

Listen to the dance music and notice the melody. It is in two parts. The first 16 measures or A section of the melody is danced with a step-hop pattern. The second 16 measures or B section is danced by winding and unwinding through an arch. These two sections are repeated over and over with instrumental variations.

Dance with the rhythm of the music. Dance the way the children of Denmark might dance.

Record 8 Side A Band 2.

Gustaf's Skoal

Swedish Folk Dance
Words by Neva L. Boyd

For more than four hundred years, kings of Sweden have been named Gustaf. "Skoal" means "We pledge a toast." The Swedish people have often danced "Gustaf's Skoal" at the King's Ball. It has been a popular folk dance in Sweden, the United States, and other countries of the world for a long time.

Listen to the dance music. Notice that the melody is in two sections. The first section is danced with dignity as the people pay respect to their king. The second section is lively as the people rejoice at the King's Ball. Notice how the repetitions of the melody are made interesting.

Learn to dance "Gustaf's Skoal" with style.

A toast we pledge to Gus-taf who is brave and true,

A toast we pledge to Gus-taf brave and true!

La la la la   la la   la   la   la   la   La la la la   la la   la   la   la   la

La   la la   la   la la   la   la   la   la   La   la   la

DANCE FORMATION: Four couples in a square. Couples one and three are head couples, two and four are side couples.

```
        3
      4   2
        1
```

As dancers sing the first section of the song, head couples walk forward three steps, bow and walk backward to place and then side couples do the same. As the first section of the song is repeated, the dance is repeated. The style is one of dignity as if paying homage to the king.

As dancers sing the first six measures of the second section of the song, side couples form arches with inside hands joined and head couples skip to center, exchange partners and skip under arch. This is done in four skips to center, release partner's hand, turn away from partner to join inside hands with opposite, skip four steps under nearest arch. Girls then go right, boys left and return to places in four skips. With the last two measures of the song, couples join both hands and swing once around clockwise in four skips. As the second section of the song is repeated, the head couples form the arches and the dance is repeated with side couples moving to center.

The entire dance is repeated five times.

When the dance is known well it can be varied by having "extras" outside the square who try to steal a partner at the time of the two-hand swing by jumping in before the original partners join hands.

Music of Your Own

The plan of discovering musical principles through exploration with classroom instruments can pay great dividends in the education of children. When children have explored the tone qualities of simple instruments, they will be more aware of tone quality in all music. When they have played rhythmic patterns which they improvise, they will be more aware of the rhythms they hear and those they see in notation, such as the expressive qualities of different rhythms, the technicalities of meter and division of beat, and the interest of the sound of two or more patterns of rhythm occurring simultaneously. When children have played their own ideas on melody and harmony instruments, they will become more aware of form, phrasing, melody line, and style. They should also become aware of the fact that further exploration with musical sounds will always be of interest and that there are many unexplored possibilities.

1. Experiment with rhythm. Refer to pages xii and xiii for ideas of ways to play percussion instruments and supplement the children's ideas if necessary. Help children discover or review the ideas of "even" and "uneven." Write rhythmic notation on the board for some of the patterns they "discover." They might play tones that sound with the beat or that are an even division of the beat in patterns such as these:

They may play uneven rhythms derived from uneven division of one beat or from combining two beats in an uneven pattern.

Attractive percussion compositions for "marching," "skipping," and "dancing" can be played by using several instruments played together or in sequence. For example, the "dance" might be a series of even patterns played on a drum, followed by uneven patterns played on maracas or castanets. The first section of the composition might

Music of Your Own

A good way to learn more about music is to explore the sounds of your classroom instruments and to compose music of your own. You can experiment with one instrument or with several instruments. You can work by yourself, with a classmate, or in groups of three or four.

You can explore the sounds of the percussion instruments and experiment with **rhythm.** You can explore the sounds of the bells and experiment with **melody.** You can explore the sounds of the autoharp and experiment with **harmony.** You can experiment with different kinds of musical **design.**

1. Discover the different tones of the percussion instruments. Which have deep tones and which have light tones?
   Find different ways of tapping or shaking the instruments to make different sounds.

   What rhythms can you play?
   Compose a rhythm that is even and one that is uneven.
   Compose a rhythm for marching, one for skipping, and one for dancing.
   Imagine a story and try to tell it by playing rhythms.

   Work with others and combine instruments and rhythms in different ways.
   Practice until you can remember your experiments.
   Share them with the class.

2. Discover the different tones of the bells.
   Play tones that are high and others that are low.

   What melodies can you play?
   Compose a melody with only the white bells.
   Compose a melody with only the black bells.
   Choose a few bells that you like to hear.
   Compose a melody with only those tones.

   Can you plan the **contour** of your melody before you play?
   Compose a melody with several phrases.
   Can you give your melody a design?
   Share your experiments with the class.

3. Discover the different chords of the autoharp.
   Play **major** chords. Play **minor** chords.
   Can you hear the harmony?
   Experiment with different ways of strumming the strings.
   Experiment with strumming different rhythms.

   Choose a few chords that you like to hear.
   Compose a chant to sing as you play the chords.
   Sing and play your chant for the class.

   Experiment by striking the strings with a mallet while
       someone presses different bars.
   Remember to use your discoveries when you accompany your
       songs on the autoharp.

be repeated for section three. A fourth section might follow in which the even and uneven rhythms are played simultaneously. Or, the fourth section might be composed of new patterns played on several other percussion instruments. If the fifth section is a repetition of the first and third, the children have composed a "percussion rondo." Children might dance to the rhythms after the composers have the composition well in mind.

2. Experiment with melody in similar ways. Assist children with experimentation and improvisation with melodic patterns played on the bells. As you begin to work with melody, many of the ideas will be new to the children. Return to this page often as scales, melodic contour, and design are studied in more detail. Help the children realize that when they compose only on the white keys, they are composing in the key of C. When they compose only on the black keys, they are composing in a pentatonic scale. In the initial lesson it is more important that the children grasp the idea of self-expression and acquire a desire for experimentation than it is that they understand the harmonic and melodic structure of their work.

3. Experiment with harmony. Working with the autoharp will be an important skill for the children to learn. Guide the children in how to hold the autoharp, the different ways of strumming the strings, the different picks that may be used, and the necessity of pressing down the chord bars firmly before each stroke. Help them to locate the major and minor chords and ask them to compare their sounds.

After the class has read the ideas about exploration of rhythm, melody, or harmony, and has participated in a sample experiment, individual children and small groups can be assigned to work at various times apart from the class, later sharing the project with the entire class. All members of the class should have many opportunities throughout the year to work in this way with the ideas presented on these pages and with extensions of the ideas such as those found on pages 127 and 183 of this book.

All through the year, you should relate the rhythms, melodies and harmonies of folk and composed music children study to the ideas children have discovered for themselves by playing "original" sounds. THIS SONG IS IN $\frac{6}{8}$ METER. IT HAS THE SKIPPING RHYTHM JOHN LIKES TO PLAY ON THE WOOD BLOCK. IN THIS COMPOSITION, THE PIANO ACCOMPANIMENT IS MADE UP OF PATTERNS OF RHYTHM THAT ARE DIFFERENT FROM THOSE OF THE MELODY YOU SING. THEY ARE SOMEWHAT LIKE THE TWO RHYTHMS JANE AND LINDA MADE UP ON THE TAMBOURINE AND TRIANGLE.

We Sing of Golden Mornings

Key: F   Starting Tone: C (5)
Meter: $\frac{4}{4}$ (♩)
Piano accompaniment on page 190

ABOUT THE SONG: The melody of this song appeared under the title "Complainer" in *Southern Harmony,* a collection of folk hymns published in 1835. William Walker compiled this book of folk hymns, mostly written by New England composers, as an outgrowth of the "Great Awakening" (an eighteenth-century revival movement led by Jonathan Edwards). The folk hymns which had religious texts but folk melodies replaced the early eighteenth-century psalm tunes of the Puritans. At the end of the eighteenth century, these folk hymns found their way into the religious life of the South and by 1815 were being published in southern collections. *Southern Harmony* is such a collection and is typical of the southern folk-hymn tunebook. The music was written in shape notes, an early form of musical notation introduced in 1798.

* **FORM:** As children are learning the song, help them to discover the like and unlike phrases. The first four measures form phrase one. There are four four-measure phrases. Phrases one, two, and four are alike (except the last two notes), and phrase three is different. This can be indicated by the symbols A A' B A'. Phrase three is the **climax** phrase. It contains the highest notes of the song, and it is sung louder than the other phrases. Assist the children to sing complete phrases on one breath. This is most easily taught by imitation of the recording or of your singing, rather than by calling too much attention to breathing.

RHYTHM: Write on the chalkboard the four patterns of rhythm found in the song, with lines to indicate relative length of the tone:

Review with the class the ideas that the quarter notes in $\frac{4}{4}$ meter move with the beat, the half notes combine two beats, the dotted quarter and eighth are an **uneven** (long-short) division of two beats. Ask class members to clap each pattern several times, to chant words from the song with each pattern, to play each pattern on percussion instruments, and finally to clap and/or play the rhythm of the entire song as they look at the notation.

We Sing of Golden Mornings

Music from William Walker's *Southern Harmony*
Words Adapted by Vincent Silliman
from a poem by Ralph Waldo Emerson

Brightly

1. We sing of gold-en morn-ings, We sing of spar-kling seas,
2. We sing the heart cou-ra-geous, The youth-ful, ea-ger mind;

Of prai-ries, val-leys, moun-tains, And state-ly for-est trees.
We sing of hopes un-daunt-ed, Of friend-ly ways and kind.

We sing of flash-ing sun-shine And life-be-stow-ing rain,
We sing the ros-es wait-ing Be-neath the deep-piled snow;

Of birds a-mong the branch-es, And spring-time come a-gain.
We sing, when night is dark-est, The day's re-turn-ing glow.

When people express their feelings in music, they often sing about the things they love most: their country, their homes, and the beauty of nature. Ralph Waldo Emerson did this in his poetry. An American, he appreciated the beauties of his country. Look through your book and notice the songs that people of different countries sing about nature.

Record 1   Side A   Band 7. VOICES: children's choir.
ACCOMPANIMENT: harmonium.
FORM: Introduction, *4 meas.;* Vocal, *vv. 1-2.*

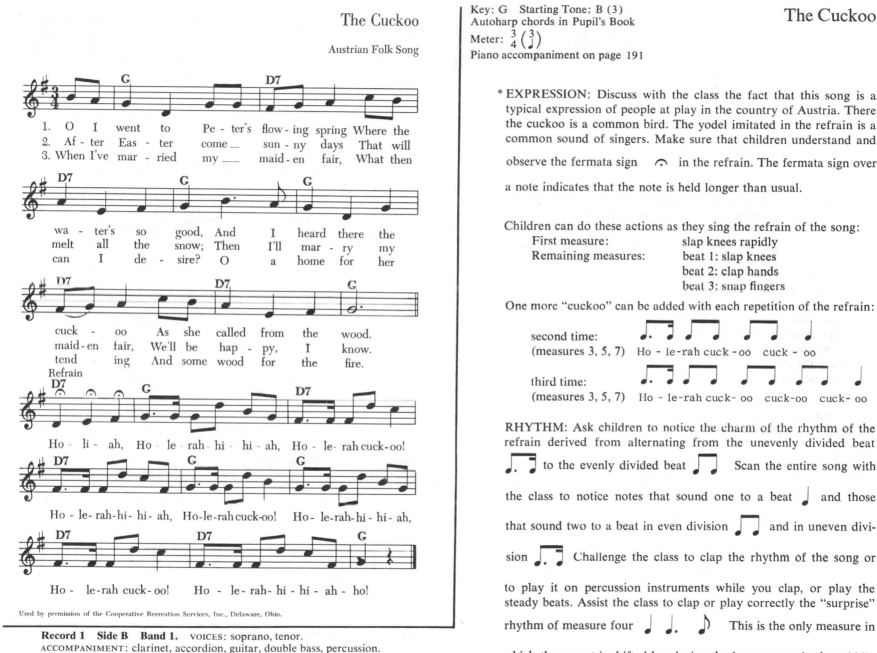

The Cuckoo

Austrian Folk Song

1. O I went to Pe-ter's flow-ing spring Where the
2. Af-ter Eas-ter come sun-ny days That will
3. When I've mar-ried my maid-en fair, What then

wa-ter's so good, And I heard there the
melt all the snow; Then I'll mar-ry my
can I de-sire? O a home for her

cuck-oo As she called from the wood.
maid-en fair, We'll be hap-py, I know.
tend-ing And some wood for the fire.

Refrain

Ho-li-ah, Ho-le-rah-hi-hi-ah, Ho-le-rah cuck-oo!

Ho-le-rah-hi-hi-ah, Ho-le-rah cuck-oo! Ho-le-rah-hi-hi-ah,

Ho-le-rah cuck-oo! Ho-le-rah-hi-hi-ah-ho!

Used by permission of the Cooperative Recreation Services, Inc., Delaware, Ohio.

Record 1   Side B   Band 1. VOICES: soprano, tenor.
ACCOMPANIMENT: clarinet, accordion, guitar, double bass, percussion.
FORM: Introduction, *1½ meas.*; Vocal, *vv. 1-3*.

Key: G   Starting Tone: B (3)
Autoharp chords in Pupil's Book
Meter: $\frac{3}{4}$ $\left(\frac{3}{\downarrow}\right)$
Piano accompaniment on page 191

The Cuckoo

* EXPRESSION: Discuss with the class the fact that this song is a typical expression of people at play in the country of Austria. There the cuckoo is a common bird. The yodel imitated in the refrain is a common sound of singers. Make sure that children understand and observe the fermata sign ⌒ in the refrain. The fermata sign over a note indicates that the note is held longer than usual.

Children can do these actions as they sing the refrain of the song:
  First measure: slap knees rapidly
  Remaining measures: beat 1: slap knees
                                      beat 2: clap hands
                                      beat 3: snap fingers

One more "cuckoo" can be added with each repetition of the refrain:

second time:
(measures 3, 5, 7)   Ho-le-rah cuck-oo   cuck-oo

third time:
(measures 3, 5, 7)   Ho-le-rah cuck-oo   cuck-oo   cuck-oo

RHYTHM: Ask children to notice the charm of the rhythm of the refrain derived from alternating from the unevenly divided beat to the evenly divided beat   Scan the entire song with the class to notice notes that sound one to a beat and those that sound two to a beat in even division and in uneven division   Challenge the class to clap the rhythm of the song or to play it on percussion instruments while you clap, or play the steady beats. Assist the class to clap or play correctly the "surprise" rhythm of measure four   This is the only measure in which the accent is shifted by placing the longest note in the middle of the measure.

A la nanita nana

Key: D minor and D major
Starting Tone: D (1)
Meter: $\frac{3}{4}$ $\left(\frac{3}{\downarrow}\right)$
Piano accompaniment on page 192

EXPRESSION: Teach the children to sing this lullaby with expression and proper phrasing and to pronounce the words lightly and clearly. Encourage the children to sing each four-measure phrase without a break. The last two lines may be sung in four phrases instead of two, with a slight ritard.

MELODY AND HARMONY: The melody of the song is typical of Spanish melodies which often change from major to the parallel minor. In this song the refrain comes first and is in the key of D minor. The D minor scale is D E F G A Bb C D. The second section of the song is in the key of D major (D E F# G A B C# D). Thus, in the descant, the children play the F natural in the first and last sections, the F sharp in the middle section. The third section of the song has the key signature of D minor and is in that key except for the last tone, which by means of the F sharp changes again to D major. Children need not be concerned with this in playing the descant because they play the tone D which is common to both scales, but they will hear the change in the piano accompaniment and will notice it in the notation of the melody.

Give children further experience with the difference in the sounds of major and minor. Play a series of triads on the piano, some that are minor, others that are major, and ask the class to identify the major and minor sounds. Ask three children to play chords on the bells such as C-E-G, C-Eb-G, F-A-C, F-Ab-C, as the class listens. Ask someone to play the first phrase of "Twinkle, Twinkle Little Star" in the key of C (c c g g a a g, f f e e d d c) and then to play it in a minor key by using E flat instead of E and A flat instead of A.

Ask children to describe the major and minor sounds. They may say that the major sound is bright, the minor sound is dark, or that the major has a bright mood while the minor has a somber mood.

A la nanita nana

Spanish Folk Melody
English Words by Beth Landis

This lullaby is sung in Spanish-speaking countries. Some of the words here are in English. The Spanish words essentially mean "Lullaby, lullaby."

A la na - ni - ta na - na, na - ni - ta
e - a, na - ni - ta e - a,
An - gels your watch are keep - ing, will hush your
weep - ing, bring peace - ful sleep - ing.
The night - in - gale is sing - ing, foun - tain is play - ing,
Your lit - tle cra - dle swing-ing in bran - ches sway - ing.

Record 1 Side B Band 2. VOICE: soprano.
ACCOMPANIMENT: alto flute, guitar, bells.
FORM: Introduction, *4 meas.;* Vocal; Coda, *4 meas.*

A la na - ni - ta na - na, na - ni - ta e - a.

A la na - ni - ta na - na, na - ni - ta e - a.

Play this descant on the bells. In which section of the song will you play F? When will you play F#?

You will need four different bells. Place them in this order:

Latin-American Instruments

The music from the West Indies known as calypso has become very popular in the United States. The following instruments are commonly used to accompany the calypso and other types of Latin-American music.

Cowbell

> The cowbell is held by its clapper. Play it by tapping with a metal rod. A comparable sound may be achieved by playing a triangle.

Bongo Drum

> A bongo is a two-headed drum which is played with the fingertips. One of the heads is of higher pitch than the other.

Conga Drum

> The conga is a deep-sounding drum played with the fingertips and the palm of the hand.

Claves (*clah'-vehs*)

> Claves are short, stubby sticks, usually made of hardwood.

Guiro (*gwee'-roh*)

> A guiro is a notched gourd. It is played by scraping a stick across the notches.

Maracas (*mah-rah'-kahs*)

> Gourd rattles are called maracas in Latin America. They often play a steady eighth-note pattern.

Following are some simplified patterns which might be adapted for use with any Latin-American song.

Blow the Wind Southerly

Key: G   Starting Tone: B (3)
Autoharp chords in Pupil's Book
Meter: $\frac{6}{8}$ $\left(\frac{2}{\text{♩.}}\right)$
Piano accompaniment on page 194

ABOUT THE SONG: This folk song comes from Northumberland, the northern county in England bordering Scotland and the North Sea. The text tells about a girl who awaits anxiously the return of her sailor sweetheart. Songs such as this were often sung by sailors at sea. There were many verses in the original ballad which made it a lengthy story told in song. Individual sailors would usually sing the story while the crew joined in on the refrain.

A "southerly" wind is one that blows from the south; "offing" refers to the ship's being in the distance; a "bark" is a three-masted, square-rigged sailing vessel; "bonny" means pretty.

* EXPRESSION: Have the class sing the song in a rather straight-forward manner, without sentimentality but with a few planned dynamics. It is usually more difficult to sing a controlled decrescendo than to sing a crescendo, so assist the children to sing the last phrase gradually softer but with tone that is firm and flowing.

* RHYTHM: Discuss $\frac{6}{8}$ meter with the class, pointing out that the **eighth** note is the note that moves with the beat. The melody derives much of its flowing quality from the succession of eighth notes moving in even rhythm throughout the song. Ask the class to count the beats as they hear the recording: 1,2,3,4,5,6 with light accents on 1 and 4. Then ask the children to use the conductor's beat and interpret the rhythm in an up-and-down swing as they sing the song or listen to it.

FORM: The melody is in A A B C form with four measures in each section. Point out that this is not the usual form for a folk song. Most of the folk songs they have learned have been in A B A form.

Compose new verses for the song. You might ask one group to write new verses that give the song a sad ending; another group might write a happy ending. Stimulate ideas by discussion and questions. WHAT IF THE WIND SHOULD STOP BLOWING? WHAT IF SHE SHOULD SEE THE SHIP?

Blow the Wind Southerly

Northumberland Folk Song

Blow the wind south- er - ly, south- er - ly, south- er - ly,

1. Blow the wind south o'er the bon - ny blue sea;
2. Blow, bon - ny breeze o'er the bon - ny blue sea;

Blow the wind south - er - ly, south - er - ly, south - er - ly,

Blow, bon - ny breeze,__ my lov - er to me. They
Blow, bon - ny breeze,__ and bring him to me.

Record 1   Side B   Band 3. VOICE: baritone.
ACCOMPANIMENT: accordion.
FORM: Introduction, *4 meas.;* Vocal, *v. 1;* Interlude, *2 meas.;* Vocal, *v. 2;* Coda, *2 meas.*

18

Here is one poet's impression of the sea.

Sea Fever

by John Masefield

I must go down to the seas again, to the lonely sea and the sky,
And all I ask is a tall ship and a star to steer her by,
And the wheel's kick and the wind's song and the white sail's shaking,
And a gray mist on the sea's face, and a gray dawn breaking.

I must go down to the seas again, for the call of the running tide
Is a wild call and a clear call that may not be denied;
And all I ask is a windy day with the white clouds flying,
And the flung spray and the blown spume, and the sea gulls crying.

I must go down to the seas again, to the vagrant gypsy life,
To the gull's way and the whale's way where the wind's like a
    whetted knife;
And all I ask is a merry yarn from a laughing fellow-rover,
And quiet sleep and a sweet dream when the long trick's over.

All Beautiful the March of Days

Key: F   Starting Tone: C (5)
Meter: 4/4 (♩)
Piano accompaniment on page 196

* **FORM:** Before the children have opened their books, ask them to listen to the recording of the song. Then lead a discussion about the type of song they have heard, the mood, and the general meaning of the text. Ask them to listen again and to discover by ear the like and unlike phrases. Help the children discover that the form is A A B A. (Each phrase is four measures in length.)

* **EXPRESSION:** With books open, help the class discover the groups of words that paint pictures—words that describe the beauties of the seasons, the loveliness of day and night, and the works of a supreme being.

Vaughan Williams has written a beautiful accompaniment to be used with group or congregational singing. On the recording this accompaniment is played by an organ.

It is important to focus on singing by phrases. Sing each phrase with continuous movement and on one breath. Try for beautiful interpretation. Interpret the first stanza in this way:

Phrase 1   p < mp > p

Phrase 2   mp < mf > mp

Phrase 3   mf < f > ff

Phrase 4   pp < p > pp

Help the class develop different interpretations for the phrases of the other stanzas. Keep the climax of each phrase in mind. Guide the children to discover that the dynamics are natural and inherent in the music.

Practice singing those words that have two notes to a syllable. Listen for distinct movement to each note and correct any tendency to slide between tones on such words as "march" and "of."

All Beautiful the March of Days

"Forest Green"
Traditional English Melody
Arranged by Ralph Vaughan Williams
Words by Frances W. Wile

1. All beau-ti-ful the march __ of __ days,
2. O'er white ex-pan-ses spark-ling __ pure
3. O thou from whose un-fath-omed __ law

As sea-sons come and go;
The ra-diant __ morns un-fold;
The year in __ beau-ty flows,

The hand that shaped the rose __ hath __ wrought
The sol-emn splen-dors of __ the __ night
Thy-self the vi-sion pass-ing __ by

The crys-tal __ of the snow,
Burn bright-er __ through the cold.
In crys-tal __ and in rose,

Hath __ sent the hoar-y __ frost __ of __ heaven,
Life __ mounts in ev-ery __ throb-bing __ vein,
Day __ un-to day __ doth __ ut-ter __ speech,

Record 1   Side B   Band 4.   VOICES: children's choir.
ACCOMPANIMENT: organ.
FORM: Introduction, *4 meas.;* Vocal, *vv. 1-3.*

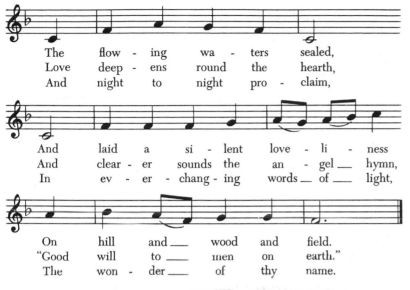

The   flow - ing   wa - ters   sealed,
Love   deep - ens   round   the   hearth,
And   night   to   night   pro - claim,

And   laid   a   si - lent   love - li - ness
And   clear - er   sounds the   an - gel — hymn,
In   ev - er - chang - ing   words — of — light,

On   hill   and — wood and field.
"Good   will   to — men   on earth."
The   won - der — of thy name.

The Composer Johannes Brahms

Born in Hamburg in 1833, the son of a double bass player in the Hamburg Opera Theater, Brahms was a nineteenth-century German composer. Early in his career he was championed by Robert Schumann as the new genius of romanticism. However, he had great regard for the classical forms and continued in the tradition of Beethoven. He might therefore be called a classic-romanticist in style.

Brahms was a fine pianist in his youth. He was a prolific composer. Among his best-known works are a violin concerto, a double concerto for violin and cello, four symphonies, the great German Requiem, the Hungarian Dances, two piano concertos, more than 300 songs, and numerous chamber works.

The melodic style of Brahms was profoundly influenced by German folk music. He wrote new settings of many folk song texts and in some cases it is not known for sure which are folk melodies and which are Brahms' original melodies. In his instrumental compositions he rarely used genuine folk melodies, but many of his own have a folk sound. The lyric quality of Brahms' melodies, his mellow instrumentation, rich harmonic texture, and superbly careful workmanship in all aspects of composition have made his works favorites of performers and listeners for a hundred years.

Robert Schumann and his wife Clara, a famous pianist, were the most important of Brahms' friends. Brahms' music was influenced to some extent by the styles of Schumann, and of Franz Schubert as well. Brahms, a bachelor, lived a simple life devoted to music. He spent the last thirty-five years of his life in Vienna and died there in 1897.

Music and Other Arts

The series of lessons comparing music and the other arts begins on this page and continues on pages 70, 116, 140, 152, and 166. In these lessons, accompanied by actual illustrations of works of "other arts," the authors present a comparison of the materials and organization used by artists. Studies of painting, architecture, sculpture, poetry, and dance are presented, as well as an additional lesson specifically on design.

Through observing and discussing composed music and works of other arts, children should gain interest in and understanding of the act of creation. They should recognize a work of art as the combined result of the characteristics of the material itself, the time and place of origin, and the genius and originality of the artist. The experiences outlined in the studies in this book are meant to improve a child's power of observation of various works of art and especially to help him appreciate works produced in a great variety of periods and styles, including those of our time. It is expected that the child will gain a deeper understanding of music through comparing it with other art forms. It is expected also that the child's own work in classroom painting and design, dance, and poetry will become more artistic and more varied because of the observation and discussion of examples in this book.

Not all of the ideas written on the pupil's page 22 will be grasped at this point. The page should be referred to often throughout the year as examples of the ideas are encountered.

In the initial study, read the page with the class. Stop to discuss the meaning of each paragraph. Help the children cite examples of each idea, naming specific musical compositions, paintings, statues, buildings, and poems. With these specific examples in mind, children can attempt to analyze the materials, the artist's style of expression, his time, place, and experience. They can discuss reasons for their own enjoyment of the work of art under consideration. Examples of the children's own creations or their accounts of their attempts at creation may be helpful in the discussion.

Music and Other Arts

Music and other arts are means of expression. Music is expression through rhythm, melody, and harmony. Dance is expression through movement. Paintings, statues, and beautiful buildings use space and form with color, rhythm, and design.

Each art has its own materials. The musician arranges musical sounds. The poet works with the sounds and meanings of words. The sculptor models in clay, wood, or stone.

The artist must understand his materials. He must be able to express his own ideas with imagination. The artist often likes to find new kinds of expression.

The work of an artist usually reflects the time and place in which he lives. The artist finds meaning in his experiences. He expresses this meaning through his art. Other people understand and enjoy his art because the artist often expresses feelings and activities that they, too, have experienced.

Brittany Landscape

BY PAUL GAUGUIN (go-gan')
BORN 1848   DIED 1903

The questions on page 23 of the pupil's book are intended to help the child reinforce the concepts present on page 22. The painting should be examined with these ideas in mind.

Paul Gauguin used color, rhythm, and design in his painting of this landscape. The color is not put down as flat areas, but as short strokes of many colors. Gauguin was using a technique and theory of color initiated by Impressionist painters of his time. He captured rhythms of nature in the curves of the hills and the trunks of the trees. His over-all design is fairly simple. Starting at the top, there is blue, purple, green, purple again with a variation, and blue again with a variation. A similar musical structure might be A B C B′ A′. But the simplicity of the design is deceptive because within each color area there is a very intricate use of color strokes.

The various arts have several common elements: structure, expression, use of materials, and the application of the artistic imagination. The involvement in the act of creation and the expression of ideas and emotions within a structure are common to all artists.

In this landscape Gauguin reflects the time in which he lived in his use of Impressionist techniques, in the somewhat romantic treatment of the landscape, and even in the very fact that he chose a landscape as the subject of a painting.

Later in his life, Gauguin moved from France to the South Pacific. Once he was away from the influence of French painters, his style began to change. He used flat areas of color with strong decorative elements such as patterned cloth.

After the class has studied the rest of the poetry and music of this section of the book, review the ideas on this page again, discussing the Gauguin painting, the Blake poem, and the Brahms' music.

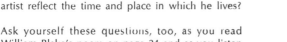

Brittany Landscape, Paul Gauguin, National Gallery of Art, Washington, D.C., Chester Dale Collection

By what means did Paul Gauguin express his ideas in the painting reproduced above? In what ways are paintings, poetry, and music similar? How does an artist reflect the time and place in which he lives?

Ask yourself these questions, too, as you read William Blake's poem on page 24 and as you listen to Johannes Brahms' music on pages 26-29.

Laughing Song

BY WILLIAM BLAKE
BORN 1757   DIED 1827

Read the poem with a happy tone of voice for the class. Conduct a discussion of the word pictures, the mood, and the word sounds. Have the class read the poem aloud in unison. Later, when the poem is memorized, conduct a discussion of the statements and questions on the pupil's page. The topic of human happiness in a setting of natural beauty and plenty is a common subject in poetry, songs, and paintings.

Blake repeats the word "laugh" many times in this poem. He gives nature the ability to laugh in order to express his own feelings of joy. Like the Gauguin painting on the preceding page, the poem expresses the artist's mood through nature.

Poets often use rhyme as part of the design of a poem. This poem's structure is three verses of four lines each, with the first line rhyming with the fourth. Not all the rhymes are perfect rhymes. The poet uses the "Ha, Ha, He!" twice as rhyme words. In doing so, he reinforces the joyous mood of the poem.

William Blake was one of the greatest figures in English poetry and art, and the volume of his creative output is astonishing. He began writing lyrical poetry at age fourteen and continued writing it for thirty years. In his later years he wrote long mystical poems. Among his best known poems are the "Songs of Innocence," of which this poem is one. He was an engraver and printer and he was a painter. In painting he was uninterested in realism. He was greatly interested in imaginative content. His subjects were often from the Bible, from Shakespeare or Milton. He often illustrated his own poetry.

Laughing Song

by William Blake

When the green woods laugh with the voices of joy,
And the dimpling stream runs laughing by;
When the air does laugh with our merry wit,
And the green hill laughs with the noise of it;

When the meadows laugh with lively green,
And the grasshopper laughs in the merry scene,
When Mary and Susan and Emily
With their sweet round mouths sing "Ha, Ha, He!"

When the painted birds laugh in the shade,
When our table with cherries and nuts is spread,
Come live and be merry and join with me,
To sing the sweet chorus of "Ha, Ha, He!"

The poem on this page was written almost two hundred years ago by an English poet. What is the topic of the poem? Is it a subject of interest to many people? What does the poem tell you about the poet?

Enjoy the sounds and ideas of this poem. Read it aloud with expression. Memorize the poem and say it together.

Record 7   Side B   Band 3.

Have you ever written a poem, painted a picture, or modeled a figure in clay or wood? Have you composed music or a dance of your own?

Each of you might create an art work to share later with the class. Use musical instruments in your classroom or an instrument you have at home. Use art materials found at home or at school. Use your own dance patterns for a dance or your own words for a poem.

Describe the materials and ideas with which you worked. Discuss with the class the pleasures and problems of creating something of your own.

As a part of the introduction to a study of the arts, plan lessons and develop projects in which the children work with the materials available to produce their own works of art. The projects should develop over an extended period of time until each member of the class has completed at least one work of which he can be proud.

A class lesson in poetry, painting, or modeling might initiate the work in each medium with all children undertaking a project in the medium presented. Or a general class introduction to two or more kinds of artistic endeavor might be followed by individual and group work with different materials. Such projects require organization so that the time available, the space, availability of materials, and general environment are conducive to doing satisfying work. If easels or floor space for painting are limited, a few children might work at painting one week and others, the next. If only one table is available for clay or wood modeling, the same plan might be used.

Children who want to compose poetry or create a dance may need various kinds of stimuli through music, pictures, poetry books, and discussion. The classroom instruments should be used by children who will work on musical compositions. The finished compositions of individuals or groups might be recorded on tape for later discussion, or practiced until they can be remembered and played at a later time. Some children may complete many different projects, especially those who like to work at such things at home as well as at school.

As projects are finished and the children begin to present their works to the class, allow time for each artist to explain his ideas and the problems he encountered in expressing them. Encourage each one to express his feelings about working in an original way on his own artistic creation. As more of the finished products are presented, help the class to develop criteria for evaluating the works. IS THE MATERIAL OF THE ARTIST (wood, paint, musical tone, movement, words) USED IN AN INTERESTING WAY? DOES IT EXPRESS CLEARLY ONE MAIN IDEA OF THE ARTIST? IS THERE ALSO CONTRAST (VARIETY)? IS THERE SOMETHING ORIGINAL IN THE WORK THAT IS THE SPECIAL EXPRESSION OF THIS SPECIAL ARTIST?

Lullaby

Key: E♭   Starting Tone: G (3)
Meter: $\frac{3}{4}$ $\left(\frac{3}{\downarrow}\right)$
Piano accompaniment on page 198

* EXPRESSION: When the children have listened to the recording of the song, discuss the suggestions in their book. Notice the phrasing (each phrase is four measures in length). Ask the children to read aloud the words of each phrase and notice the idea stated in each. Notice the four musical ideas (phrases) and the fact that all are different. Notice the dynamic marking "*p*" and discuss its meaning. The wide skip to the highest tone in the melody forms a special point of interest, the **climax** of the song. After a repetition of that skip, the melody descends in tonal pattern and dynamics to a quiet ending. After the discussion of the expressive elements of the song, ask the class to listen to the recording again, giving special attention to all that they have discussed. Discuss the piano accompaniment and in another hearing ask children to notice that Brahms' accompaniment moves in a rocking rhythm against the melody (melody tones of the accompaniment are on the "offbeat"—the second half of each beat). Point out that the accompaniment has a melody of its own which makes the song more interesting. (See page 21 for a biographical sketch on Brahms.)

* RHYTHM: The rhythm of the third measure of the song is often sung incorrectly. Ask children to notice that a longer note falls on the important word "good" rather than on the unimportant word "and." (The original German words *"Guten Abend, Gut' Nacht"* are more natural here than the English.) Write the rhythmic notation on the board for the words "Lullaby and good night" and ask the class to chant the words in correct rhythm.

FORM: The song is in **two-part** form because phrases one and two comprise one section of the song and phrases three and four the other section. The design of the two sections might be written A B; the design of the four phrases is A B C C' (C' indicates that the melody is almost the same as C). Each phrase is composed of two melodic "motives" or patterns.

Lullaby

by Johannes Brahms

This lullaby is one of the world's best-known songs. Originally sung in German, it is now sung in many other languages, too.

Lul - la-by and good-night, With ros - es be - dight,

With down o - ver - spread   Is ba - by's wee bed.

Lay thee down   now and rest,   May thy slum - bers be   blest;

Lay thee down now and rest, May thy slum - bers be   blest.

Sing the song with expression. Notice the **phrases.** Each **phrase** is a musical idea. The music and the words help you determine the phrase. How many phrases are in this song?

Record 1   Side B   Band 5.   VOICE: soprano.
ACCOMPANIMENT: piano.
FORM: vocal and piano accompaniment as written by composer.

Which subjects of interest did Brahms choose for this song and for "Lullaby"? What gives special interest to the melody of this song?

The Blacksmith

Music by Johannes Brahms
Words by William S. Haynie

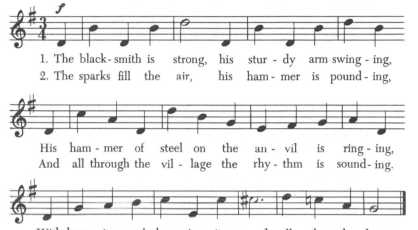

1. The black-smith is strong, his stur-dy arm swing-ing,
2. The sparks fill the air, his ham-mer is pound-ing,

His ham-mer of steel on the an-vil is ring-ing,
And all through the vil-lage the rhy-thm is sound-ing.

With bang-ing and clang-ing it sounds all the day long.
The black-smith has man-y good friends all through the town.

* EXPRESSION: Refer to page 1 and review with the class the subjects of interest found in musical compositions. THE SUBJECT OF THIS SONG BELONGS TO A PARTICULAR TIME AND PLACE. HOW IS IT DIFFERENT FROM THE SUBJECT OF THE LULLABY? (The lullaby is a subject found in all times and places.) Discuss with the children the way in which Brahms arranged the tones of the melody to give a percussive (pounding) feeling that suits the text. (He used wide skips, and returned often to the D to suggest a steady hammering.)

Help the class discover that the continuing series of quarter notes results in a driving, on-going rhythmic sound that could not have been achieved with two notes to the beat or any other division. Give special attention to the accompaniment and the ways in which it gives further interest to the song. Make sure the class sings the song in brisk tempo with full tone appropriate to the style of the song.

MELODY: The melody of the song can be played effectively on resonator bells. Suggest that children sometimes sing the melody without words, on the syllable "ho," in order to enjoy the full effect of the melodic line.

The scale tone D is very important in the song. HOW MANY TIMES DO WE SING HIGH OR LOW D? (12) Brahms makes this tone even more important by changing C, the tone before D in the scale. Notice that in one measure he makes it C sharp. This gives a feeling of pull (resolution) to the D. When the sharp is removed (by the natural sign), the melody seems to pull toward G as the home tone and the melody comes to rest on that tone.

Record 1   Side B   Band 6.   VOICE: baritone.
ACCOMPANIMENT: piano.
FORM: 2 vocals and piano accompaniment as written by the composer.

Liebeslieder Waltzes, Opus 52

BY JOHANNES BRAHMS

BORN 1833   DIED 1897

On a day when books are not in use, play the recording of the two waltzes for the class with only the statement that the music is a set of waltzes composed by Johannes Brahms and sung in German. Encourage children to enjoy the flowing waltz rhythm, the voices, and the sounds of the German words. Conduct a discussion of all that the children heard—probably they will have noticed the piano accompaniment and men's and women's voices. They may be able to notice some of the composer's musical characteristics such as the simple and appealing melodies, the piano accompaniment often moving with two tones to one tone of the melody. After the discussion, play the two compositions at least once more.

Wie des Abends schöne Röte

Later, or on another day, when children are using books, read the page with the class and study each waltz. Discuss the soprano and contralto (alto) voices as women's voices having different ranges and tone qualities. (The contralto voice has a lower range and fuller, richer quality.) The violin and viola might be compared with the two voices. Discuss the accompaniment and help children discover that the waltz is in two phrases (each in two parts) and that each is repeated exactly.

Die grüne Hopfenranke

The title means "The Green Climbing Vine." The waltz is in four phrases. Phrases one and three are sung by soprano and contralto, phrase two by tenor and bass, phrase four by all four voices. The first two phrases are repeated (with different words) and then the third and fourth phrases are repeated exactly. Brahms built the climax in the last phrase by using all four voices and by having the melody reach the highest tone of the song. There is a crescendo leading to that tone and a slight hold in the interpretation of the word on that tone. All these factors are a part of the subtle and expressive melodic climax typical of Brahms' writing.

The waltzes are numbers four and five of a set numbered from one to eighteen. Play the compositions for the class through the year on request, in review, for further study or for quiet listening enjoyment.

Liebeslieder Waltzes, Opus 52

by Johannes Brahms

Johannes Brahms was a master composer of songs. The "Love-Song Waltzes" were composed for voices and two pianos. The German words are well suited to Brahms' rhythm and melodies.

Wie des Abends schöne Röte

This waltz begins with a phrase which means "Like the evening's crimson beauty, wish I to glow with beauty." Listen to the **soprano and alto duet.** Notice the movement given to the rhythm of the song by the use of two notes in the **piano accompaniment** to each melody note of the singers. How did Brahms lengthen the short song?

Die grüne Hopfenranke

This waltz tells of a maiden who cannot be happy while her love is away. Listen to the song. Notice that the first and second phrases are repeated. The third and fourth phrases are also repeated. Notice the waltz accompaniment composed of chords which follow the voice parts. The second phrase is a **tenor and bass duet.** Which voices sing the first and third phrases? The fourth phrase is the **climax** of the song. By what means did Brahms build the climax?

Record 8   Side A   Band 4.
V. Tyler, soprano; R. Sarfaty, mezzo;
C. Bressler, tenor; J. Boyden, baritone;
Gold and Fizdale, pianists.

28

Trio in A Minor, Opus 114

Third Movement

by Johannes Brahms

In the *Trio in A Minor* for clarinet, cello, and piano, the composer Brahms gives us beautiful melodies for instruments. He wrote many compositions for instruments, including four **symphonies**, works for piano, and **chamber music** such as the *Trio in A Minor*.

Listen to the third movement called "Andante grazioso." This is a musical term which gives instructions to the performer about how the music should be played. As you listen to the music, decide what the term means.

Listen again to the music. Can you follow the melody all the way through as it moves from one instrument to another? Which instrument plays this melody at the beginning?

When one instrument plays the melody, the other instruments also play interesting and important parts. Listen for various kinds of accompaniment beneath the melody. Listen for two instruments to join in a little duet. Notice when two instruments play **"question-answer"** passages. Listen for an instrument to play an interesting melody of its own against the main melody. Listen for new notes to be added to the main melody.

Why do we like to hear some phrases repeated near the end of the music exactly as they were played at the beginning?

Record 8   Side B   Band 1.
Sidney Forrest, clarinet
Bernard Greenhouse, cello
Erno Balogh, piano.

Trio in A Minor, Opus 114
Third Movement

BY JOHANNES BRAHMS
BORN 1833   DIED 1897

(See page 21 for information about the composer.) When the children have heard the recording, help them describe the character of the music and the tempo (graceful, moderate) in their own words and then to learn that the Italian word "Andante" is used in music to indicate moderate (walking) tempo or speed. The Italian word "grazioso" means gracefully. Such words are often written by the composer at the beginning of a work or movement to help the players know how it should be played. These words often become a kind of title for the music as well.

The movement begins with the clarinet playing the melody above a plucked accompaniment on the cello and descending chord patterns on the piano. Children sometimes will hear an accompaniment pattern of one chord per measure; sometimes an instrument will play another melody against the main melody. Often the cello and clarinet or clarinet and piano play short duets. A series of "question-answer" passages are presented by the clarinet and cello.

◉

At the end of the first section of the composition, listen for the piano to play a passage leading to a new melody by the clarinet.

The other instruments provide a subdued accompaniment. The second part of the section is characterized by running eighth notes played by clarinet, then cello, then piano. The piano once more plays the new melody.

◉

Children should recognize the return to the music of the first section, introduced this time by the cello with piano accompaniment. The design of the movement is A B A Coda. IS THE SECOND A AS LONG AS THE FIRST? The return to A is less than half as long. The symmetry which the composer achieves by returning to the original material after a contrasting portion is esthetically satisfying and pleasing to the ear. It is not necessary to hear as much of the material the second time because the listener is already familiar with it.

Girl with Lantern

BY SUZUKI HARUNOBU
BORN 1725   DIED 1770

Art from England, France, Italy, Germany, and our own country is what most of us are accustomed to. When we start looking at Japanese art, we begin to think we are looking at something more exotic. The same is true when we listen to Japanese music (as the class will appreciate when they hear the unfamiliar instruments on pages 57, 58, and 59). The reason for the exotic appearance or sound is that art and music from countries like Japan have had long traditions of development that are very different from the European tradition to which we belong. During the last century we have come to learn more about the arts in faraway countries, but it is still exotic to us.

The picture on page 30 is a woodblock print by Suzuki Harunobu. He was one of the great masters of woodblock printing and was responsible for perfecting a method of making prints using more colors and subtler tones than previous artists had used. Woodblock printing is an art medium for which Japan has always been famous. Even now artists go to Japan to study print making.

Harunobu lived in Tokyo and was one of the great artists of a style that dealt with scenes of the fleeting world, that is, everyday scenes of everyday people engaged in their usual activities. Most of Harunobu's prints dealt with young girls in and around their homes.

The print in the book shows a young girl lighting a lantern in her garden. The artist emphasized the girl's delicacy by the use of subtle shades of peach in the girl's robe, her face and small hands, and in the blossoms on the tree. The decorative repeated pattern on her robe, and the pattern made by the flowers show a sense of a small design with a large one.

The exotic quality of the painting is not created simply by the girl's costume or features. The striking black background is something we would rarely encounter in Western art. The kind of off-center balance found in this picture is something we have only recently learned from art such as this.

Harunobu *Girl with Lantern*, The Metropolitan Museum of Art, Fletcher Fund 1929

The songs and instrumental selections in this section are from other lands: Latin America, Europe, and the Orient. As the children read this page, ask them to look through the unit and locate songs from various countries. Find the countries on a world map.

Read paragraph two; look for examples of the various types of songs which are mentioned. Play examples of music from countries which are represented in this section. Talk about the differences in melody, rhythm, instrumentation. Some choices which might be played are "Stodola Pumpa," page 48, from Czechoslovakia; "Vreneli," page 52, from Switzerland; "Koto and Tsuzumi," page 58, from Japan; and "Serranilla," page 65, from Spain.

Look through the book and find examples of music written by composers from various countries. Draw attention to examples of other kinds of art from different countries, including the painting on the facing page, the photograph of the Rheims Cathedral on page 71, the leaf from the choir book on page 88, and the African sculpture on page 117.

As the children discuss the ideas presented on this page, help them begin to realize that people all over the world express similar feelings through music and participate in music in the same ways that we do. The music of other lands can indeed be meaningful to us.

Children may plan a bulletin board display based on the ideas presented in this section. As they study new songs from different lands, ask them to locate pictures in magazines that describe life in those countries. Arrange the pictures with the titles of the songs; group them by the type of song. For example, arrange the titles of work songs with pictures of people working. Invite children to look in other books for songs which are representative of particular countries. Add these titles to the bulletin board list.

Music from Far Away

We like to sing the songs of our own country. We also like to sing songs from other countries, imagining life as it is there. We like to dance to music from different places and learn rhythms and dance patterns other people know.

Different countries have developed music with different sounds. Each country has melodies and rhythms that seem to belong especially to that country. Yet people everywhere have songs of work and songs of play. They sing as they worship. Their songs express love of country and love of home.

Artists often use materials and ideas that they find in their own lands. Their music and other works of art are the result of imagination and of life in the places where they live.

As you explore music of the people and the artists of different lands, look for expression of similar thoughts and feelings. Listen for sounds that are different. Enjoy the music of many places.

The Happy Plowman

Key: G   Starting Tone: G (1)
Autoharp chords in Pupil's Book
Meter: 2/4 (2/♩)
Piano accompaniment on page 202

*EXPRESSION: Review the discussion on page 31. WHAT TYPE OF SONG IS THIS? IN WHAT COUNTRY IS IT SUNG? To answer the second question, help children discover that they may look directly below the title of the song. They will always find the composer or source of the music here. Ask children to read the title and the words to the song to decide that it is a work song. THIS IS A SONG ABOUT WORK; IT MAY HAVE BEEN SUNG BY THE PLOWMAN AS HE GUIDED HIS HORSE ALONG THE FURROW, OR AT THE END OF THE DAY, AS HE WAS RESTING.

FORM: Listen to the recording; discover that there is a verse and a refrain. HOW MANY PHRASES ARE IN EACH? (Two.) HOW MANY PHRASES ARE IN THE ENTIRE SONG? (Four.) WHICH PHRASES ARE EXACTLY ALIKE? (Two and four.) WHAT PHRASE IS ALMOST THE SAME AS PHRASES TWO AND FOUR? (One.)

MELODY: Notice that each phrase is made up of short patterns, or **motives.** Examine phrase one. Find the first motive ("Near a home in a wood.") Compare it with the second motive. ("with a horse very good.") Notice the similarities and differences. Practice singing: 1-low 5; 1-low 6. Ask children to sing the two motives with words. Compare phrase one with phrase two. They begin with the same two motives. Look at phrase three. The entire phrase is made up of two motives. The second motive has the same melody as the first, but it sounds one step lower. This is called a **sequence**.

Play the recording, singing these motives softly as you hear them. Listen to the melody of the remainder of the song.

*RHYTHM: When children have studied page 34, "Let's Explore Rhythm," study the rhythm of this song. Clap these patterns:

Review the relationship of the notes within the patterns to the beat, and to each other.

The Happy Plowman

Swedish Folk Song
Translated by Mrs. Elbert Magnuson

Record 1   Side B   Band 7.   VOICES: soprano, baritone.
ACCOMPANIMENT: woodwind quintet.
FORM: Introduction, *4 meas.;* Vocal, *v. 1;* Interlude, *3 meas.;* Vocal, *v. 2;* Coda, *3 meas.*

When children have studied "Let's Explore Rhythm" on page 34, include some of the following activities in subsequent music classes. Help children become more aware of the function of the meter signature and the relationship of the various notes to each other.

Clap a rhythm pattern one measure long. At first clap patterns made up of two kinds of notes. Put the two notes on the chalkboard; clap the pattern and ask children to notate it. Following are some examples:

Later, clap patterns which are made up of three kinds of notes.

Put the rhythm of the first phrase of a familiar song on the chalkboard. Ask children to notate it several times, each time using a different note as the beat-note. Remember that the top figure of the meter signature will never change. Help the children realize that each pattern will sound the same when clapped because the relationship between notes always remains the same. Here is an example using "All Beautiful the March of Days," page 20.

Play "Add a Note." The first child chooses a meter signature. Each child takes his turn choosing a note for the rhythm. Anyone who chooses a note which makes the pattern longer than a measure must drop out. For example, in 4/4 time:

Child one chooses: 𝅗𝅥

Child two chooses: ♩

Child three must choose: ♩ or ♪ not 𝅗𝅥

Child four begins a new measure or adds ♪ depending on child three's choice.

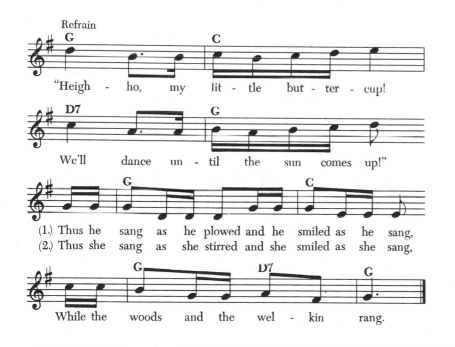

Refrain

"Heigh - ho, my lit - tle but - ter - cup!

We'll dance un - til the sun comes up!"

(1.) Thus he sang as he plowed and he smiled as he sang,
(2.) Thus she sang as she stirred and she smiled as she sang,

While the woods and the wel - kin rang.

Let's Explore Rhythm

Read the directions in the pupil's book aloud and turn to "Donkey Riding" on page 36. Follow each suggestion concerning this song.

Tap the beat:

Tap the accent:

Tap the rhythm of the melody:

Emphasize the fact that the beat is even and regular and sounds continuously throughout the song. The accent also recurs regularly. The rhythm of the melody keeps changing. It may be even or uneven.

In answer to the questions in paragraph three, discover that there are two beats in each group and that the first beat sounds heavy and the second beat sounds light. The regularly recurring accents (the heavy beats) cause the beats to sound in groups. To be sure that children grasp this concept, review other songs which move in twos or in threes. Decide how each moves. ("Lullaby," page 26; "The Blacksmith," page 27.)

Discuss the purpose of the **meter signature.** Stress the fact that one can tell whether the rhythm of a song moves in twos or in threes by listening or by looking at the meter signature.

Emphasize the relationship of the quarter note to the beat by asking children to listen again to the song and clap the beat. ON WHAT WORDS DID YOU CLAP WITH THE BEAT? (Donkey.) WHAT KIND OF NOTES REPRESENT THE RHYTHM FOR THIS WORD? (Quarter notes.) THAT IS WHY THE QUARTER NOTE IS CALLED THE BEAT NOTE IN THIS SONG. IT WILL SOUND WITH THE BEAT.

When children have clapped the rhythm pattern given at the bottom of the page, help them answer the questions. Children should be familiar with the names of the various notes. If not, draw the notes and write the names of each on the chalkboard so that children may review them.

The half note is twice as long as the quarter note.

The dotted half note is three times as long as the quarter note.

Let's Explore Rhythm

When you hear rhythm in music, you hear **beat, accent,** and **pattern.** Listen to "Donkey Riding" on page 36. Tap the beat as you listen. Listen again and tap the accents. Listen a third time and tap the rhythm of the melody. Notice that it is made up of different patterns.

Discuss the difference between the sound of the beat, the accent, and the rhythm of the melody.

Listen again and tap the beats. Notice that they sound in groups. How many beats are in each group? Why do the beats sound in groups?

The grouping of beats in music is the **meter.** You can discover the meter of a song by looking at the **meter signature.** Look at the meter signature of "Donkey Riding." The upper number tells you that the beats will sound in groups of two. The lower number tells you that the quarter note sounds with the beat.

Rhythm patterns are made up of notes of different lengths. Divide the class into two groups. Clap these rhythm patterns while one person plays the beat on a drum.

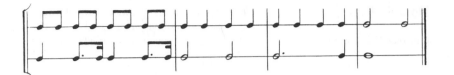

When you have clapped the patterns, answer these questions.

Which note is twice as long as the quarter note (♩)?
Which note is three times as long as the quarter note (♩)?
Which note is twice as long as the eighth note (♪)?
Which note is twice as long as the sixteenth note (♬)?
Which note is three times as long as the sixteenth note (♬)?

Look at the notes of "Donkey Riding." Find some of the patterns you clapped. Tap the rhythm of the song while someone taps the beat.

Cherries So Ripe

Traditional Round

Look for rhythm patterns in this work song. Which of the rhythm patterns above and opposite are found in this song?

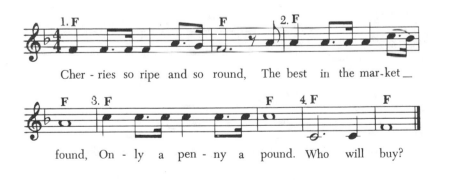

Cher - ries so ripe and so round, The best in the mar-ket _ found, On - ly a pen - ny a pound. Who will buy?

Record 2   Side A   Band 1.   VOICES: children's choir.
ACCOMPANIMENT: piccolo, oboe, French horn, tuba.
FORM: Vocal (unison); Vocal (4-part round); Instrumental (4-part round).

The quarter note is twice as long as the eighth note.   ♩ = ♫

The eighth note is twice as long as the sixteenth note.   ♪ = ♬

The dotted eighth note is three times as long as the sixteenth note.   ♪. = ♬

Cherries So Ripe

Key: F   Starting Tone: F (1)
Autoharp chords in Pupil's Book
Meter: 4/4 (4/♩)
No piano accompaniment

* EXPRESSION: This work song is different from many others. It is a street call that the market women sing as the people walk through the market. Street calls were a primitive kind of advertising! In this work song the music does not help the worker with physical work, as a sailor's chantey might; it helps him do the work of selling his products.

* RHYTHM: Review page 34 as children study the rhythm of this song. Discover that the meter moves in fours. Ask a child to establish a steady beat pattern in fours. Discuss the importance of keeping each beat even and regular. Remind the children that the first beat in each group of four must sound heavier: heavy-light-light light, heavy-light-light-light.

Help children locate various rhythm patterns in this song that are found in the patterns given on pages 34 and 35. To help children be sure that they are clapping the dotted pattern correctly, suggest that they clap a steady sixteenth-note pattern:

Then ask them to clap only on the first and fourth notes in each group. Listen carefully to the uneven pattern. Chant the words of the song in rhythm; chant lightly, stressing the accents. One child may play a steady beat as the rest chant.

* MELODY: Discover that the entire melody is based on 1 3 5 and low 5. Review the placement of low 5. Remind children that 1 can also be called 8. To find low 5, count down from F. The children will readily recognize this as middle C.

When children know the song well, they may sing it as a four-part round.

Donkey Riding

Key: E♭ Starting Tone: E♭ (1)
Autoharp Key: F Starting Tone: F (1)
Autoharp chords not in Pupil's Book
Meter: $\frac{2}{4}$ ($\frac{2}{\text{♩}}$)
Piano accompaniment on page 203

* EXPRESSION: Discuss the paragraph in the pupil's book. Certain engines used at the docks are so small that they have less than one horsepower, so they are called "donkey" engines. This song was sung by the dock workers as they loaded ships. HOW SHOULD THE SONG BE SUNG? Agree that it should be sung with a rhythmic swing and strongly accented to help the workers move in rhythm as they help to lift the heavy loads of ore or lumber.

* MELODY: Scan the melody; discover that the phrases one and two are similar. Notice that the melody moves primarily by steps. Encourage children to sing phrases one and two with numbers. Discuss the differences between the endings of the two phrases. WHICH PHRASE SOUNDS UNFINISHED, AS THOUGH THE SONG MUST CONTINUE? WHICH PHRASE SOUNDS COMPLETE? Agree that the second phrase sounds complete because it ends on 1, the home tone. Phrase one must go on because it ends on the second step of the scale. Review the definition of the term "home tone."

* RHYTHM: Follow the directions on pages 34-35 and study the rhythm.

Donkey Riding

Canadian Folk Song

This work song from Canada is not about a ride on an animal. The "donkey" is the little engine used around docks to haul cargo.

1. Were you ev - er in Que - bec,
2. Were you ev - er in Car - diff Bay,

Stow - ing tim - ber on a deck,
Where the folks all shout, "Hoo - ray!

Where there's a king with a gold - en crown,
Here comes ___ John with his three months' pay,

Rid - ing on a don - key?
Rid - ing on a don - key"?

Refrain

Hey - ho! A - way we go! Don - key rid - ing, don - key rid - ing,

Hey - ho! A - way we go, Rid - ing on a don - key!

Record 2 Side A Band 2. VOICES: men's ensemble.
ACCOMPANIMENT: percussion.
FORM: Introduction, *2 meas.*; Vocal, *vv. 1-2.*

36

The words of this round mean "The broom, the broom, what do you do with it? We sweep the floor!" As you sing, add interesting movements for each section of the song to show the design.

De bezem

Dutch Round

Look at the meter signature. What does it tell you about the rhythm of this song? Listen to the song on the recording. Does the rhythm sound as you thought it would?

Look for patterns of rhythm in this song. Find notes that sound with the accented beats. Notice uneven rhythms that include quarter and eighth notes. Clap the patterns that you find.

1. De be zem, de be - zem,

2. Wat doe je er mee? Wat doe je er mee?

3. Wij ve - gen er mee, Wij ve - gen er mee,

4. De vloer aan, de vloer aan!

Record 2 Side A Band 3. VOICES: children's choir.
ACCOMPANIMENT: clarinet, trumpet, trombone, double bass.
FORM: Vocal (unison); Vocal (4-part round); Instrumental (4-part round).

De bezem

Key: E♭   Starting Tone: E♭ (1)
Autoharp Key: F   Starting Tone:
   F (1)
Autoharp chords not in Pupil's Book
Meter: $\frac{6}{8}$ $\left(\frac{2}{\cdot}\right)$
No piano accompaniment

* RHYTHM: Follow directions in the pupil's book. As the children look at the meter signature, they will decide that the song moves in sixes. When they listen to the song on the recording, they may recognize that it moves in twos. Discuss the fact that music which is written in the $\frac{6}{8}$ meter signature often sounds in twos if it moves at a quick tempo. Practice clapping a $\frac{6}{8}$ rhythm very slowly, so that each beat is heard: 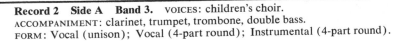 Speed up the pattern, accenting 1 and 4 until it is moving quickly enough to sound in twos.

Discover that the dotted quarter sounds with the accented beats. We might write this meter signature thus: $\frac{6}{8} = \frac{2}{\cdot}$. Notice that the song is made up of two different rhythm patterns:

(Note that each pattern begins on the last beat of a measure.)

* MELODY: This song is based entirely on 1-3-5-8, the tones of the I chord. Practice singing 1-3-5-8-5-3-1. Sing the song with numbers, then listen to the recording to learn the Dutch words.

HARMONY: When the song is familiar, sing it as a round. Children may easily accompany this song on the autoharp, as it uses only the I chord. Suggest that they play the autoharp in an interesting rhythm:

Call John the Boatman

Key: E♭   Starting Tone: G (3)
Autoharp Key: F   Starting Tone:
  A (3)
Autoharp chords not in Pupil's Book
Meter: $\frac{6}{8}$ $\left(\frac{2}{\text{♩.}}\right)$
No piano accompaniment

* EXPRESSION: Discuss the question in the pupil's book. Help the children to discover that some kinds of work are done in all countries; other kinds of work depend on the geography of a country. In this song the steady $\frac{6}{8}$ rhythm, strongly accented, helps the boatmen pull together on the oars. WHY IS IT BETTER TO HAVE THE BOAT SONG WRITTEN IN $\frac{6}{8}$ THAN $\frac{2}{4}$? Tap both patterns:

In $\frac{6}{8}$ meter the rhythm seems to sway gently, suggesting the rise and fall of the boat on the waves.

FORM: Study the structure of the song. Discover that there are six phrases; each two are grouped together to form a complete musical thought. Two phrases which form a complete musical idea are called a **period**. Guide children to recognize that no two phrases are the same.

* RHYTHM: Determine the meter signature and the beat note. Review the discussion regarding $\frac{6}{8}$ meter on page 37. WILL THIS SONG SOUND IN SIXES OR IN TWOS? Probably in twos because it will need to move quickly enough to make a good tempo for rowing. The dotted quarter will sound as the beat note.
Find different patterns of $\frac{6}{8}$ rhythm. Clap each pattern.

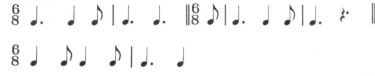

HARMONY: This song may be sung as a round. However, since it is quite long and the melody is complex, children must be very familiar with the melody. Sing it first as a two-part round, later as a three-part round.

Call John the Boatman

English Round

As you study this work song and the one opposite, discuss the kinds of work in different countries. How does music help a worker complete his task?

1. Call John the boat - man, call, call a - gain,
For loud roars the tem - pest and fast falls the rain.
2. John - ny is a good man, he sleeps so ver - y sound;
His oars are at rest and his boat is a - ground.
3. Red rolls the riv - er, so rap - id and so deep;
Well, the loud - er you call him, the fast - er he'll sleep!

Record 2   Side A   Band 4.   VOICES: children's choir.
ACCOMPANIMENT: woodwind quintet.
FORM: Vocal (unison); Vocal (3-part round); Instrumental.

The songs that people sing reflect their way of life and the lands in which they live. This fishing song is from Greece. A fishing song from England is opposite. Find Greece and England on a map. Why would people from these countries sing about work on the ocean?

Sponge Fishing

Greek Folk Song

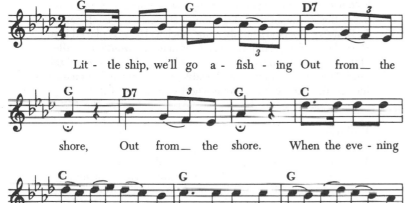

Lit - tle ship, we'll go a - fish - ing Out from_ the

shore, Out from_ the shore. When the eve - ning

bell_ is_ ring - ing, Man - y spong-es we'll_ be_ bring - ing,

And we'll sail for home_with_ sing - ing, O - lo lo

lo, _____ o - lo lo _____ lo.

Record 2 Side A Band 5. VOICE: baritone.
ACCOMPANIMENT: clarinet, bouzoukee, guitar, tambourine, drum.
FORM: Instrumental; Vocal; Instrumental.

Key: A♭ Starting Tone: A♭ (1)
Autoharp Key: G Starting Tone: G (1)
Autoharp chords not in Pupil's Book
Meter: $\frac{2}{4}\left(\frac{2}{\downarrow}\right)$
Piano accompaniment on page 204

Sponge Fishing

* EXPRESSION: Give children the opportunity to express their ideas about the question in their book. People in these countries will sing about work on the ocean because Greece and England are largely on bodies of water. Many of the people earn their living by fishing, working on the docks, or by doing other work connected with the sea.

Compare the two songs, "Sponge Fishing" and "Call John the Boatman." Notice that the latter has a much stronger rhythmic flow than the former. What might be the reason for this? Children may suggest that the Greek boat is a sailboat, and the song does not need a strong rhythm to help anyone pull oars.

* RHYTHM: Listen to the recording; notice the constantly changing rhythm. Discuss the purpose of this sign:  HOW MANY EIGHTH

NOTES DO YOU USUALLY SING DURING ONE BEAT IN THIS SONG? (Two, because the quarter note is the beat note; therefore, two eighth notes will sound with the beat.) WHY DO YOU SUPPOSE THERE IS A THREE OVER (OR UNDER) THIS GROUP OF EIGHTH NOTES? Discover that there are five eighth notes in the measure; the last three have been grouped together to show that they must be sung on one beat. This sign is called a **triplet**. It tells us to sing three notes to the beat instead of singing two notes to the beat. Practice clapping two, then three, eighth notes to a beat:

Look for other measures that have interesting rhythms. Clap these patterns:

As children listen to the recording, they may hear that the word "shore" is held longer than one beat. (Measures four and six.) WHAT DO YOU SEE ON THE SONG PAGE THAT MIGHT TELL YOU TO HOLD THIS WORD? Locate the **fermata** . Review the function of the fermata.

Hary Janos Suite

BY ZOLTAN KODALY (koh'-dah-ee)
BORN 1882

This suite of instrumental compositions is taken from an opera which is often performed in European countries. The opera is based on a folk legend and is more like an operetta than grand opera.

Prelude

The "sneeze" is suggested by the rising chromatic scales played by strings and woodwinds followed by a downward glissando on the piano. The theme is played as described in the children's book. The five-note descending motif, played as described, results in further suggestion of humor. The entire theme is played again by French horns against a shimmering sound of the strings. The oboe and flute play the theme the last time in a quiet statement "now the tale begins." The intervals of the melody, the tempo, harmony, and instrumentation contribute to the mood of mystery.

Viennese Musical Clock

The main theme is played by the woodwinds and French horns. The trumpets and French horns are heard in variations that add humor and excitement. The strings are not used in the composition. In discussion alternating with listening to the music, the class can discover that the woodwind theme is played four times with the brass variations between. The composition is a rondo in the form A B A C A D A with a brief coda.

Most members of the class might stand in a circle representing the face of a clock. As mechanical figures, they might come to life when the main theme begins, doing various dance steps and "tricks" in place. The hands of the clock might be represented by two short lines of children who move forward and backward (clockwise and counterclockwise) in some humorous marching "drills" to the music of the brass instruments.

Another interpretation might be dramatized as children "march" and do "tricks" as they move in four lines in square formation to represent movement of the figures around the tower of the building. The

Hary Janos Suite

by Zoltan Kodaly

Zoltan Kodaly, an important Hungarian composer of our time, based this music on the tales about a Hungarian folk character. In Hungary a person's family name, such as Hary, is placed first. Hary Janos, for whom the music is named, would be called "Johnny" in English. He is a lovable person who likes to tell tall tales. The tales are quite unbelievable, but Johnny always makes himself the hero and everyone who listens is amused.

Prelude

There is a superstition in Hungary that, if a storyteller sneezes while speaking, every word of the story will be true! The prelude is unusual music composed of an orchestral "sneeze" and one little ten-note melody. Listen to the composition and discuss how the "sneeze" is produced by the orchestra. Discuss all the ways in which the melody is played.

Can you hear the theme played in turn by the double basses, cellos, violas, and violins? Can you hear only the first five notes of the theme played by the clarinet, oboe, flute, and strings? What instrument plays the entire theme again?

What gives the music a mood of mystery? How does the music seem to say "And now the tale begins"?

Record 8   Side B   Band 2.
Philadelphia Orchestra,
Eugene Ormandy, conductor.

Viennese Musical Clock

When Johnny went to Vienna, he saw the famous clock on the tower. As you might expect, Johnny's description of it was different from that of anyone else. For him the mechanical figures not only marched around, but they also did tricks!

In the musical description of Johnny's tale, the composer used percussion instruments to imitate the clock: bells, chimes, triangle, snare drums, gong, celesta, and piano. Which group of orchestral instruments plays the main theme? Which instruments play passages that add humor and excitement?

When you know the music, compose a group dance. What formation might you use to represent the mechanical figures of the clock? How will you show the many repetitions of the main theme? How will you make your dance humorous?

The Battle and Defeat of Napoleon

In this musical description, you will be able to hear Johnny's next big adventure. He and his awkward peasant army come upon the French army led by Napoleon. Johnny and his men draw their swords, and the French begin to fall in battle. Finally Napoleon must face the brave and tall Johnny. According to Johnny, Napoleon was shaking with fright and begging for mercy

Listen to the music and follow the story through the interesting use of instruments: the snare and bass drums in the introduction, three trombones to represent Johnny and his men, trombones and tuba sounding the theme of Napoleon's forces, the trumpet call to battle, the mournful funeral music of the alto saxophone.

sections of the music played on brass instruments might then be dramatized by movement in place as children stop the march each time the A section of the music is finished. Some experimentation and discussion should lead to use of imagination in the drama. Movements should be rather small.

The Battle and Defeat of Napoleon

After the class has studied the music, noticing that again the strings are not used in the composition, the boys might develop a comical dance drama. One boy may be Janos, another Napoleon, another the trumpeter who gives the call to battle. Janos and Napoleon will be joined by their "armies." Each army and leader should experiment with ways of marching. Janos and his men should find movements that are awkward and completely out of formation. The other group should have its own characteristic way of marching.

After some preliminary experimentation with movement, the pantomime of the duel should be carefully planned. Make the battle look real by deciding on a position on the stage for each boy. Each might have a battle partner. As the French soldiers fall, they might form a line which moves back slowly. Finally Janos and his men march forward with the funeral dirge as Napoleon and his men back away.

Although some foolishness is inevitable in developing the humor of the drama, suggest to the boys that such acting does, in fact, require great control. As the boys become more and more familiar with the music and as their interest in complete dramatization of it grows, they will develop concentration and acting that is controlled.

An interesting presentation of the entire lesson can be developed by playing the "Prelude" after a verbal explanation by one of the class members and following this with the two dances. The clock music might be dramatized by the girls and the battle music by the boys.

The contemporary Hungarian composer, Kodaly, is one of the most noted of music educators and has spent his life composing, collecting folk music, and devising methods of teaching music to young people. With the composer Bartok, he has done a great deal to preserve true Hungarian music and to bring it to the attention of the world. His choral work "Psalmus Hungaricus" based on a Hungarian text has been translated into eight languages. Many of his chamber works and orchestral works are also well known.

Riding with the Cavalry

Key: D minor   Starting Tone: D (1)
Meter: $\frac{4}{8}$ $\left(\frac{4}{\text{♩}}\right)$
No piano accompaniment

*FOLK STYLE: The melody of "Riding with the Cavalry" is a folk tune. Discuss the differences between this song from Hungary and songs of our country. Notice that there is a little repetition in the melodic line of "Riding with the Cavalry." Some children may recognize that the melody is in minor. The rhythms are more complex than many of our songs.

The accompaniment was written by Kodaly, the composer of *Hary Janos*. He collected many Hungarian folk songs and arranged piano accompaniments for them. He thought the music of his country was beautiful and wanted people everywhere to be able to enjoy it.

Brahms is another composer the children have studied who has written accompaniments for folk songs. Review pages 26 and 27.

*HARMONY: Draw attention to the interesting accompaniment which does not always move with simple chords as we are accustomed to hearing in American folk songs. Discuss the fact that it is sometimes hard to be sure of the home tone. Some children may be able to sense the momentary change to D major at the end of the third phrase. Listen for the accompaniment in the left hand. By the middle of phrase four, the song has returned to D minor.

RHYTHM: Notice the interesting rhythms. In answer to the directions in the pupil's book, measures with even rhythms are 3, 5, 7, and 10. Measures for uneven rhythms are 1, 2, 4, 6, 8, 9, 11, 12, 13, 14, 15, 16. Many measures begin with a short note followed by a longer note. Discuss the fact that most often measures in songs we know begin with a long tone followed by a shorter one (♩ ♪) or by two tones of equal length (♩ ♩). A short-long pattern (♫.) is called **syncopation**. Practice the syncopated patterns. To help children tap them correctly, tap four sixteenth notes: ♬♬

Then clap only the first two of each group: ♬♬ = ♫.

Riding with the Cavalry

Music by Zoltan Kodaly
Words by Beth Landis

This composed song is based on a folk melody. Listen to Kodaly's accompaniment on the recording.

Ya-yi! ya-yi! Head in sky!__ Rid-ing with the cav-al-ry!

1. Hoofs are danc-ing, My horse pranc-ing Proud-ly with the cav-al-ry;
2. Hoof beats are my mu-sic sound-ing Wild-ly with the cav-al-ry;

Rid-ing o'er the land and shout-ing, Ya-yi-yi! We ev-er will be free!
Sa-bre flash-ing, met-al clash-ing, Ya-yi-yi! We ev-er will be free!

Ya-yi! ya-yi! Head in sky!__ Rid-ing with the cav-al-ry!

Study the interesting rhythm of this song.
Find measures in which notes sound two to a beat in **even** rhythm.
Find measures in which they sound two to a beat in **uneven** rhythm.

Chant the rhythms with the words of the song. Clap them.
Play them on percussion instruments.

Azért, hogy én huszár vagyok by Zoltan Kodaly from Magyar népdalok. Copyright by Zenemukiado Vallalat. Reprinted by permission of Boosey and Hawkes, Inc., Sole Agents for Kultura.

Record 2   Side A   Band 6. VOICE: baritone.
ACCOMPANIMENT: piano.
FORM: Vocal, *v. 1;* Interlude, *4 meas.;*
Vocal, *v. 2.*

Listen to the recording to learn the Spanish words to this song about a burro. What else in this song sounds different from songs of other countries?

El burro de Villarino

Spanish Folk Song

1. Ya se mu-rió el bu-rro que a-ca-rre-a-ba el vi-na-gre.
2. Es-ti-ró la pa-ta, a-rru-gó el ho-ci-co,

Ya lo lle-vó Dios de es-ta vi-da mi-se-ra-ble.
con el ra-bo tie-so de-cí-a "A-diós Pe-ri-co."

Que tu-ru-ru-ru-rú, que tu-ru-ru-ru-rú.

Que tu-ru-ru-ru-rú, que tu-ru-ru-ru-rú.

3. Él era valiente,
   él era mohino.
   Él era el alivio
   de todo Villarino.
   Que tu-ru-ru-ru-rú,....

4. Todas las vecinas
   fueron al entierro,
   la tía María
   tocando el cencerro.
   Que tu-ru-ru-ru-rú,....

Record 2   Side A   Band 7. VOICE: tenor.
ACCOMPANIMENT: trumpet, marimba, guitar, double bass.
FORM: Instrumental; Vocal, v. 1; Vocal, v. 1 (singer pauses after each phrase, instruments repeat each phrase); Vocal, vv. 1-4.

El burro de Villarino

Key: A minor   Starting Tone: A (1)
Meter: $\frac{2}{4}$ ($\frac{2}{\quad}$)
Piano accompaniment on page 205

* RHYTHM: Before listening to the recording, ask children to scan the notation and learn to clap the rhythm. Discover that the song moves in twos and the quarter note is the beat note. Find different patterns of rhythm:

Tap the patterns; then tap the rhythm of the complete melody. Listen to the song and learn the melody and the Spanish words. As an aid in learning the Spanish words, the song has been recorded in a special way, the vocalist sings a phrase; it is then repeated without words. The complete song is performed in this manner. When children have listened to the recording carefully several times, they may echo the vocalist during each repeated instrumental passage.

FOLK STYLE: In answer to the question in the pupil's book, draw children's attention to the accompaniment. Listen for instruments that are typical of Spanish music. Notice the rhythm in the accompaniment. Notice the trumpet, guitar, marimba, and double bass on the recording. Listen for the trumpet as it plays the melody on the repeated phrases of the paused version. In verse four the trumpet plays a second melody. Help children decide that this song is different in mood from the Spanish folk song, "San Sereni," on page 178.

Ask children to make up their own accompaniment. Encourage them to do research to determine which instruments (in addition to those on the recording) are typical of Spanish music. The tambourine, castanets, or high-pitched drums would be appropriate.

The words of the song mean:

1. The burro that used to carry
   The vinegar is dead.
   God took him
   From this miserable life.

2. He stretched out his leg,
   And wrinkled his snout.
   With his tail stiff, he said,
   "Good-bye, Perico."

3. He was brave,
   And he was a good burro.
   He was a help
   To all Villarino.

4. All the neighbors
   Went to the funeral,
   Tía María
   Ringing his bell.

Pretty Little Pony

Key: F   Starting Tone: F (1)
Meter: $\frac{2}{4}$ ($\frac{2}{\downarrow}$)
Piano accompaniment on page 206

COMPOSER'S STYLE: Edvard Grieg is often referred to as a nationalistic composer because his music reflects the mood and character of his country, Norway, and its people. He loved the folk music of his country, and his own music often sounds similar to folk music. In the bass part of the piano accompaniment he imitated the sound of the Norwegian Hardanger fiddle. The Hardanger fiddle has more strings than the fiddle we know, and it plays a drone bass in fifths below the melody.

* **FORM:** This is an art song, that is, a type of composed song rather than a folk song. Help the children to recognize that the accompaniment plays an important part in the form of the song. Listen to the **introduction** and to the **interludes** between the various sections of the song. Notice also that Grieg provides a new melody for the final verse, although he uses the same melodic motives. Other art songs are found on pages 28, 74, 76, 162.

EXPRESSION: Discuss ways of singing the song expressively. Experiment with changes of tempo and dynamics, helping children to discover the changes that best express the music and text. Study all marks of expression. (See page 75 for definitions.)

Pretty Little Pony

What other songs have you had like this one? Notice the interesting piano accompaniment in the recording.

Music by Edvard Grieg
Words by William S. Haynie

Edvard Grieg, the composer of this song, lived in Norway. He loved the folk music of his country because it reflected the lives of the people. Many of his own songs are like folk songs.

1. Pret - ty lit - tle po - ny, Come in - to your
2. Pret - ty lit - tle po - ny, You shall have some

lit - tle barn, You shall have a blan - ket warm,—
oats and hay, You have had a long, hard day,—

Pret - ty lit - tle po - ny.
Pret - ty lit - tle po - ny.

You are ver - y tired now, You have climbed the
I'll tell you a se - cret, Would you like to

hills so high, You have walked the moor so wide, My
hear it now? You can rest to - mor - row morn, My

Record 2   Side B   Band 1. VOICE: tenor.
ACCOMPANIMENT: piano.
FORM: 3 vocals and piano accompaniment as written by the composer.

pret - ty   lit - tle   po - ny.
pret - ty   lit - tle   po - ny.

very calmly   *slow down little by little to the end*

3. Dream now   of   to - mor - row, Dream of   all   the

oats   and   hay,   You   shall   have   a   pleas - ant   day,   My

pret - ty   lit - tle   po - ny.

Developing Musical Independence

An important objective of classroom music is musical independence of the individual class members. Independent activities and individual and small group practice are essential in this development. Also essential is willingness of the teacher to provide leadership in initial study of a song or other compositions and, thereafter, to exert less and less leadership. Conducting, although it is occasionally useful, should not be a regular part of the teacher's role in the elementary classroom. It may lead to mechanical singing and too much dependence upon the teacher.

The following questions may be of help as you plan and observe the development of musical independence in your class.

Can class members take responsibility for preparatory steps as well as for performance of a song: can they set the tempo, play an introduction, find the starting pitch? Can they sing songs they know with good intonation, interpretation, diction, and appropriate style without undue reminding? Can they play accompaniments and various kinds of instrumental embellishments?

Do class members know and enjoy songs well enough to sing them outside the classroom? Can they explain to parents with some degree of accuracy and detail what they have learned about the instrumentation and form of an orchestral composition?

Do children who play orchestral instruments sometimes take responsibility for working out a harmony part to play with class singing? Do they sometimes learn to play themes of orchestral compositions for the class?

Are class members developing the freedom and poise necessary to compose an original dance as a part of the music class or apart from it? Can they dance folk dances they have learned, making their own preparation, and with a minimum of organization by the teacher?

Do class members show ability to use the elements of music and various musical devices as they improvise or as they experiment with original musical ideas?

Do children assist in keeping instruments and musical materials in good condition and in a convenient place? Can they prepare the setting for the class music period, making sure that necessary equipment is ready?

Once

Key: C   Starting Tone: C (1)
Autoharp chords in Pupil's Book
Meter: $\frac{2}{4}$ ($\frac{2}{\text{♩}}$)
Piano accompaniment on page 208

Once

Israeli Folk Song

Notice these signs:

| 1. | 2. | How do they tell you what to sing in the first two lines of music?

RHYTHM: Before children follow the instructions in their book, have them study the rhythm of the song. Notice that it is made up of tones that move with the beat, tones that move two tones to a beat, and tones that are held for two beats. Draw attention to the first and second endings. Help children to decide that these signs tell them to sing the first phrase with the words and music under the bracket marked 1. Then they must repeat the first phrase with new words and music. This time they omit the music under the first bracket and sing the music which is included under the bracket marked 2. Notice that the last eight measures are repeated. WHAT SIGN TELLS YOU TO REPEAT THESE PHRASES? (Repeat sign.) Find the repeat signs at the beginning and end of this section: ‖: :‖

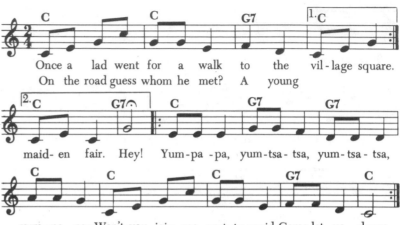

Once a lad went for a walk to the vil-lage square.
On the road guess whom he met? A young maid-en fair. Hey! Yum-pa-pa, yum-tsa-tsa, yum-tsa-tsa, yum-pa-pa. Won't you join me, pret-ty maid, Come let us dance.

Play the melody on the bells. Do you know how to find the bells that you will need? You can find them easily if you know the **letter names** of the **lines** and **spaces** of the **staff**.

Look at the notes of the melody. Find the bells that have the same letter names as the notes. Put the bells in order from low to high. Read the notes and play the melody.

* MELODY: Discuss carefully the ideas presented in the pupil's book. Examine the staff; discuss the fact that each line and space has a specific letter name. Notice that only seven different letters are used. That is because there are only seven different tones in a major scale. (The first and eighth tones "sound the same," therefore they have the same name. To help children sense this, play two C's simultaneously; then play C and B, seven steps above. Notice the difference in sound. The first two tones sound "right" together; the last two are somewhat displeasing.)

Ask the class to name the different notes which are included in the melody of "Once." One child may locate the proper bell as they are named: C D E F G A C. Discuss the fact that only the B bell is missing from the C scale.

Discuss the last paragraph. It is important that children understand that when we say a song is in a certain key, we are saying that the melody is made up of tones from the scale which begins on the letter that names the key.

Review the meaning and function of the **home tone**. Play the recording of this song and others. Ask children to determine the home tone by listening. Point out that they can identify the correct tone because it has a feeling of "rest" and completion when heard at the end of a phrase. Other tones give us a desire for the melody to move on; when we reach the home tone we are satisfied.

This song is in the **key of C** because the melody is made up of tones of the **C scale**. **C** is the **first step** of this scale. **C** is the **home tone** of this melody.

Record 2   Side B   Band 2.   VOICES: baritone, children's choir.
ACCOMPANIMENT: 2 trumpets, French horn, tuba, percussion.
FORM: Introduction, 8 meas.; Vocal; Instrumental (vocal beginning on "hey").

People often sing as they hike. It is one way to enjoy music at play. What other hiking songs do you know? In what other ways do people in different countries enjoy music for recreation?

Holla-Hi! Holla-Ho!

German Folk Melody
Translated by Peter Kunkel

1. Who comes up the mead-ow way?
2. Peo - ple say with twin-kling eyes,
} Hol - la - hi! Hol - la - ho!

Sure - ly 'tis my sweet-heart gay;
Love is blind but age makes wise;
} Hol - la - hi - a - ho!

She goes by the __ o - pen door,
Lit - tle heed I __ when they tease,
} Hol -la - hi! Hol - la - ho!

Must not love me __ an - y - more,
I may love just __ whom I please,
} Hol - la - hi - a - ho!

This song is in the same key as "Once" on page 46. What is the home tone? Which notes make up the scale? Study the notation and find patterns made up of steps of the scale. Play these patterns on the bells.

Record 2 Side B Band 3. VOICES: children's choir.
ACCOMPANIMENT: clarinet, accordion, guitar, double bass, percussion.
FORM: Introduction, *2 meas.;* Vocal, *vv. 1-2;* Coda, *2 meas.*

Key: C   Starting Tone: C (1)
Autoharp chords in Pupil's Book
Meter: $\frac{4}{4}$ ($\frac{4}{\downarrow}$)
Piano accompaniment on page 209

Holla-Hi! Holla-Ho!

* EXPRESSION: In answer to the first question in the pupil's book the children may recall the song "Hiking, Laughing, Singing" on page 6 or the hiking song, "We're All Together Again," which they learned in third grade. Discuss the features which the songs have in common that make them good hiking songs. Both songs in this book move in an even rhythm with the quarter note as the beat note. The melodies have a light-hearted lilt that suggests the mood of gaiety which people often have as they set out on a hike. The children may name many ways in which music is used for recreation. These could include dancing, singing games, boating, etc.

* MELODY: In answer to the questions at the bottom of the page in the pupil's book, agree that C is the home tone; therefore this melody is in the key of C. The melody is made up of these notes: C D E F G A B C D. The first measures of phrases one and two are made up of a step-wise pattern. Play this pattern on the bells. Sing it with numbers, then with words. Listen to the recording and learn the remainder of the song.

* DESIGN: Examine the design of the song. There are four phrases. Each phrase is made up of two motives in a question and answer form. When the class knows the melody, they may wish to sing the song in this fashion. Group I sings the question; group II answers with "Holla-hi! Holla-ho!"

HARMONY: Choose a few children to learn the following descant which may be sung with the last two phrases of the song. The descant may also be played on the bells.

Hol-la - hi,   Hol-la - ho,   Hol-la - hi,   ho!

Hol-la - hi,   Hol-la - ho,   Hol-la - hi - a - ho.

Stodola Pumpa

Key: C   Starting Tone: G (5)
Autoharp chords in Pupil's Book
Meter: $\frac{4}{4}$ ($\frac{4}{4}$)
Piano accompaniment on page 210

EXPRESSION: Talk about what makes this an interesting song. The contrast between the verse and refrain gives variety. The verse moves slowly, with a flowing melodic line; it has a wide range and moves primarily by skips; the rhythm is primarily even. The refrain, in contrast, moves at a quick tempo; the melody uses only a few tones and progresses by steps, with a repetitious rhythm.

SING IN A STYLE THAT SHOWS YOU RECOGNIZE THE CONTRASTING SECTIONS. The verse should be sung in a **legato** style, while the refrain should be sung **staccato,** quickly and exuberantly. Caution the children to be ready to change mood with the "Hey!" which occurs between verse and refrain. It must be short and quick and must not interrupt the rhythm of the beat.

* RHYTHM: Observe that there are two meter signatures, $\frac{4}{4}$ and $\frac{2}{4}$. The movement in fours is appropriate for the verse which moves smoothly. In contrast, the movement in twos is appropriate for the refrain; the strong accents mark the dance rhythm.

Learn the dance that is traditionally performed with this song:

Formation: Partners stand side by side in a double circle facing counterclockwise; girls on the right; partners hold crossed hands.

Verse: Measures 1-6: Walk with slow, sauntering steps.

Measure 7: Drop hands; turn in a circle away from partner.

Measure 8: Join inside hands with partner, strike a pose with outside hands in air, shout "hey."

Refrain: Measures 1-4: Begin with outside foot; heel goes forward; toe backward.

heel toe   step step step hop   step step step hop   step step step hop

Measures 5-8: Repeat, beginning now with inside foot.

heel toe   step step step hop   step step step hop   stamp stamp stamp

Stodola Pumpa

Czechoslovakian Folk Melody
Words by A. D. Zanzig

The refrain of this dance from Czechoslovakia suggests the sound made by the village pump. When the dance is over, the boys pump cool water for the girls to drink.

1. Walk - ing at night a - long the mead - ow way,
2. Near - ing the wood, we heard the night - in - gale,

Home from the dance be - side my maid - en gay.
Sweet - ly it helped me tell my beg - ging tale.

Walk - ing at night a - long the mead - ow way,
Near - ing the wood, we heard the night - in - gale,

Home from the dance be - side my maid - en gay. *Hey!*
Sweet - ly it helped me tell my beg - ging tale. *Hey!*

Refrain

Sto - do - la, sto - do - la, sto - do - la pum - pa,

Sto - do - la pum - pa, sto - do - la pum - pa, pum, pum, pum.

Record 2   Side B   Band 4.   VOICES: 2 sopranos, 2 tenors.
ACCOMPANIMENT: clarinet, accordion, double bass.
FORM: Introduction, *2 meas.;* Vocal, *vv. 1-3.*

48

Let's Explore Melody

Begin on middle C and play a **major scale** on the bells. How many bells will you play? What is the letter name of each bell?

Rearrange the bells and start on F. Play up eight steps: F G A B C D E F. Which bell must be changed to make the sound of a major scale? Experiment until you find the correct bell.

Now start on G and experiment until you find the bells that make up the G major scale.

Only certain bells sound right to you because all major scales follow the same pattern of whole and half notes. You are used to hearing this pattern, and you know immediately when any part of it is incorrect.

Play the C major scale very slowly on the bells. Discover the steps of the scale. Make a chart showing the pattern of whole and half steps for the complete scale.

Play the F and G scales. Say the words "whole step" or "half step" as you play. Notice that these scales follow the same pattern of whole and half steps you discovered when you played the C scale.

Start on D. Follow the pattern of whole and half steps and discover the tones that make up the D scale.

Start on E flat. Decide which tones make up the E flat scale.

Let's Explore Melody

Study the page carefully. Read each instruction and discuss the ideas presented. In answer to the first question, the children will need to play eight bells: C D E F G A B C. Notice that all seven letters of the musical alphabet are used, although not in the usual order, that is, not starting with A.

When children rearrange the bells, beginning on F, they will discover that the fourth step B needs to be altered. Ask the class to decide whether it should be higher or lower. Allow them to experiment until they decide that B flat, a half step lower, is the correct bell. WE CALL THIS B FLAT BECAUSE IT SOUNDS A HALF STEP LOWER THAN B.

Rearrange the bells, beginning with G: G A B C D E F G. Help the children realize that the seventh step must now be altered; this time the tone needs to be higher. THIS NOTE IS CALLED F SHARP BECAUSE IT SOUNDS A HALF STEP HIGHER THAN F.

Before following the instructions in paragraph five you may wish to be sure that the children can hear the difference between whole and half steps. Play C-D, then C-D flat. Discuss the difference. Ask the class to sing whole steps, then half steps from a given tone.

When children have explored the difference in sound between whole and half steps, determine the sequence of these steps which makes up the major scale. Make a chart as suggested in the pupil's book and put it on the bulletin board so that it can be referred to as needed.

1	2	3	4	5	6	7	8
whole	whole	half	whole	whole	whole	half	

When children have made the chart, invite them to begin on the note of their choice and build a scale. Suggest that they can use their ears as well as their new knowledge of whole and half steps to determine the tones of the scale. Turn to the keyboard in the back of the pupil's book and show the class how to find whole and half steps on a keyboard. Two keys which are immediately adjacent will form a half step (G-G♯, B-C, E-F). Whole steps occur when there is a black or white key between any two keys (C-D, D-E, E-F♯, F-G, etc.). Remind the children that in order to find the sharp or flat of a given note, they must move by half steps. They must move one half step to the right for sharps, and a half step to the left for flats.

Swiss Roundelay

Key: G Starting Tone: D (5)
Autoharp chords in Pupil's Book
Meter: $\frac{3}{2}$ ($\frac{3}{\text{♩}}$)
No piano accompaniment

* RHYTHM: Discuss the meaning of the meter signature—the music will move in threes, and the half note will be the beat note. Scan the notation; notice that it often moves with quarter notes. HOW WILL THE QUARTER NOTE SOUND IN RELATION TO THE BEAT? (Two quarter notes to a beat.) Notice that this ♩. ♪ pattern will equal one beat.

Now guide the children to follow the directions in the pupil's book.

* MELODY: As children listen to the recording, draw attention to the melody. It moves primarily by skips. This is typical of the songs of the Alps in Switzerland, Austria, and Germany. Compare it with "Holla Hi! Holla Ho!" on page 47. It is also a yodeling song.

HARMONY: Locate the bells needed for the descant: D F♯ G A B C D. Play the descant; sing it with numbers. Some classes may wish to make up words so that they can sing the descant. Choose individuals to learn to play the descant on the bells. Give them an opportunity to practice alone before playing the descant with the class.

The children can easily learn the autoharp accompaniment for the song. They will feel the natural accent of the song on the first beat of the measure. Help them decide that the autoharp should be played on that accent (unless there is a chord change within a measure). Remind the children that they must press down the chord bars firmly and strum the strings with a sweeping stroke that goes across all of the strings.

Swiss Roundelay

Swiss Folk Melody
Words by Beth Landis

Study the notation and chant the words of the song in rhythm. Listen to the recording. Did you chant the words in the correct rhythm?

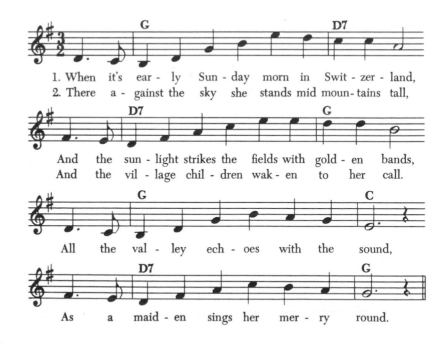

1. When it's ear-ly Sun-day morn in Swit-zer-land,
2. There a-gainst the sky she stands mid moun-tains tall,

And the sun-light strikes the fields with gold-en bands,
And the vil-lage chil-dren wak-en to her call.

All the val-ley ech-oes with the sound,

As a maid-en sings her mer-ry round.

Record 2   Side B   Band 5. VOICES: soprano, men's ensemble.
ACCOMPANIMENT: 3 French horns.
FORM: Introduction, *8 meas.;* Vocal, *v. 1;* Interlude, *2 meas.;*
Vocal, *v. 2;* Coda, *8 meas.*

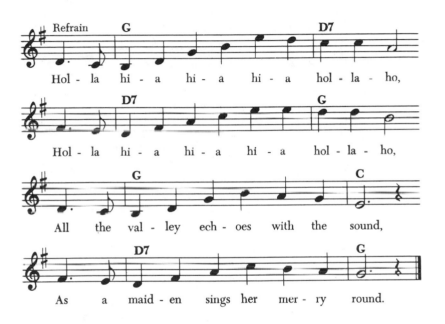

Learn to play this descant on the bells. What bells will you need?

Lyrics from music:

Hol - la hi - a hi - a hi - a hol - la - ho,

Hol - la hi - a hi - a hi - a hol - la - ho,

All the val - ley ech - oes with the sound,

As a maid - en sings her mer - ry round.

Review of Melodic Concepts

Help children become more aware of the function of key signatures and melodic notation. Include some of the following activities in music class after the children have studied pages 49, 54, and 56.

Give children staff paper on which key signatures and the numbers for simple melodic patterns have been placed. Ask them to place the notes in the proper lines or spaces. Then sing and play the patterns. The worksheet might look like this:

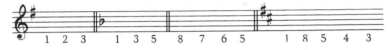

1 2 3   1 3 5   8 7 6 5   1 8 5 4 3

Another time, play simple patterns on the bells or piano using steps or skips based on 1-3-5. Ask the children to write the numbers of the patterns you play. Following are some examples:

Later, some fourth-graders may be able to notate the patterns you play. Write the key signature and the starting tone on the chalkboard; ask the children to complete the pattern that they hear.

Have a "Mystery Tune of the Day." Write the melody of a familiar song on a chart. Put it on the bulletin board. When children know the name of the song (or think they do), they may write the title and their own name on a piece of paper and attach it to the chart. During music time, check to see how many children have identified the tune correctly. One child may choose the next "Mystery Tune."

Play "Melody Spell Down." Divide the class into two groups. The teacher, or a child acting as leader, writes a key signature on a staff on the chalkboard. He then gives the numbers for a three-tone pattern. The first child in group 1 must place the notes in the right spaces on the staff; the first child in group 2 must play the three tones on the bells, or sing them. When a child misses, he must drop out of the game.

Vreneli

Key: E♭   Starting Tone: B♭ (5)
Autoharp Key: F   Starting Tone:
  C (5)
Autoharp chords not in Pupil's Book
Meter: 4/4 (4/♩)
Piano accompaniment on page 212

* RHYTHM: Observe that the rhythm is made up primarily of alter-

nating **even** and **uneven** patterns: ♩♩ and ♩.♪ As one child main-

tains a steady beat, the class may tap the rhythm of the melody. Review the relationships of the various notes to each other and to the beat. Locate the measure where the rhythm moves with the beat. (Next to last measure.) Sing the song crisply, with marked rhythm and clear enunciation so that the contrasting rhythmic patterns can be heard distinctly.

* FORM: This is a dialogue song; the verse is made up of three phrases. Decide which phrase should be sung by the boys, which phrases by the girls. The refrain is made up of short **motives.** A motive is a short distinctive melodic or rhythmic pattern. (See page 101.) Follow the directions on page 53 in the pupil's book for creating harmony.

EXPRESSION: Call attention to the **fermatas** ⌢ at the begin-ning of the refrain. Listen to the recording. Review the function of these signs. They tell the singer to hold the tone longer than the value of the note indicates.

Discuss the musical purposes of the fermata. Help children realize that the lengthening of the tones at this point helps provide a climax for the song. They have noticed climaxes in other songs which were created by dynamics or by the melodic contour. Another way to pro-vide a climax is to emphasize that point by interrupting the rhythmic flow of the melody, as the fermata does in this song. Notice that the climax also occurs at the highest point in the melodic line.

Vreneli

Swiss Folk Song

1. "O Vren - e - li, my pret- ty one, Pray tell me where's your home?"
2. "O Vren - e - li, my pret- ty one, Pray tell me where's your heart?"
3. "O Vren - e - li, my pret- ty one, Pray tell me where's your head?"

"My home it is in Swit-zer-land, It's made of wood and stone."
"O that," she said, "I gave a- way, Its pain will not de- part."
"O that, I al- so gave a- way, 'Tis with my heart," she said.

"My home it is in Swit- zer-land, It's made of wood and stone."
"O that," she said, "I gave a- way, Its pain will not de- part."
"O that, I al- so gave a- way, 'Tis with my heart," she said.

Record 2   Side B   Band 6. VOICES: 2 sopranos, 2 tenors.
ACCOMPANIMENT: clarinet, accordion, guitar, double bass, percussion.
FORM: Introduction, *2 meas.;* Vocal, *vv. 1-3.*

52

Yo, ho, ho, tra - la - la - la; Yo, ho, ho, tra - la - la - la;

Yo, ho, ho, tra - la - la - la; Yo, ho, ho, tra - la - la - la;

ho, tra - la - la - la, Yo, ho, ho.

The boys may sing "yo, ho, ho" each time that these words are repeated. Hold the last tone of each pattern while the girls sing "tra-la-la-la." Listen to the interesting harmony created by the combined tones.

Yo, ho, ho _____ Yo, ho, ho _____

tra - la - la - la   tra - la - la - la

The Symphony Orchestra

Orchestras, as we think of them today, were first heard nearly two hundred years ago, about the time that George Washington lived. These orchestras had only about twenty or thirty members. All the members of the string family were present but in much smaller numbers than are used today. The woodwinds and brasses were also represented in smaller numbers than are used today. Tubas were never found in these early orchestras. The variety of percussion instruments was not great; the timpani were the most frequently used. How different from the orchestra of today with as many as a hundred players and a wide variety of instruments!

Following is the instrumental makeup of a typical modern orchestra.

Strings	16 first violins
	16 second violins
	12 violas
	10 cellos
	8 double basses
	1 harp
Woodwinds	3 flutes, 1 piccolo
	3 oboes, 1 English horn
	3 clarinets, 1 bass clarinet
	3 bassoons, 1 contrabassoon
Brass	4 French horns
	3 trumpets
	3 trombones
	1 tuba
Percussion	Timpani, snare, tenor, and bass drum, glockenspiel, celesta, piano, xylophone, triangle, wood blocks, and tambourine.

All of these instruments are not necessarily heard in every composition. Their use depends on the specific needs of the piece. The percussion section may be expanded by a variety of special kinds of instruments. For special compositions a larger brass section is needed. Sometimes saxophones are added for special effects.

Echo Yodel

Key: G   Starting Tone: D (5)
Meter: $\frac{2}{4}$ $\left(\frac{2}{\text{♩}}\right)$
No piano accompaniment

* MELODY: Before the children read the first paragraph on page 55 in their books, set out the bells G A B C D E F G. Review the activities that the class completed when studying page 49. Help the class recall that the seventh step F had to be raised to F♯ to make these bells sound like a major scale.

When children have played the G scale, read the first two paragraphs on page 55. Stress the fact that this discussion gives them another, quicker way to find the **home tone.** Read the rule (words in bold face) aloud. Look at the key signature. Observe that the ♯ is on the F line, the note which the children have already determined was the one which needed to be altered. Count from the G on the second line to discover that F is definitely the seventh step of the G scale.

Follow instructions and sing the scale with letters, then with numbers. Discuss with the children the fact that the sharp affects all F's, not just the F on the top line of the staff.

1	2	3	4	5	6	7	8	1	7	6	5
G	A	B	C	D	E	F♯	G	G	F♯	E	D

Assign some children to learn to play the melody on the bells. Listen to the recording and learn the words which are in German dialect and mean, "I wish I had you."

At another time, place these key signatures on the chalkboard. Ask children to determine the key of each by applying their rule.

Echo Yodel

German Canon

Study this two-part canon carefully. Find the places where the voices imitate each other exactly and the places where the melodies are different. Follow the directions on the next page and discover the home tone for this song.

Hätt' i di, hätt' i di, Hätt' i di, ja du - li -

Hätt' i di, hätt' i di, Hätt' i di, ja

ri - ja, Hab' i di, hab' i di, Hab' i di, ja du - li -

du - li - ri - ja, Hab' i di, hab' i di, Hab' i di, ja

ri - ja. Hab' i di! _____

du - li - ri - ja. Hab' i di! _____

Record 2   Side B   Band 7.   VOICES: children's choir.
ACCOMPANIMENT: bells.
FORM: Vocal (bells on upper part, voices on lower part); Vocal (voices on upper part, bells on lower part); Vocal (voices on both parts).

In order to play a melody, you must know the scale on which the melody is based. You must discover the **home tone.** To find the home tone, you can look at the key signature at the beginning of the song.

Look at the key signature to determine the home tone. When a **key signature** is made up of **sharps**, remember that

the last sharp in the key signature is the seventh step of the scale. Count up or down from this sharp to find the home tone.

This is the **key signature** for the **key of G. G** is the **home tone. G** is the **first step** of the **G scale.**

Play the G major scale on which the melody of "Echo Yodel" is based.
Sing the scale with letters and with numbers.
Sing the melody of the song with numbers.
Sing the melody with letter names.
Play the melody on the bells.

When they have named the keys, ask them to write the notes for the scales on the staff and put numbers and letters beneath. Play and sing each scale.

```
1  2  3  4  5  6  7  8        1  2  3  4  5  6  7  8
D  E  F# G  A  B  C# D        E  F# G# A  B  C# D# E
```

* HARMONY: This song may be played or sung as a canon. The second part follows the first very quickly (after one beat) so the children will need to know the melody very well before attempting to sing it as a canon. The quick repetition gives the effect of an echo, as though one might be hearing one's own yodel echoing back from the distant mountain. DOES THE SINGER EVER "GET YOU!" AS THE WORDS OF THE SONG SUGGEST? (Yes, at the very end, when both parts sing simultaneously.)

Mon merle

Key: F   Starting Tone: C (5)
Meter: 𝄴 (4/♩)
Piano accompaniment on page 213

RHYTHM: Ask children to learn this song independently by studying the notes. Draw attention to the cumulative verses. Determine how the song will move by studying the meter signature; identify the beat note. Call attention to this sign: 𝄴 It is often used to indicate 4/4 meter. Scan the notation for different rhythm patterns. Ask one child to establish a beat pattern that moves in fours:

𝄴 ♩ ♩ ♩ ♩ | As he taps the beat, ask the class to tap the

rhythm of the melody. Notice the quarter rests. A rest indicates silence in music. The quarter rest receives the same time value as the quarter note. (See page 96 for a detailed discussion of rests.)

MELODY: Follow the same sequence of activities outlined on page 54. Place these bells in order: F G A B C D E F. Ask children to exchange bells to make the pattern sound like the F scale. Discover that the B must be exchanged for B flat. Look at the key signature of the song. Discover that the flat is on the B line, the fourth step of the scale of F. Read the rule for finding the home tone in flat keys.

Follow instructions and sing the F scale with letters, then with numbers.

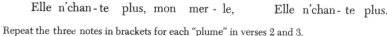

```
1   2   3   4   5   6   7   8
F   G   A   B♭  C   D   E   F
```

When children can sing the melody correctly with numbers and with letters, listen to the recording and learn the French words. They mean, "My blackbird has lost one feather. She doesn't sing anymore." Each verse adds a feather.

Place other key signatures on the chalkboard. Ask children to apply the rule and determine the home tone for each key signature. Find the correct bells for each scale and play them. Put the notes for each scale on the staff.

Mon merle

French Folk Song

When a **key signature** is in **flats**, remember that **the last flat in the key signature is the fourth step of the scale. Count up or down from this flat to find the home tone.**

This is the **key signature** for the **key of F**. F is the **home tone**. F is the **first step** of the F scale.

1. Mon mer - le a per - du une plu - me,

Mon mer - le a per - du une plu - me

Elle n'chan - te plus, mon mer - le,   Elle n'chan - te plus.

Repeat the three notes in brackets for each "plume" in verses 2 and 3.

2. Mon merle a perdu deux plumes,
   Mon merle a perdu deux plumes, une plume,

3. Mon merle a perdu trois plumes,
   Mon merle a perdu trois plumes, deux plumes, une plume,

Play the F major scale on which the melody of "Mon merle" is based.
Sing the scale with letters and with numbers.
Sing the melody of the song with numbers.
Sing the melody with letter names.
Play the melody on the bells.

Record 2   Side B   Band 8.   VOICE: child's voice.
ACCOMPANIMENT: accordion, guitar, double bass.
FORM: Introduction, *2 meas.;* Vocal, *v. 1;* Interlude, *1 meas.;*
Vocal, *v. 2;* Interlude, *1 meas.;* Vocal, *v. 3.*

Variations on "Sakura"

by Kimio Eto

"Sakura" is probably the Japanese folk song best known in the United States and in other countries. Listen to "Variations on 'Sakura.'" After the playing of the melody, tell how many complete **variations** you heard. What changes were made to form each variation?

The composition was written and performed by Kimio Eto, a Japanese musician of the present time. He is one of Japan's finest koto players. He gives concerts in many parts of the world because he wants people everywhere to enjoy the music of Japan.

The **koto** has been the most popular instrument in Japan for a thousand years. It has thirteen strings which can produce great variety in individual pitches and in combinations of tones. The performer sits on the floor and plucks the strings with picks attached to the thumb and first and second fingers of his right hand. With his left hand he plucks the strings with bare fingers or presses the strings to change the pitch. He can produce another kind of sound by gliding his fingers or a pick along the strings.

Record 9   Side A   Band 1.
Kimio Eto, koto.

Variations on "Sakura"

BY KIMIO ETO
BORN 1926

The melody of the folk song is played in its original form. This is followed by three complete variations on the melody.

◉

The first variation is almost twice as fast as the statement of the theme. The accompaniment pattern consists of four notes to each beat.

◉

In the second variation the tempo is the same as the statement of the theme. The melody tones are sometimes changed. Patterns from the original melody and rhythm are sometimes moved to different beats and sometimes appear in the accompaniment rather than in the melody.

◉

In the third variation the tempo is the same as that of the first variation. The melody is much like the original except the last line, which is changed and which leads into a coda or ending for the composition. The coda lends itself to the playing of decorative pitches and rhythms surrounding melody tones, and this is a chief element of these variations.

Children may remember the song from the third grade. Review it with them. In their third-grade book it appeared with Japanese and English words with the title "Cherry Blossoms." Sing it now with Japanese words. Pronounce them phonetically: a (ah), i (ee), o (oh), u (oo).

Sa - ku - ra   Sa - ku - ra   Ya - yo - i   no

so - ra___ wa   Mi - wa - ta - su

ka - gi - ri   Ka - su - mi   ka   ku - mo___ ka

Ni - o - i   zo   i - zu - ru

Song of Itsuki

Tonality: Pentatonic (F G A C D)
Starting Tone: C
Meter: $\frac{3}{4}$ ($\frac{3}{\quad}$)
Piano accompaniment on page 215

This song has been recorded with instruments typical of Japanese music. Help the children identify the koto as it plays on the introduction. (Refer back to page 57 for a discussion of the koto.) Listen to the recording to learn the pronunciation of the Japanese words.

Haiku Poetry

The sea in the dusk
is green, and the sky is green
as a field of rice.

After the bells hummed
and were silent, flowers chimed
a peal of fragrance.

As part of the Japanese unit presented on these pages, these haiku poems might be studied. Japanese haiku poems do not rhyme. Each verse contains three lines of five, seven and five syllables, respectively. The poems are child-like descriptions of small marvels of nature. The translation of these verses provides a basis for discussion of the Japanese love of the beauty of nature. Children should notice the imagery and liveliness of description achieved in few words. They might write some "haiku poetry" of their own.

Song of Itsuki

Japanese Folk Song

A - do - ma Kan - jin Kan - jin An - hi - to
A poor beg - gar am I, poor beg - gar

Ta - cha Yo - ka - shu Yo - ka - sha Yo - ka
here Till days of Bon, But some like you have

O - - bi ___ Yo - ka Ki - mo - no.
O - bi fine and fin - est Ki - mo - no.

Koto and Tsuzumi

Japanese Folk Melody
Words by Beth Landis

This song from Japan names some of the musical instruments of that country. Can you find their names in the song?

O ko - to, ko - to, ko - to, Hear the sound we strum,

O tsu - zu - mi, O tsu - zu - mi, Play up - on the drum.

Record 3 Side A Band 1. VOICE: soprano.
ACCOMPANIMENT: recorder, koto, xylophone, drum, cymbal, temple blocks.
FORM: Introduction, *4 meas.;* Vocal (Japanese); Instrumental; Vocal (English); Instrumental fade-out.

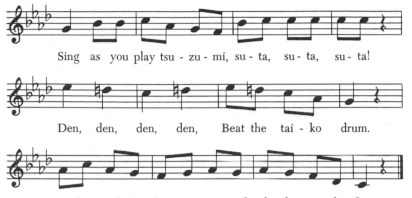

Sing as you play tsu-zu-mi, su-ta, su-ta, su-ta!

Den, den, den, den, Beat the tai-ko drum.

Sweet-ly sounds the sham-i-sen and soft-ly sings the flute.

When you know the song, play this accompaniment.

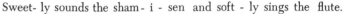

Autoharp

Small Drum — Large Drum

Flute or Bells

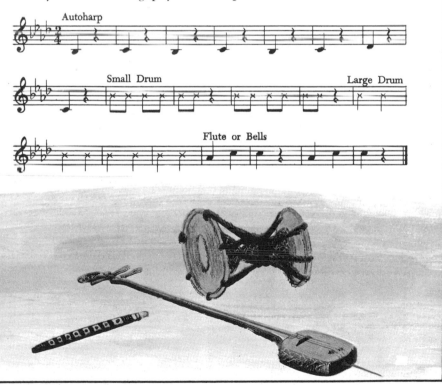

Record 3   Side A   Band 2. VOICES: children's choir.
ACCOMPANIMENT: koto, tsuzumi, taiko, shamisen, bells.
FORM: Instrumental; Vocal; Instrumental.

Based on a pentatonic scale
   Starting Tone: B♭
Meter: $\frac{2}{4}$ $\left(\frac{2}{\text{♩}}\right)$
No piano accompaniment

Koto and Tsuzumi

*FOLK STYLE: The songs on this and the following pages are from Japan. As transportation becomes swifter and as people with the armed forces and with various American companies travel and live in different countries, the world seems to grow closer together. We enjoy living in other countries, learning the people's customs, and discovering such aspects of their culture as music. As the children study Japan's music, stress the fact that although the musical sounds may be different from ours, people in Japan enjoy music and use it in much the same way that we use music in this country: for dancing, for other forms of recreation, for work, and for worship.

The **koto** is a harplike instrument, played horizontally. It has thirteen strings stretched over a sound box which serves as the resonator. The **tsuzumi** is a small, double-headed drum, pictured in the pupil's book. It is usually held over the shoulder or at the knee. The **taiko** is a larger drum with a deeper sound than that of the tsuzumi. The **shamisen** is pictured in the pupil's book. It is a three-stringed instrument which is played by plucking. Flutes in Japan are called **fue.** They are usually made of bamboo.

Authentic Japanese instruments are used in the recording of this song. The song is heard three times on the recording. The first two times Japanese instruments play the accompaniment given in the pupil's book. The shamisen plays the autoharp part. The tsuzumi plays the small drum part and the taiko the large drum part. Japanese bells together with the shamisen play the flute-and-bells part. The first time the song is played the koto plays the melody except for the words "Sweetly sounds the shamisen," which is played by the shamisen. The third time the song is heard, all the instruments play a free variation of the song. This is typical of the style in which it would be played in Japan. Also typical is the clap of the woodblocks which ends the song.

FORM: Study the design of the song. It is made up of five four-measure phrases. Observe that no two phrases are exactly alike in either rhythm or melody. Repetition is more often used in the folk songs of the Western world than in the music of the Orient.

A Good Day in Japan

Tonality: Pentatonic (Db Eb F Ab Bb)
Starting Tone: Db
Meter: $\frac{4}{4}$ ($\frac{4}{\text{J}}$)
No piano accompaniment

* **EXPRESSION:** Read the opening paragraph aloud with the children. Stress the fact that this is not Japanese music, but was composed in the style of the music of that land. It was written by a woman whose husband was stationed in Japan with the United States Air Force. Some children in your class may have lived in either Japan or Europe because their father had been stationed there.

Discuss the fact that visits to other countries provide wonderful opportunities to learn the customs, language, and music of other people. One of the things we discover is that, though the music of other countries may sound somewhat different, it is often enjoyed in the same way that we enjoy music.

* **MELODY:** Before children are assigned individual parts, have the class study the music of each part. Discuss the way the music is set up on the page. The lines above and below the five line staffs are percussion staffs. The four staffs are tied together by a line at the beginning of each score or line of music. This indicates that all parts are to be performed at the same time.

Answer the question in the pupil's book on page 61 regarding the melody. This five-tone pentatonic scale, Db (low), Eb, F, Ab, Bb, Db (high), is typical of many Japanese folk songs. Play the melody on one set of resonator bells.

Discover that the part for bells or piano also uses tones from this pentatonic scale, D flat and A flat. If a second set of bells is not available, play this part on the piano.

Wind chimes are usually available in many novelty shops. If not, the children may play a **glissando,** gliding quickly from one tone to another on the bells or the black keys of the piano. Call attention to the symbol for the glissando (*gliss.*).

A Good Day in Japan

Words and Music by Peg McClelland

In our world of today, faraway places seem very close. People travel quickly from country to country. Some people from the United States now live in Japan. They make new friends and learn Japanese customs, language, and music. This music was written by an American woman who lived in Japan for a long time.

Work in groups of four to perform this composition. Practice each part separately. Play the parts together.

Record 3   Side A   Band 3. VOICES: children's choir.
ACCOMPANIMENT: wood blocks, bells, wind bells.
FORM: Introduction, 4 meas.; Vocal.

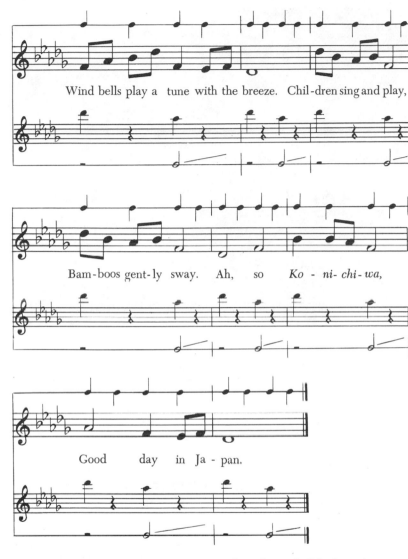

Wind bells play a tune with the breeze. Chil-dren sing and play,

Bam-boos gent-ly sway. Ah, so Ko - ni- chi- wa,

Good day in Ja - pan.

How many different notes are used in the melody? Place the notes in order from low to high and play them on the bells. This is a **pentatonic scale.**

*RHYTHM: Chant the words of the song in rhythm; tap the pattern so that the children have the rhythm well in mind before practicing the melody.

Notice that the wood blocks play on the beat throughout the song. Beats one and three should be high; beats two and four are low. Experiment with the wood block; find two places to tap which produce different pitches.

The bell or piano part plays consistently on every first and third beat. Review the function of the rest.

Strike the wind chimes gently with a stick, or shake them, on the last two beats of each measure.

*HARMONY: As suggested in the pupil's book, divide the class into groups of four and assign each child a part. Give each group an opportunity to practice the composition. When they have prepared it, allow them to play it for the class.

Later, invite individuals to improvise another bell part, using the tones of the pentatonic scale.

O Give Me a Cot

Key: C Starting Tone: G (5)
Autoharp chords in Pupil's Book
Meter: $\frac{3}{4}$ ($\frac{3}{\downarrow}$)
Piano accompaniment on page 216

* **EXPRESSION**: Read the words of this song and "Snug 'neath the Fir Trees" aloud. Discuss the ideas presented in the pupil's book. People like their homes and think home is a wonderful place to be. Ask children if they know any American songs which tell of love of home. Some may recall "Home, Sweet Home."

* **MELODY**: Help children remember, in answer to the question on page 63 in their book, that this song is in C. When there are no sharps or flats in the key signature, we know that the song is in C. Scan the melody; find the places where the melody moves as described in their book, using tones C E and G (at the beginning of each phrase). Discover places where the melody moves by skips using other tones of the scale (measures 3, 10, 14, 19). Find patterns which move by steps (measures 2, 6, 11, 15, 16, 18, 22).

Sing up and down the C scale; sing 1-3-5-8-5-3-1. Encourage children to sing the song with numbers, then with words. Have the class listen to the recording and correct their errors.

Follow the suggestion in the pupil's book. Give interested children an opportunity to practice the melody on the bells. A few children might learn the autoharp accompaniment. A firm stroke played on the first beat of each measure will help establish the strong rhythm of this song.

FORM: Discover that this song is made up of eight phrases. There are only six phrases printed in the book. HOW DO WE KNOW THAT THERE ARE EIGHT PHRASES IN THE SONG? Guide children to locate the repeat sign at the end of the second phrase. Review its function. (See page 46.)

O Give Me a Cot

Welsh Folk Song
English Words by
Florence Hoare

This song is from Wales. The song on page 64 is from Finland. The words of the songs show that the people of both countries love their homes. They think that home is the best of all places to be!

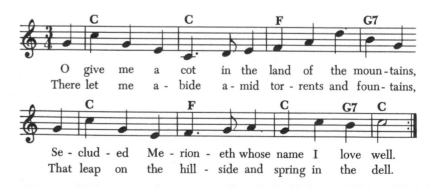

O give me a cot in the land of the moun-tains,
There let me a-bide a-mid tor-rents and foun-tains,

Se-clud-ed Me-rion-eth whose name I love well.
That leap on the hill-side and spring in the dell.

Record 3 Side A Band 4. VOICE: baritone.
ACCOMPANIMENT: harp.
FORM: Introduction, *2 meas.;* Vocal.

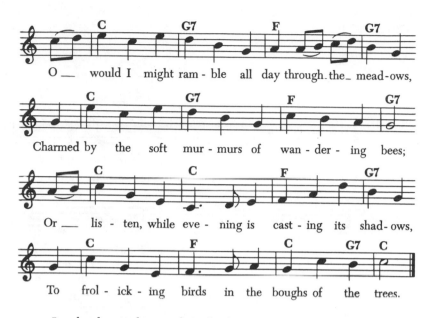

O __ would I might ram - ble all day through. the_ mead - ows,

Charmed by the soft mur - murs of wan - der - ing bees;

Or __ lis - ten, while eve - ning is cast - ing its shad - ows,

To frol - ick - ing birds in the boughs of the trees.

In what key is this song? Study the notation. Notice how the melody centers around C, E, and G which are 1, 3, and 5 of the C scale. Read the notes and learn to play the melody on the bells.

Make New Friends

Traditional Round

1. Make new friends, but keep__ the__ old;__

3. One is sil - ver and the oth - er gold.

Record 3   Side A   Band 5.   VOICES: children's choir.
ACCOMPANIMENT: flute, English horn, bass clarinet, bells.
FORM: Vocal (unison); Vocal (4-part round); Instrumental (4-part round).

Key: E♭   Starting Tone: E♭ (1)
Meter: $\frac{4}{4}$ ($\frac{4}{4}$)
No piano accompaniment

Make New Friends

* EXPRESSION: Read the words aloud and discuss their meaning. WHAT MIGHT THE PHRASE "ONE IS SILVER AND THE OTHER GOLD" mean? (Both groups of friends are valuable and pleasant to have although the old friends are more valuable.) Sing the two phrases lightly and rhythmically.

* RHYTHM: Draw attention to the curved lines which connect the eighth notes and the two quarter notes in the second measure. Ask children to listen to the recording and decide what these curved lines tell us to do. Help the children hear that each of the words "keep the old" are sung on two different tones. THE CURVED LINE IS CALLED A <u>SLUR</u>. IT TELLS US TO SING ONE SYLLABLE OR ONE WORD ON TWO TONES.

* MELODY: Observe the contour of the melody; notice the skips and steps. Study the key signature; determine the home tone (E flat). If necessary, have the children review page 56. Sing 1-3-5-3-1-low 5-1. Sing the song on a neutral syllable; watch for the steps and skips. Listen to the recording to be sure the children have sung the melody correctly.

HARMONY: Sing this song as a round. At first divide the children into two groups. Later the class may sing it as a four-part round.

Snug 'neath the Fir Trees

Key: A♭ Starting Tone: E♭ (5)
Meter: 2/4 (2/♩)
Piano accompaniment on page 218

* **RHYTHM:** Notice the repeated **uneven** pattern, ♩ ♪.♪. Review the relationship of the dotted eighth to the sixteenth (three times as long). Find measures where the rhythm is even, moving with the beat (♩ ♩), moving with two tones to a beat (♫ ♫), or moving in some combination of these patterns (♩ ♫).

* **MELODY:** Review the rule for key signatures as found on page 56. Help children determine that this melody is based on the scale of A flat. Have the children study the notation. DO YOU FIND MELODY PATTERNS COMPOSED OF STEPS, SKIPS, OR BOTH? (Most patterns in the song are a combination of steps and skips.) The song begins with a pattern that is primarily built on 1-3-5. Other tones of the scale occur on the short, unaccented notes (the B flat at the end of measure one). Notice that phrase two moves primarily step-wise. Except for the last two measures of phrase four, phrases three and four are a repetition of phrases one and two.

Discover the **sequence** at the beginning of the refrain. Review page 32 in this teacher's edition for a definition of a sequence.

Using the children's knowledge of steps and skips, invite the class to sing the first two phrases on a neutral syllable, then with words. Listen to the recording and correct errors. Remind the children that, since phrases three and four are almost the same as phrases one and two, they should now be able to sing all four phrases. Follow the same procedure and learn the refrain: sing it on a neutral syllable; listen to the recording; sing the refrain again.

HARMONY: Some children may sing the following descant during the refrain. It may also be played on the bells.

Hoi - la___ Hoi - la___ Hoi - la___ Hoi-la la la

This folk melody was used by the composer Ferruccio Busoni in his *Finnish Folk Songs, Opus 27*, written for piano (four hands). If possible, play a recording of this work and challenge the children to see if they recognize the melody.

Snug 'neath the Fir Trees

Finnish Folk Song

1. Snug 'neath the fir trees my cot - tage lies hid - den
2. Deep in the for - est the song of the cuck - oo

Deep in the qui - et of the Finn - ish wood.
Ten - der - ly prais - es the charm of his mate.

High o'er the tree - tops the moun - tains are loom - ing
Tones of the wald - horn re - ced - ing, re - sound - ing,

Blue in the light of the glow of the morn.
Come to my ears from a - far___ and near.

Refrain

Hoi - la - ri, la - ri, la. Hoi - la - ri, la - ri, la.

Ech - o your an - swer, my Finn - ish wood! wood!

Record 3 Side A Band 6. VOICES: soprano, tenor.
ACCOMPANIMENT: 3 flutes.
FORM: Introduction, *4 meas.;* Vocal, *v. 1;* interlude, *4 meas.;* Vocal, *v. 2;* Instrumental fade-out.

Follow the steps on page 56 and discover the key of this song. Study the notes. Do you find patterns that are composed of steps of the scale? Do you find any patterns that are composed of skips, using 1, 3, and 5 of the scale?

Serranilla

Castilian Folk Song

1. En lo al - to de a - que - lla mon - ta - ña yo
quie - ro a un la - bra - dor - ci - llo que

cor - té u - na ca - ña, yo cor - té u - na flor,_____
co - ja las mu - las y se va - ya a - rar,_____

pa - ra el la - bra - dor, la - bra - dor ha de ser.___ 2. Que
ya la me - dia no - che me ven - ga a ron - dar.___ Con

las cas - ta - ñue - las, con el al - mi - rez

y la pan - de - re - ta que re - tum - be bien._____

Some class members should play an accompaniment as the rest sing. Tap the castanets against your palm playing with the beat. Shake the tambourine in an arc on the first beat of each measure.

Record 3   Side A   Band 7. VOICES: soprano.
ACCOMPANIMENT: guitar, piano, bells, castanets, marimba, tambourine.
FORM: Instrumental; Vocal, *vv. 1-2;* Vocal, *vv. 1-2* (singer pauses after each phrase; instruments repeat each phrase); Vocal, *vv. 1-2.*

Key: F   Starting Tone: A (3)
Autoharp chords in Pupil's Book
Meter: $\frac{3}{8}$ ($\frac{3}{♪}$)
No piano accompaniment

Serranilla

* RHYTHM: Notice the meter signature. HOW WILL THE RHYTHM MOVE? (In threes.) HOW WILL THE RHYTHM OF THE MELODY SOUND? (With the beat most of the time because the eighth note is the beat note in this song.) This song is recorded in the same manner as "El burro de Villarino," page 43, as an aid in teaching the Spanish words.

When children have learned the song, follow the suggestions in their book and add a percussion accompaniment. The almirez (found in the words of the song) is a kitchen utensil which, in this song, is used as a rhythm instrument. It might consist of a pot lid which makes a pleasing sound when struck with a wooden spoon; it could be two spoons or knives struck together. The children may enjoy adding this instrument to their accompaniment. As children make up patterns for the accompaniment, remind them that they must sound in threes, with the meter of the song. When the children have composed their patterns, help them determine the notation.

MELODY: Scan the notation. Discover that the melody is very repetitious. Much of it is based on these two patterns:

5   3   5   5   4   6

Find measures made up of other melodic patterns and practice singing these. In answer to the question in the pupil's book, step-wise patterns can be found in measures 8-9, 10-11, 17-18, 19-20; the skips use only 3 and 5 and are found in measures 1, 3, 5, 14.

Following is a literal translation of the words:

1. High on that mountain
   I cut a reed,
   I cut a flower,
   For the farmer.
   It is for the farmer.

   And who goes plowing;
   Who at midnight
   Comes to serenade me,
   With castanets,
   With the almirez
   And the tambourine that
   resounds.

2. For I love a little farmer
   Who drives mules

HARMONY: Some fourth-graders will be able to play the autoharp accompaniment. The children should practice playing with one stroke per measure.

As the Sun Goes Down

Key: C   Starting Tone: G (5)
Autoharp chords in Pupil's Book
Meter: **C** ($\frac{4}{\downarrow}$)
Piano accompaniment on page 220

* EXPRESSION: Although this is a composed song, it is based on musical sounds that Josef Marais heard in South Africa. The words express the same love of home and friends that we found in the songs of Spain, Finland, and Wales.

Notice ways that the music supports the idea expressed in the words. The first section tells of evening time and the setting sun. The overall melodic movement is downward. Compare this with the melody of the next section, which moves primarily upward. WHY DOES THE MELODY MOVE THIS WAY IN THIS SECTION? (Because the words suggest activity—riding all night.)

* RHYTHM: Draw attention to the meter signature. Ask children to look at the rhythm of the song and decide what this meter signature means. Help them discover the fact that each measure usually contains four beats: **C** ♩ ♫ ♫ ♫ |. The song therefore probably moves in fours. Listen to the song and determine that this is correct. Tap the beat lightly; listen and decide which note moves with the beat (the quarter note). Conclude that this sign **C** stands for the meter signature $\frac{4}{4}$.

* MELODY: WHAT IS THE KEY OF THIS SONG? (C) Ask one child to establish the key of C for the class by playing 1-3-5-8-5-3-1 on the bells. Scan the notation. CAN YOU LOCATE PATTERNS WHICH INCLUDE SKIPS USING 1, 3, OR 5? WHERE DOES THE MELODY MOVE DOWN BY STEPS? Challenge children to sing the melody with numbers, with "loo," with words.

MUSICAL SYMBOLS AND TERMS: Explain the meaning of the *D.C. al Fine*. The children have seen this sign before but may not understand its meaning. WHAT DO YOU THINK THIS SIGN TELLS YOU TO DO? (It tells you to go back to the beginning and sing to the *Fine*.)

As the Sun Goes Down

Words and Music by Josef Marais

I think of my dar - ling as the sun goes down,
I'll see my dear dar - ling as the sun comes up,

The sun goes down, the sun goes down;
The sun comes up, the sun comes up;

I think of my dar - ling as the sun goes down,
I'll see my dear dar - ling as the sun comes up,

Down, down be - low the moun - tain.
Up, up a - bove the moun - tain.

Record 3   Side B   Band 1. VOICE: tenor.
ACCOMPANIMENT: banjo, guitar, double bass, percussion.
FORM: Introduction, *2 meas.;* Vocal; Coda, *2 meas.*

I'll ride, I'll ride, I'll ride, I'll ride, I'll ride all night,

When the moon is bright, When the moon is bright;

I'll ride, I'll ride, I'll ride, I'll ride, I'll ride all night,

I'll get there in the morn-ing.

Building a Lifetime Song Repertoire

The *Exploring Music* series is carefully planned to include a cumulative repertoire of songs and other compositions which will become a lifetime possession of children who study from the books. For this reason, it is suggested that the list below be used as a guide for the selection of songs from Book 3 which should be a part of the children's permanent repertoire.

Ask the children to contribute to the list. They may suggest songs that they particularly enjoyed in the third grade. Challenge them to sing the songs selected from memory.

Carillon
from *L'Arlésienne Suite No. 1*

BY GEORGES BIZET (bi-zay')
BORN 1838   DIED 1875

Play the opening bars of the composition and ask children to listen for the three-tone pattern described in their book. It is played by French horns and harp. As children listen a second time, suggest that they hum softly. Put the bells for the E major scale in order and allow them to experiment until they locate the correct pattern: G♯ E F♯ (3 1 2).

The composer builds his music to a climax near the end of the A section in several ways. The bell pattern becomes more prominent; the French horns are now answered by flute, clarinet, and bassoon. Against this insistent pattern the rest of the orchestra sustains full chords; and the dynamic level increases to fortissimo.

◉ The theme of the B section is announced by the flutes.

Contrast between the A and B sections is created in several ways: the melody of this peaceful, pastoral section is now in minor; it moves primarily by steps over a narrow range, in direct contrast to the sweeping violin melody of the A section. The meter has changed from $\frac{3}{4}$ to $\frac{6}{8}$. The tempo in the B section is somewhat slower; the dynamic level is consistently soft.

◉ The clue that warns of the return of A may be heard in the French horn which appears beneath the flute melody; at first it simply hints at the original bell pattern; gradually the sound becomes more insistent until the tempo and meter of the A section is definitely re-established. Notice that this time the oboe plays the melody originally assigned to the violins.

Little Bells of Westminster

Key: G   Starting Tone: D (5)
Meter: $\frac{2}{4}$ $\left(\frac{2}{\text{♩}}\right)$
No piano accompaniment

The compositions on pages 68-69 have bells as their theme. The recording of this particular song was made on the Laura Spelman Rockefeller Memorial Carillon, Riverside Church, New York City. During the first part of the recording, the improvisation on the tune is played by James R. Lawson.

Carillon

from *L'Arlésienne Suite No. 1*

by Georges Bizet

A **carillon** is a set of bells hung in the steeple of a tall tower and played by means of a keyboard. The earliest carillons had four bells. A modern carillon may have as many as fifty bells.

In Bizet's composition called "Carillon," the orchestra imitates the sound of the bells. Listen to the opening section. The three-tone pattern of the bells is played by the horns. Can you decide which steps of the scale are used in this pattern?

Violins play a melody against the repeated bell pattern.

Notice how the composer builds his music to a **climax** near the end of this section.

Discuss ways in which the middle section contrasts with the opening section. Which instruments now have the main melody? What differences do you notice in the rhythm and the melody?

What clue tells you that the opening section is going to be repeated as the third section of the composition? Do you hear anything new in this section?

Little Bells of Westminster

Westminster is a famous cathedral in London.

Traditional Round

The lit-tle bells of West-min-ster go ding, dong, ding, dong, dong.

Record 9   Side B   Band 1.
Philadelphia Orchestra,
Eugene Ormandy, conductor.

Record 3   Side B   Band 2A.
Carillon improvisation.

Record 3   Side B   Band 2B.   VOICES: children's choir.
FORM: Vocal (unison); Vocal (4-part round—two times).

Learn to play the melody of this round on the bells. When the song is performed as a round, play one part on the bells while the other two parts are sung.

The Bell Doth Toll

Traditional Round

The bell doth toll, its ech - oes roll, I know the sound full well,

I love its ring - ing, for it calls to sing - ing

With its bim, bim, bim, bom, bell. Bim, bom, bim, bom, bell.

This round names four famous cathedrals of France.

French Cathedrals

Traditional French Round

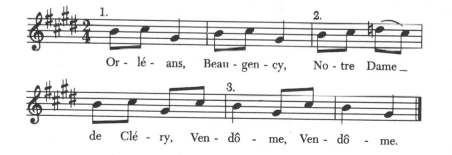

Or - lé - ans, Beau - gen - cy, No - tre Dame _

de Clé - ry, Ven - dô - me, Ven - dô - me.

Record 3   Side B   Band 3.   VOICES: children's choir.
ACCOMPANIMENT: bells.
FORM: Vocal (unison); Voice (twice as 3-part round).

Record 3   Side B   Band 4.   VOICES: children's choir.
ACCOMPANIMENT: oboe, French horn, harp, chimes.
FORM: Vocal (unison); Vocal (4-part round); Instrumental (4-part round).

Key: F   Starting Tone: C (5)
Meter: $\frac{4}{4}$ ($\frac{4}{\quarternote}$)
No piano accompaniment

The Bell Doth Toll

* MELODY: Determine the key signature (F). Discover that this melody is made up of seven different pitches (considering low C and high C as one pitch). Sing up and down the F scale; sing 1-low 5-1. Sing the song with numbers, then with words.

RHYTHM: Scan the notation. Find measures that include uneven rhythms, measures that move with the beat, and measures that move with tones that are longer than the beat. Remind the children that they must sing with a strong, steady rhythm so that the three parts will sound well when sung as a round. Accent the first beat in each measure to suggest the strong tolling of the bell.

* HARMONY: As suggested in the pupil's book, this melody may be performed as a three-part round, with one part played on bells.

Key: E   Starting Tone: B (5)
Meter: $\frac{2}{4}$ ($\frac{2}{\quarternote}$)
No piano accompaniment

French Cathedrals

* MELODY: As explained in the pupil's book, the words of this song name four famous cathedrals. Assign a child to do research and locate each of the cathedrals. Look for pictures of the cathedrals. Discuss their design.

The melody uses only four tones. Some children may notice the

sign (♮) preceding D in the third measure. This is a **natural sign.**

It tells us to sing D natural instead of D sharp as is indicated by the key signature. Practice singing the melody on "loo." Then sing it with words.

* HARMONY: Sing the song as a three-part round. If more than one set of bells is available, this song sounds well played as a three-part round on the bells.

Music and Other Arts
Architecture

As the class reads this page, take time to discuss each idea. Have the children look for pictures of buildings from Mexico, Japan, and other lands. Discuss the ways in which those buildings are different from buildings here. Design, materials, and century play a part in making buildings different. Discuss some of the reasons for the differences. Among the reasons will be geography, materials readily available, tools people had to work with, tradition of design, and engineering skills.

For example, pictures from Mexico may include examples of traditional Spanish colonial buildings, new skyscrapers, university buildings with Mosaic work, ancient Indian pyramids, and even adobe homes. Spanish colonial buildings are usually of stucco with thick walls, high ceilings, and pantile roofs. These help keep the buildings cool despite a hot sun. They also carry on the Spanish tradition in Mexico. The skyscrapers are all recent. They became necessary as the cities grew and space became scarce. They indicate engineering skills and equipment that only recently became available. Discuss the other kinds of buildings, noting design, materials, and century.

Study the photograph of the cathedral with the children. Have them notice the ways the architect achieves unity: the peaked arches of the doorways are repeated over each window: the pattern of the towers is repeated exactly on each side, and so on. Have the children notice the contrasts: circular shapes in the center section, the center spire set apart from the other towers and of a different shape. Ask children to locate smaller climax points in the design.

Review the design of "Carillon" on page 68. Discuss again the definition of an A B A design in music. Compare it to the A B A design of the cathedral.

Study pictures of other buildings: identify those which have a three-part, or A B A design. Look for other buildings which seem to follow other designs which can be found in music: two-part, A B, or rounds, A B A C A B A, etc.

If there are interesting buildings in the community, visit them and study the design of the architecture. Children might also like to draw their own architectural designs. Discuss them in relation to repetition, contrast, climax points, etc.

Music and Other Arts

Architecture

Designs of buildings in other countries are often different from those that you are accustomed to seeing. What kind of architecture would you expect to see in Mexico? in Japan? Look for pictures of buildings from different lands. Discuss the design of each building.

An architect creates his work of art with wood, metal, or stone. A composer creates a composition by organizing musical sounds. Both artists search for ways to arrange their materials in a design that is pleasing to the ear or eye.

Look at the photograph of the French cathedral opposite. Can you find repetition in the architect's design? Notice how the center section of the cathedral gives contrast.

Listen again to "Carillon" on page 68. Notice that the design of this composition is A B A. The design of the cathedral might be described in the same way. Discuss the ways in which each artist arranges his materials to create a good design.

The **three-part form, A B A,** is only one of many designs which architects and composers use in their compositions.

Rheims Cathedral

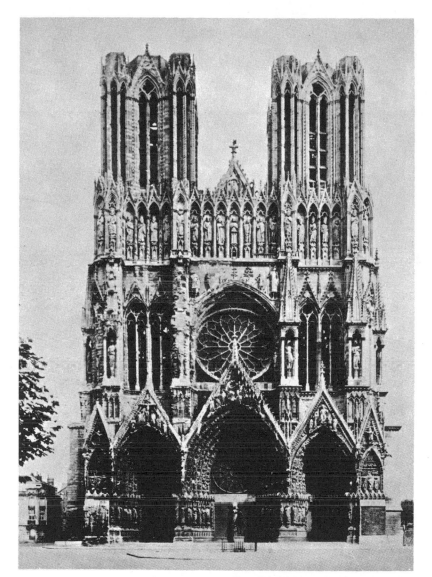

Rheims Cathedral, Courtesy of French Govt. Tourist Office

Rheims is a city about ninety miles northeast of Paris. For centuries it was the coronation place of French kings. When an older church burned down, the people of Rheims decided to build a great cathedral worthy of their kings. Work began in 1211. It continued for about a century. The entire building was not actually completed as we know it until 1430. Although damaged during World War I, it was restored, and is a fine example of Gothic architecture.

The word "Gothic" was first used in Italy by men who disliked the style. They considered pointed arches to be a degenerate form of the arch. They blamed the pointed arch on invading barbarians, such as the Goths. Today, of course, we admire such architecture.

The pointed arch is a major element in Gothic architecture. It is structurally less self-sufficient than the round arch and needs more external support. It is, in a way, a product of the conflict between round and vertical forms.

From left to right, this building has a symmetrical A B A form. From ground to towers it is a study in the interplay of two themes: the round and the vertical.

At the ground level, the piers and statues flanking the doors state the vertical theme. The rounded arches and the circular form over the central door state the round theme. But each rounded arch is topped by an inverted V peak. These peaks direct our eyes to the vertical lines on the next level. Here the structures at the sides have achieved a vertical emphasis by substituting double windows for the ground level's single door frames. These two vertical areas flank a rose window, a perfectly circular structure which strongly brings back the circular theme. But even the perfect circle has a slightly pointed form just above it. Once our eyes move to the next level, the vertical theme becomes dominant. The regularly spaced niches with upright statues emphasize the verticality, and finally in the two towers the vertical theme has won out. This verticality fits the spiritual aim of the building. It raises the eyes upward.

The structure of a building may be likened to that of a musical composition, but there is a major difference. The entire facade of a building is before the viewer at the same moment in time. A piece of music, on the other hand, must be heard serially from beginning to end. Because the cathedral's facade can be before us as a whole, the positions of elements contribute to the degree of emphasis. The magnificent rose window, in its strategic central position, can assert the circular theme with great strength against all the verticality.

Violin Concerto in D Major, Opus 61
Third Movement

BY LUDWIG VAN BEETHOVEN (bay'-toh-vin)
BORN 1770   DIED 1827

Read the first paragraph in the pupil's book. Recall other designs that the children have studied, such as the A B A design of Georges Bizet's "Carillon."

Listen to the A section and answer the question in the pupil's book. The theme is heard three times; it is played twice by the solo violin with only a light string accompaniment; then it is played by the full orchestra.

Before playing the complete composition, give the children an opportunity to become familiar with the B and C themes and to answer the questions in their book. These themes may be located by the two visible intermediate bands on the recording.

The B theme begins with a skip down and up similar to the one at the beginning of the A theme; it continues with many rapid scale passages and arpeggios.

The C theme is more thoughtful and quiet than the other two. The melody is in minor; it is sustained and song-like.

As children hear the complete composition, help them to determine the design and write it in letters as given below. On repeated hearings draw children's attention to additional details in the music: the instrumentation, changes in dynamics, key, variations within the different sections, etc.

A: Theme announced by solo violin; repeated two octaves higher; then stated by full orchestra which prepares the way for the B section with five chords, which grow gradually softer.

Violin Concerto in D Major, Opus 61

Third Movement

by Ludwig van Beethoven

Listen to the last movement of the *Violin Concerto in D Major*. There are seven sections in the design. You will hear three different themes. Each theme is first played by the solo violin.

As you listen to the first section, decide how many times the A theme is played. How are the repetitions of the theme different from the first statement?

Can you tell when a new section is about to begin? Listen for rapid scale passages played by the solo violin during this section. Here is the B theme:

The mood of the C section is different from the mood of sections A or B. Can you describe the difference?

Record 9   Side A   Band 2.
Isaac Stern, violinist
New York Philharmonic,
Leonard Bernstein, conductor.

Listen to the rest of the composition. Do you hear themes you have heard before? When you have listened to the entire composition, write the design in letters. This design is called a **rondo.**

Listen for the **cadenza** played by the solo violin near the end of the rondo. A cadenza is a section which demonstrates the skill of the performer. This cadenza is based on one of the three themes you heard during the rondo. Can you decide which one? Listen for the **trill** which signals the end of the cadenza.

B: Against the main melody played by solo violin, countermelodies may be heard first played by the French horns, then by oboe, clarinet, and bassoon. Listen to the dialogue between solo violin and orchestra; the violin plays double stops, bowing two strings at the same time.

A: Notice that the orchestral statement is slightly altered at the end, to prepare for the C section which is in G minor.

C: Listen for the theme played by solo violin, imitated by the bassoon. Notice the duet between two oboes near the end of the section.

A: As in the beginning.

B: Repetition of original statement; the end is slightly altered to introduce the cadenza, based on the A theme. The cadenza ends with a long trill; underneath it the cellos and double basses play fragments of the A theme.

A: This section is heard in altered form. Notice that the second statement of the theme alternates between violin and oboe. The movement ends with a coda consisting of brilliant arpeggios in the violin and accompanied by syncopated chords played by the entire orchestra.

Mister Urian

Key: A minor and A major
Starting Tone: E (5)
Meter: $\frac{3}{4}$ ($\frac{3}{\downarrow}$)
Piano accompaniment on page 222

* EXPRESSION: Read the words of this delightful song aloud to the children. Mister Urian is the storyteller, a most remarkable one. Children may like to make up more tales for Mister Urian to tell when they know the song.

Read the paragraphs in the pupil's book regarding **marks of expression.** Emphasize the idea that learning to follow the tempo and dynamic markings of a song is just as important as singing the right melody and rhythm. When a composer writes a song, he is trying to create a specific mood. He often knows exactly how he wants the song to be sung. The marks of expression are his directions to the performer. Discuss the meaning of each term given in the pupil's book. Find three of these marks in the music. Listen to the recording. DOES THE PERFORMER INTERPRET BEETHOVEN'S MUSIC AS HE INDICATED IT SHOULD BE PERFORMED? As children sing, remind them to be sure they are observing each expression mark.

Discuss the fact that this composition is written by the same man who composed the *Violin Concerto in D Major, Opus 61,* page 72. Although Beethoven is most famous for his instrumental compositions, he also wrote many songs.

* MELODY: Notice that a new **key signature** is introduced at the refrain. Ask children to listen to the song and decide what difference in sound occurs when the new key signature is introduced. Some children may sense that the melody changes at this point from **minor** to **major.** The first section is written in A minor; the second section changes to A major.

When children are familiar with the melody, one child may be "Mister Urian" and sing the verse while the class sings the refrain.

Mister Urian

Music by Ludwig van Beethoven
Words Translated by Ronald Duncan

This lighthearted song was written by the composer of the beautiful "Rondo" from the *Violin Concerto in D Major* on page 72.

Record 3   Side B   Band 5.   VOICES: tenor, children's choir.
ACCOMPANIMENT: piano.
FORM: Vocal, *vv. 1-6.*

3. Then off I went to Timbucktoo
   With pockets full of carrots.
   I couldn't find a donkey there;
   I sold them to some parrots.
   Refrain

4. Of course I went to Paris, too,
   To eat some frogs and garlic.
   But it was dark when I arrived —
   I dined on dogs in aspic.
   Refrain

5. In Spain I tried to find Berlin
   But found that they had moved it;
   I bought a map of Italy
   Which only went to prove it.
   Refrain

6. From there I went to Pimlico
   To try my hand at crime, sir.
   I landed up at Wormwood Scrubs
   And there I learned to rhyme, sir.
   Refrain

When a composer creates a song, he indicates how the melody, rhythm, and harmony should sound by writing the music in notes. He gives instructions to help the performer create an expressive performance.

The composer gives directions about the **tempo**, or speed, of the composition. He also indicates **dynamics**, or how loudly or softly the song should be sung.

p, piano — soft
pp, pianissimo — very soft
mp, moderato piano — moderately soft
f, forte — loud
ff, fortissimo — very loud
mf, moderato forte — moderately loud

⟶ *crescendo*   gradually growing louder

⟵ *decrescendo* — gradually growing softer

moderato — at a moderate tempo
staccato — crisply, not connected

These directions are called **marks of expression.**

Children will enjoy this poem after they have sung "Mister Urian."

He Thought He Saw

from *Sylvie and Bruno*

BY LEWIS CARROLL

He thought he saw a Buffalo
   Upon the chimney-piece:
He looked again, and found it was
   His Sister's Husband's Niece.
"Unless you leave this house," he said,
   "I'll send for the Police!"

He thought he saw a Rattlesnake
   That questioned him in Greek:
He looked again, and found it was
   The Middle of Next Week.
"The one thing I regret," he said,
   "Is that it cannot speak!"

He thought he saw a Banker's Clerk
   Descending from the 'bus:
He looked again, and found it was
   A Hippopotamus.
"If this should stay to dine," he said,
   "There won't be much for us!"

He thought he saw a Kangaroo
   That worked a coffee-mill:
He looked again, and found it was
   A Vegetable-Pill.
"Were I to swallow this," he said,
   "I should be very ill!"

He thought he saw a Coach and Four
   That stood beside his bed:
He looked again, and found it was
   A Bear without a Head.
"Poor thing," he said, "Poor silly thing!
   It's waiting to be fed!"

He thought he saw an Albatross
   That fluttered round the lamp:
He looked again, and found it was
   A Penny-Postage-Stamp.
"You'd best be getting home," he said:
   "The nights are very damp!"

The Butterfly

Key: E♭ Starting Tone: B♭ (5)
Meter: $\frac{2}{4}$ $\left(\frac{2}{\text{♩}}\right)$
Piano accompaniment on page 224

* COMPOSER'S STYLE: Discuss the similarities and differences between this composed song and folk songs. The subjects are often the same, as pointed out in the pupil's book. The music of composed songs is sometimes more complex, and melodies may be more elaborate, with less repetition. The accompaniments have been written by the composer expressly to support the mood of the words. These songs are sometimes called **art songs** to distinguish them from folk songs.

* EXPRESSION: Listen to the recording of "The Butterfly." Hear the melody which moves lightly up and down over a wide range. Draw attention to the piano introduction. HOW DO THE INTRODUCTION AND INTERLUDE HELP SET THE MOOD OF THE SONG? (The short, quick notes suggest the movement of the butterfly's wings.)

As children hear, and later sing, "The Butterfly," draw attention to the marks of expression. Notice the crescendo and decrescendo marks in phrases three and four. WHY DOES THE COMPOSER DIRECT YOU TO SING GRADUALLY LOUDER, THEN GRADUALLY SOFTER AT THESE POINTS? (Perhaps to emphasize the rise and fall of the melodic line.) WHICH CRESCENDO SHOULD BE THE GREATEST? (The one at "sweeter, ever.") This is the **climax** of the song. Notice that the melody moves in an arc and the rhythm contrasts with the rhythm of the remainder of the song. Melody, rhythm, and dynamics all help to create a climax at this point in the song.

DESIGN: Study the design of the composition. It begins with a five-measure introduction. The first section of the song is composed of four phrases. Phrases one and two are the same, except for one note and a slight change in rhythm. The third phrase is made up of two identical motives, or patterns. Phrase four contrasts rhythmically and melodically with the other phrases. The second section is made of two phrases. The first is the same as the first phrase of the first section. Listen for the **interlude** between verses and the **coda** at the end of the second verse.

The Butterfly

Music by Franz Schubert
Words Translated by Iris Rogers

Notice that these songs are about play, nature, and worship—the same subjects found in folk songs.

1. I dance — in the sun - shine So free - ly and light - ly, And through — wav-ing branch - es Col - ors shim - mer bright - ly. Bright - er, ev - er bright - er, See my wings are glow - ing; Sweet - er, ev - er — sweet - er Scent - ed buds are blow - ing.

2. What joy — to be danc - ing, As care - free I wan - der From morn - ing to eve - ning O - ver hills and yon - der. When the sun is sink - ing, Breez - es mur - mur light - ly; Woods and fields — are — green - er, Flow - ers glow more bright - ly.

I plun - der their trea - sure, And feast — at my plea-sure,

Record 3 Side B Band 6. VOICE: soprano.
ACCOMPANIMENT: piano.
FORM: 2 vocals and piano accompaniment as written by the composer.

I plun - der their trea - sure, And feast__ at my plea - sure.

Music for Special Times

Come, Ye Thankful People, Come

Music by George J. Elvey
Words by Henry Alford

1. Come, ye thank-ful peo - ple, come, Raise the song of har-vest home;
2. All the world is God's own field, Fruit un - to his praise to yield;

All is safe - ly gath- ered in, Ere the win - ter storms be - gin;
Wheat and tares to- geth - er sown, Un - to joy or sor - row grown;

God, our Mak- er, doth pro - vide For our wants to be sup- plied;
First the blade, and then the ear, Then the full corn shall ap - pear;

Come to God's own tem - ple, come, Raise the song of har- vest home.
Lord of har- vest, grant that we Whole-some grain and pure may be.

Record 3   Side B   Band 7.   VOICES: mixed choir.
ACCOMPANIMENT: trumpet, organ.
FORM: Instrumental; Vocal, vv. 1-2.

The songs on pages 77-87 are about special times or seasons of the year. Most of the songs are from Europe. Some are composed songs. The children will enjoy adding these to their repertoire of holiday music.

Key: F   Starting Tone: A (3)
Meter: 4/4 (4/♩)
Piano accompaniment on page 226

Come, Ye Thankful People, Come

* EXPRESSION: Many fourth-graders will be familiar with this Thanksgiving hymn. Read the words together and discuss their meaning.

Listen to the recording. The instrumental is played by trumpet and organ. Point out the trumpet descant during the second verse.

Ask children to decide what marks of expression might be added to this song. Have them listen again to the recording. Give the children time to study the words and the melody line silently. Children may decide that the song should be sung at a moderate tempo (moderato). At the beginning it should be moderately loud (mf). Notice that the melody of the third phrase begins low and gradually moves upward.

Children may decide to indicate a gradual crescendo (————)

for this phrase, beginning with "God, our Maker," and continuing to the beginning of phrase four. The last phrase should be sung loudly (f) because it is the climax of the song.

RHYTHM: Notice the repetition of this uneven rhythmic pattern:

♩. ♪♩ ♩ Find two-measure patterns where the rhythm moves

evenly (measures 7-8, 15-16). Remind children to make a clear distinction between the even and uneven rhythms as they sing the words.

SCORED FOR INSTRUMENTS: This song is scored for band and orchestral instruments. Select instrumentalists and give them time to practice the parts before they attempt to accompany the class.

 Scored for instruments.
See "Exploring Music Instrumental Supplement."

O Savior Sweet

Key: A   Starting Tone: A (1)
Meter: $\frac{3}{4}$ ($\frac{3}{\downarrow}$)
Piano accompaniment on page 228

* EXPRESSION: Assist the children to sing the song expressively and in legato style as directed in their book. Humming the melody as they listen to the recording of the song may help them develop a smooth legato tone. Vocalizing scale or arpeggio tones on the vowel sounds a, e, i, and o may help develop correct singing of these sounds. Remind children that a feeling of tenderness will be expressed in their singing if they think of the meaning of the words as they sing.

* MELODY: Study the melodic notation as children learn the song and help them discover that the legato feeling is derived from the many patterns of *even* rhythm. They should notice that *uneven* rhythm occurs in two measures only (measures 1 and 19). These give variety to the melody and should be sung accurately. The legato feeling is also due to the melodic contour which moves up or down gradually with few wide skips.

Ask children to discover the sequence phrase—a phrase which contains the same melodic intervals as the preceding phrase, but begins on a lower or higher tone. (Phrase three has the same intervals as phrase four, but four begins three tones lower.)

O Savior Sweet

German Folk Melody
Arranged by
Johann Sebastian Bach
Words by Beth Landis

Sing this song in **legato style.** Let your voices move smoothly from one tone to the next. Sing through each phrase with one breath. The vowel sounds are important in this song. Sing each vowel sound clearly.

1. O Sav - ior sweet, O Sav - ior dear,
2. O Sav - ior sweet, O Sav - ior dear,

On this glad day we feel ___ thee near.
Thy chil - dren would to thee ___ be near.

We cel - e - brate thy ho - ly birth
We serve thee best with deeds of love

With thank - ful hearts and joy and mirth,
And ask thy bless - ing from a - bove,

O Sav - ior sweet, O Sav - ior dear.
O Sav - ior sweet, O Sav - ior dear.

Record 3   Side B   Band 8.   VOICES: children's choir.
ACCOMPANIMENT: organ.
FORM: Instrumental; Vocal, *vv. 1-2.*

O Come, All Ye Faithful

Music from John F. Wade's "Cantus Diversi"
Translated by Frederick Oakeley

Sing this lovely Christmas hymn with dignity, as though you were marching in a procession.

1. O come, all ye faith - ful, joy - ful and tri - um - phant,
2. Sing, choirs of an - gels, sing in ex - ul - ta - tion,

O come ye, O come __ ye to Beth - le - hem;
Sing, all ye cit - i - zens of heav'n __ a - bove!

Come and be - hold him, born the King of an - gels;
Glo - ry to God, all glo - ry in the high - est;

Refrain

O come, let us a - dore him, O come, let us a - dore him,

O come, let us a - dore him, __ Christ, __ the Lord!

Record 4 Side A Band 1. VOICES: children's choir.
ACCOMPANIMENT: organ.
FORM: Introduction, *8 meas;* Vocal, *vv. 1-2* (English); Vocal, *vv. 1-2* (Latin).

Key: A   Starting Tone: A (1)
Meter: $\frac{4}{4}$ ($\frac{4}{4}$)
Piano accompaniment on page 230

O Come, All Ye Faithful

* **EXPRESSION:** This processional hymn should be sung with dignity, as suggested in the pupil's book, but in a tempo that allows proper phrasing. Make sure that children understand the meaning of the text. Study the notation of the melody. Notice that the third phrase is the climax phrase of the verse and begins with the highest note in the song. The phrase therefore is sung with more volume and with a special emphasis.

When words are repeated in poetry or songs, the repetitions are often said or sung differently to give emphasis or special effect. Ask the class to experiment with various ways of singing the repeated phrase in the refrain of the song.

RHYTHM: This hymn is used for processionals partly because the rhythm is especially appropriate. Allow children to practice walking as they sing the hymn. Instruct the class to take two steps to a measure with the left foot stepping on the first beat of the measure. Review the rhythmic lengths of quarter, half, dotted quarter, and eighth notes. Remind the class of the importance of singing the rhythm accurately and without changing the tempo when the song is used for a procession.

SCORED FOR INSTRUMENTS: The instrumental accompaniment for this hymn can be treated as a special assignment for a few children. It can be performed in a special Christmas program either for parents or another class.

The children may enjoy learning the Latin words.

Adeste fideles,
Laeti triumphantes,
Venite, venite in Bethlehem:
Natum videte
Regem angelorum:
Refrain
Venite, adoremus, venite, adoremus,
Venite, adoremus Dominum.

En grege relicto,
Humiles ad cunas.
Vocati pastores approperant:
Et nos ovanti
Gradu festinebus:
Refrain
Venite, adoremus, venite, adoremus,
Venite, adoremus Dominum.

Scored for instruments.
See "Exploring Music Instrumental Supplement."

The Yodlers' Carol

Key: F   Starting Tone: C (5)
Meter: $\frac{3}{4}$ ($\frac{3}{\downarrow}$)
Piano accompaniment on page 232

* **MELODY:** Listen to this two-part carol. Lead the class in a discussion of the melody. Have the children look for repetitions of melodic patterns, such as those in measures 9-10 and 13-14. Notice the many skips. When children have listened to the recording several times and discussed the words, ask them to sing the melody softly on "loo." Listen again to the recording, then sing the song with words.

* **HARMONY:** When the melody is familiar, choose a few children to sing the descant. Have the children listen as you play the descant on the piano or bells. Stress the importance of holding the half notes for two full beats. Give the selected children time to practice the descant before they sing it with the class.

FOLK STYLE: The melody for this carol comes from Austria. It was arranged by a contemporary composer. Compare this melody with other folk songs from the same mountainous area in Europe, including Switzerland and Germany. (See "Swiss Roundelay" on page 50 and "Vreneli" on page 52.) Notice that the melodies are often based on major scales with skips using tones from the I and V7 chords. These are typical of the folk music from this part of Europe, as is the yodeling pattern.

The Yodlers' Carol

Austrian Folk Melody
Arranged by Mary E. Caldwell
Words by Mary E. Caldwell

Yodeling is a familiar sound in Switzerland, Austria, and Germany. A composer of our time has used yodeling as a part of this Christmas song.

3. We have found   lit - tle Je - sus,   and we

1. From the   snow - crowned moun - tain mead - ows,   from the
2. Lit - tle   stars shall   be   our   can - dles   as we
3. We have   found him,   lit - tle Je - sus,   and we

kneel   by   his   bed.   The   star   o'er his

green wood - ed   heights,   We   shall   seek   for   the___
jour - ney   this   night___   Ti - ny   dia - monds   in the
kneel   by   his   bed.   See   the   bright star   o'er his

cra - dle,   how   it   crowns   his   head!   We'll sing

man - ger   on   this   calm,   ho - ly   night.   Let's sing
heav - ens___   we'll not   want   for   a   light.   We   sing
cra - dle;   ra - diant light   crowns   his   head!   We'll sing

Record 4   Side A   Band 2.   VOICES: children's choir.
ACCOMPANIMENT: organ.
FORM: Introduction, *3 meas.;* Vocal, *v. 1;* Interlude, *3 meas.;*
Vocal, *v. 2;* Interlude, *3 meas.;* Vocal, *v. 3;* Coda, *3 meas.*

80

"Hol - di - ri - o" for a

"Hol - di - ri - o" for a car - ol sweet and clear,
"Hol - di - ri - o" for a car - ol sweet and clear,
"Hol - di - ri - o" for a lit - tle lul - la - by,

soft lul - la - by. Ah,

"Hol - di - ri - o" as on we go; Then comes "Hol - di - ri - o"
"Hol - di - ri - o" as on we go; Then comes "Hol - di - ri - o"
"Hol - di - ri - o" so soft and low. Now on tip - toe go,

not a sound, home a - cross the snow.

for an ech - o soft and clear, far a - cross the snow.
for an ech - o soft and clear, far a - cross the snow.
do not make a sin - gle sound; then home a - cross the snow.

Children may enjoy reviewing these carols from grades 2 and 3.

Silent Night

Music by Franz Gruber
Words translated by John F. Young
from the German by Joseph Mohr

Silent night, holy night,
    All is calm, all is bright.
Round yon virgin mother and child.
    Holy infant, so tender and mild,
Sleep in heavenly peace,
    Sleep in heavenly peace.

O Little Town of Bethlehem

Music by Lewis H. Redner
Words by Phillips Brooks

O little town of Bethlehem,
    How still we see thee lie.
Above thy deep and dreamless sleep,
    The silent stars go by;
Yet in thy dark streets shineth
    The everlasting light;
The hopes and fears of all the years
    Are met in thee tonight.

Bring a Torch, Jeannette, Isabella

French Carol
Words Adapted

1. Bring a torch, Jeannette, Isabella,
    Swiftly to the cradle run.
   Christ is born, good folk of the village,
    Light a torch that you may see him.
   Ah, ah, beautiful is the mother,
    Ah, ah, beautiful is the child.

2. Gently now the babe is sleeping,
    Mary rocks him in her arms.
   Come, oh, come and see him in slumber,
    Quietly now stand by the manger.
   Hush, hush, see how he sleeps so sweetly,
    Hush, hush, peacefully sleeps the babe.

Jesus the Christ Is Born

Dorian Mode   Starting Tone: E
Autoharp Key: D minor
    Starting Tone: D (1)
Autoharp chords not in Pupil's Book
Meter: $\frac{2}{4}$ $\left(\frac{2}{\text{♩}}\right)$
Piano accompaniment on page 234

* EXPRESSION: Many of our carols come to us from various European countries where they have been sung for hundreds of years. "O Savior Sweet" comes from Germany. "Sing a Merry Noel" comes from France. "We Wish You a Merry Christmas" is English. This carol, however, comes from our own country. It was sung in the Southern Appalachian Mountains where Christmas was celebrated on January 6, the date on which Christmas fell according to the old Julian calendar. Our present calendar, the Gregorian, was adopted in 1752. In some sections of the Appalachians, people refused to change to the "modern" way of counting days and continued for many years to celebrate Christmas on January 6.

John Jacob Niles is a collector of American folk songs as well as a famous composer. There are two performances of this composed carol on your record. The first one is sung by Mr. Niles. He shows the freedom a folk singer takes with a song as he sings in a high key and accompanies himself on the dulcimer, an old folk instrument. The second recording follows the rhythm and melody that appear in your book.

* MELODY: Listen to the plaintive melody; notice that it sounds minor. The song is actually sung in an ancient **mode**, a type of scale that was used for centuries before the **major** and **minor** scales were developed.

Notice the over-all contour of the melody. It moves mostly by skips. The general contour of the first phrase is repeated in the second phrase and again in the fourth phrase. The third phrase is completely different and is the climax of the song.

HARMONY: Add the following descant. It should be sung softly and in legato style.

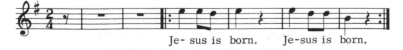

Je-sus is born.   Je-sus is born.

Jesus the Christ Is Born

Words and Music by John Jacob Niles

1. Je - sus the Christ is born,
2. Ye might - y kings of earth,

Give thanks now, ev - ery one.
Be - fore the man - ger bed,

Re - joice ye great ones and ye small,
Cast down, cast down your gold - en crown

God's will, it hath been done.
From off your roy - al head.

3. For in this lowly guise
The Son of God doth sleep;
And see the Queen of Heaven kneel,
Her faithful vigil keep.

4. Two angels at His Head,
Two angels at His feet;
Beside His bed the flower red,
Perfuming there so sweet.

5. Jesus the Christ is born,
Give thanks now, every one.
Rejoice ye great ones and ye small,
God's will, it hath been done.

Record 4   Side A   Band 3A.   VOICE: John Jacob Niles.
ACCOMPANIMENT: dulcimer.
FORM: Vocal, *vv. 1-5.*

Record 4   Side A   Band 3B.   VOICE: baritone.
ACCOMPANIMENT: piano.
FORM: Introduction, *2 meas.;* Vocal, *v. 1;* Interlude, *2 meas.;* Vocal, *v. 2;* Interlude; Vocal, *v. 3;* Interlude; Vocal, *v. 4;* Interlude; Vocal, *v. 5.*

When you know the melody, the boys may sing the part of Joseph. The girls may sing the part of Mary.

Joseph Dearest, Joseph Mild

Old German Carol
Words Adapted

Mary: "Jo - seph dear - est, Jo - seph mild,
Joseph: "I will glad - ly, la - dy mine,

Help me rock my lit - tle child.
Help thee rock the child di - vine,

God will give you your re - ward in heav'n a - bove,"
God's pure light on thee will shine from heav'n a - bove,

So prays the moth - er Mar - y.
As we both rock the ba - by"

Record 4   Side A   Band 4. VOICES: soprano, baritone.
ACCOMPANIMENT: viola, piano.
FORM: Instrumental; Interlude, *1 meas.;* Vocal;
Interlude, *5 meas.;* Vocal; Coda, *12 meas.*

Key: F   Starting Tone: C (5)
Autoharp chords in Pupil's Book
Meter: $\frac{6}{4}$ ($\frac{6}{\downarrow}$)
Piano accompaniment on page 235

Joseph Dearest, Joseph Mild

* RHYTHM: Draw attention to the meter signature. It tells us that the quarter note is the beat note, and that the rhythm moves in sixes. Notice that the same rhythm pattern is used throughout the song: $\frac{6}{4}$ ♩ ♩ ♩ ♩ | ♩ ♩ ♩. | . Discuss the reason for this—it gives a "rocking" quality to the music, thus helping to express the words of the song.

* MELODY: Determine the key (F). Notice that the melody for phrase one and phrase two is exactly the same. It uses primarily 1, 3, and 5. Phrases three and four move mostly by steps. Ask one child to establish tonality by playing 1-3-5-3-1 on the bells. Invite the class to sing the melody on "loo." Remind them to study the notes carefully as they sing, observing the skips and the step-wise patterns.

* EXPRESSION: Sing the song as suggested in the pupil's book. Discuss appropriate tempo, dynamics, and singing style. Sing in a **legato** style. Review the meaning of this word (see page 78, "O Savior Sweet").

Sing a Merry Noel

Key D: Starting Tone: F# (3)

Meter: $\frac{6}{8}$ ($\frac{2}{}$) $\frac{9}{8}$ ($\frac{3}{}$)

Piano accompaniment on page 237

*EXPRESSION: Many of the ancient carols were dance songs, as the words of this song suggest. The Christmas season was a time for rejoicing, and dances were an important part of the celebration. WHAT IN THIS MUSIC SUGGESTS THAT THIS IS A GOOD SONG FOR DANCING? Children may respond with suggestions that the uneven rhythm, the lilting melody and sprightly tempo make this a danceable song.

*RHYTHM: Observe that there are two meter signatures in this song. Discuss the differences. In $\frac{6}{8}$ time there will be two strong pulses per measure (♩. ♩.); in $\frac{9}{8}$ time there will be three strong pulses (♩. ♩. ♩.). Someone may tap these accented beats on a tambourine while the class lightly whispers the words. Enjoy the sound of the interesting rhythm. Remind children to pay careful attention to the dotted rhythms.

HARMONY: The children may enjoy playing their own percussion accompaniment for this song. Following are some suggested patterns used on the recording:

See pages 89a to 89d for a discussion of ancient instruments.

Sing a Merry Noel

French Folk Carol
Words by Beth Landis

This carol comes from a place near the Mediterranean Sea. The people there have many lovely songs and dances. Learn this carol and make up a dance.

Refrain

Danc - ing and play - ing make mer - ry your sing - ing,

Danc - ing and play - ing this glad Christ - mas Day.

Sing a mer - ry no - el, Sing a mer - ry no - el!

Verse

1. Sing to the Child as he peace - ful - ly slum - bers,
2. Play on your drum as you dance for the moth - er,

Sing a sweet song to the moth - er and child.
Play on your flute as the lit - tle one smiles.

Record 4 Side A Band 5. VOICES: soprano, tenor.
ACCOMPANIMENT: 2 recorders, viola da gamba, regal organ, hand bells, drum, tambourine, triangle.
FORM: Instrumental; Vocal, vv. 1-2.

We Wish You a Merry Christmas

English Folk Song

We wish you a mer-ry Christ-mas, we wish you a mer-ry Christ-mas,

Fine

We wish you a mer-ry Christ-mas and a hap-py New Year.

Good tid - ings we bring for you and your kin:

Good tid - ings of Christ - mas and a hap - py New Year.

1. Now bring us some fig - gy pud - ding, now
2. We won't go un - til we get some, we

bring us some fig - gy pud - ding, Now
won't go un - til we get some, We

(after verse 2, D.C. al Fine)

bring us some fig - gy pud - ding, and bring some right here.
won't go un - til we get some, so bring some right here.

Record 4 Side A Band 6. VOICES: children's choir.
ACCOMPANIMENT: string quartet.
FORM: Introduction, *8 meas.;* Vocal, *vv. 1-2.*

Key: A♭ Starting Tone: E♭ (5)
Meter: 3/4 (♩)
Piano accompaniment on page 239

We Wish You a Merry Christmas

* EXPRESSION: The custom of caroling comes to us from England. Children may wish to tell of times when they have gone caroling. The children may plan to carol for the other classrooms in their school. They might look for pictures of English caroling groups and plan simple costumes.

Discuss the words of the verses. "Figgy pudding" (fig or plum pudding) was an English delicacy, traditionally served at Christmas time. As the words suggest, the carolers would refuse to leave until they had been fed or rewarded with gifts of money.

* DESIGN: Observe the design of the song. Notice that the refrain, "We wish you a Merry Christmas," is sung at the beginning and again at the end of the second verse. Compare the melody of the first and third sections with the melody of the contrasting middle section. Notice the difference in rhythm. This section should be sung at a slightly slower tempo, and more smoothly.

Cuckoo Carol

Key: F   Starting Tone: C (5)
Meter: 3/4 (3/♩)
Piano accompaniment on page 240

* MELODY: Examine the melodic notation of this carol from Czechoslovakia. Find patterns in the melody which use the tones of the I chord, F-A-C (measures 1, 3, 5, 7, 9, 11, 12, 13, 15, 16, 17, 19). Ask the children to locate the many repetitions of melodic patterns which occur in the melody. Establish tonality and sing the song lightly on "loo." Omit the echo patterns (those marked "*p*"). Sing the song with words. Then choose a few people to be the "echo." They should sing the "cuckoo" pattern marked "*p*" and the last two measures of the song.

* EXPRESSION: When children know the melody, read the paragraph which is in their book concerning marks of expression. Help children recall that "*p*" means "soft" and "*f*" means "loud." Have the children return to page 75 for a review of expression marks. Help the children pronounce the Italian words for "*p*," "*f*," "*mp*," and "*pp*." Remind the children to follow the expression marks for this song carefully, so that the echo is truly an echo.

HARMONY: When children have learned to play the echo on the bells, suggest that they add the echo ("cuckoo") pattern as an accompaniment throughout the song. Play on the first beat of every other measure:

Cuckoo Carol

Czechoslovakian Carol

1. Walk-ing a-long the road, I bear a hap-py load;
2. Wise Men who came from far, Guid-ed by one bright star,

One cuck-oo do I to the Christ Child take,
Bring on their cam-els won-d'rous gifts for you:

This will a pret-ty pres-ent for him make,
Myrrh, frank-in-cense, and gold of shin-ing hue;

This bring I for his sake.)
Glad shep-herds came — too.)

Refrain
Cuck-oo, Cuck-oo, Cuck-oo, Cuck-oo!

Oh, from your bas-ket
Oh, Christ Child, like my

Record 4   Side A   Band 7.   VOICE: soprano.
ACCOMPANIMENT: flute, oboe, clarinet, French horn.
FORM: Instrumental; Vocal, *vv. 1-2.*

don't es - cape, ⎫
gift the best, ⎬   Cuck- oo,   Cuck-oo, Cuck-oo,   Cuck-oo!

Hap - py   the Christ Child will   a - wake,
Soft   let   your fin - gers on   him rest,

Hap - py   the Christ Child will   a - wake.
Soft   let   your fin - gers on   him rest.

Pay careful attention to the marks of expression as you sing
this song. What do *p* and *f* mean?

Here are other marks of expression.
mp, moderato piano — moderately soft
pp, pianissimo — very soft

Notice how the expression marks help to give the effect of an
echo. Learn to play the "echo" section on the bells.

Children may enjoy reviewing the following carols, which they
learned in third grade. Remember that "Christmas Is Here" is a
three-part round.

Christmas Is Here

Christmas is here,
Best time of year,
When we remember all our
Friends far and near.

Deck the Halls

1. Deck the halls with boughs of holly, Fa la la la la la la la la.
   'Tis the season to be jolly, Fa la la . . . .
   Don we now our gay apparel, Fa la la . . . .
   Troll the ancient Yuletide carol, Fa la la . . . .

2. See the blazing Yule before us, Fa la la la la la la la la.
   Strike the harp and join the chorus, Fa la la . . . .
   Follow me in merry measure, Fa la la . . . .
   While I tell of Yuletide treasure, Fa la la . . . .

3. Fast away the old year passes, Fa la la la la la la la la.
   Hail the new, ye lads and lasses, Fa la la . . . .
   Sing we joyous all together, Fa la la . . . .
   Heedless of the wind and weather, Fa la la . . . .

Complete leaf from a Fifteenth-Century choir book

The photograph shows a leaf from a book almost three feet high which was used by church choirs in the fifteenth century. Because early books had to be laboriously written by hand, they were valuable and scarce. One large book placed high on a stand had to serve for the entire choir.

The monks who copied the music prided themselves on the beauty of their art work. The first letters of words at the beginning of each chant were elaborately ornamented, sometimes even with miniature paintings of religious scenes or historical events and persons. This system of notation used neumes, variously shaped notes grouped to indicate melodic contour and vocal production. (In reading the vertical two-note groups, the lower note is sung first.) At the beginning of each four-line staff is an early version of an F clef. There were also clefs to indicate C and G; all of the clef signs originated from the use of the old Gothic letters for these pitches. The notes with tails at the end of each staff show what the first notes will be on the next line.

Today Gregorian chant sung in the Roman Catholic Church continues to be written in notation employing neumes on a four-line staff.

Complete leaf from a fifteenth century choir book, Lombardy, C. 1450, Courtesy of Buryl A. Red

Music of Long Ago

People of all times have similar thoughts and feelings which they express in music. People of each generation have songs of work and of play. Since primitive times, people have sung in worship. They have always expressed their love of home and country in music.

The music of the composer is based on musical ideas and designs known in his time. The composer's music includes new ideas found in the musical explorations of his day. The music of the people and of the composer is passed on to the next generation.

We enjoy music of different times by noticing the special musical sounds and designs. The dances of Hindemith (which you will study on page 182) do not sound like the dances of Bach. The music of Kodaly does not sound like that of Brahms. In each period of history, special musical ideas have been developed. As you study, you can trace the story of man through his music.

As you explore music of long ago, imagine the life of people from their folk songs. Discover ways in which the composers used rhythm, melody, and harmony in their compositions. Hear the sounds of the instruments first used in former times.

Read the page with the class and conduct a discussion of the ideas written there. From the songs in the book, find examples of similar thoughts and feelings which people have expressed in music. These examples might include sailor songs of different times and places, pages 18, 99, 100; hiking songs of different times and places, pages 6, 148, 165; songs of worship of people of different times and religions, pages 20, 78, 128, 134. Listen to the recordings of a few of the songs children have not yet learned and listen for the special sounds of music of the people of different times. Discuss the life of the people as it might be imagined from such songs as "Yangtze Boatman's Chantey," page 5, "The Blacksmith," page 27, "Riding with the Cavalry," page 42, and "Swiss Roundelay," page 50.

In the next lesson, read the page again and give special attention to composed music in relation to periods of time. Play all or part of the Hindemith "Fugue and Three Old-Fashioned Dances" and the Bach "Gavotte." Ask children to compare the sounds of a composition by a present-day composer with those of a composition by Bach who lived nearly three hundred years ago. In comparing the two dances, help the children to analyze differences in the use of melody, differences in rhythm and harmony, and the differences in the use of instruments. Play all or part of "The Battle and Defeat of Napoleon" from *Hary Janos Suite* by Kodaly and the third movement from *Trio in A Minor* by Brahms, as examples of twentieth-century and nineteenth-century compositions.

In comparing the Kodaly and Brahms, again consider the harmony. Consider musical design, noting that Brahms used considerable repetition while Kodaly's materials change frequently. Consider how the people of Brahms' time might have felt about the Kodaly composition. Not all the characteristics the children will mention are dependent solely on a consideration of the period in which the composer worked. A composer's style is a result of his conscious or unconscious choices from a wide range of possibilities. His final choices may have been due to the tastes of his particular audience, the instruments to which he was attracted, the availability of performers, his own experiments, or the innovations of other composers.

Return to the page occasionally as the section is studied and as examples are encountered which support the ideas on the page.

Ancient Musical Instruments

Musical instruments of the modern orchestra achieved their form, brilliance, and tone quality no earlier than the first half of the nineteenth century, for the most part. The wealth of Western music reaching back half a millenium and more all was expressed with quite a different sound made by instruments that are now obsolete or have been completely transformed. Within these centuries of medieval, Renaissance, and Baroque music-making, changes in taste and style also superannuated instruments. This complex history makes the term *ancient instruments* an over-simplification; at the least, Renaissance instruments must be distinguished from Baroque. In the recordings for this book, modern replicas of some instruments of these periods are used and are shown in the accompanying photographs.

Harpsichord: The hand-plucked dulcimer or psaltery when fitted with a mechanism in the early years of the fifteenth century became the harpsichord. In its simplest form each key controls a jack or plectrum that plucks rather than strikes (as in the piano) one string. By the sixteenth century this essential form began to be modified by the addition of more strings to each key and by stops to achieve variation in tone color. Eventually, two manuals, six or eight stops, pedals (to enable shifting stops without interrupting playing), and five strings to a key became fashionable, before the harpsichord was replaced by the piano and Romantic music. The modern example shown uses pedal stops, unknown to the Renaissance or even the high Baroque.

Portative Organ: Slung from the neck, the simple, one-rank organ used flue pipes, like a pennywhistle, for simple accompaniment to singers. The player pumped a bellows in the rear with one hand while playing the keyboard with two fingers of the other. Since only one pipe is attached to a key, only a simple succession of notes can be sounded.

Harpsichord
(harp'-si-kord)

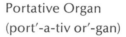

Portative Organ
(port'-a-tiv or'-gan)

Photographs from the album, "The Renaissance Band," by Decca Records. Used by permission.

Regal Organ   (ree'-gal or'-gan)

Viola da gamba
(vee-oh'-la da gahm'-ba)

Lute courtesy of Christopher Williams, Pro Musica. Photo by Ted Russell.

Regal Organ: This organ used reed pipes to create its easily recognizable snarling tone, popular in the Renaissance but out of favor in the Baroque. The reed is the beating (clarinet) type, not the free reed of the harmonium. The wooden resonators shown in this modern replica act to stop the pipes, that is, the notes sound an octave lower. While electricity supplies the air to this version, hand-pumped bellows in the rear were used in the fifteenth century, the heyday of the regal. Reed pipes on full organs are called regal stops.

Viola da gamba: The viol and violin families of bowed stringed instruments have separate and rival histories. In the sixteenth and seventeenth centuries the viol was the instrument of serious and courtly music, the violin of dance and rustic music. Viols were held between the legs (gamba means leg), and violins were held under the chin. All viols of the family or "chest" are constructed and played similarly. They are marked by a flat back, sloped shoulders, have six (rarely seven) strings tuned in fourths, a fretted neck for finger placement, and are bowed underhand, that is, with palm upward. Without this type of bowing, it is not possible to bring out the almost reedy tone of the instrument; correct style is nonvibrato so the total tonal effect is quite different from that of the violin family.

Lute: An ancient instrument similar to the modern guitar, the lute was originally brought to Europe from Persia. Interest in the instrument gradually spread over the entire continent. Schools of lute performers and composers flourished in Spain and Italy and, later, in France and England.

The body of the lute is shaped like a pear cut in half, the stem of the pear representing the fingerboard. Unlike the violin, the lute has no bridge, and the fingerboard has frets; that is, raised strips of wood which facilitate finding finger positions for the notes. The strings were plucked by the fingers, producing a gentle subdued tone. Members of the lute family varied in size from very large to quite small.

Lute   (loot)

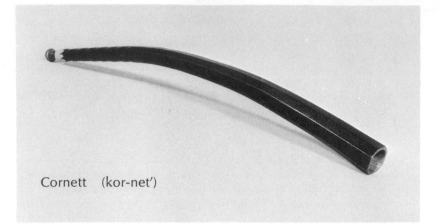

Cornett   (kor-net')

Cornett: The cornett or zink is a wooden trumpet that flourished from 1500 to 1650, although it remained well enough known in Germany for Bach to use it in some of his earlier cantatas. Like other Renaissance instruments, it was made in a family of sizes and ranges; the most commonly used was the treble, shown here. A curved piece of wood was split in half, grooved, then glued and planed to an octagonal outside surface, and wrapped in leather. A detachable cup mouthpiece of ivory or metal gave the player great control over tone as well as agility; modern experience with replicas rarely achieves the reported beauty of sound—it is the most difficult of the Renaissance winds. Its six holes and a thumbhole give it a range of two and a half octaves, with a fingering that is very much like that of the recorder. A few examples of straight cornetts have also survived, as well as a mute cornett in which the mouthpiece is carved directly into the wood giving an unusually soft tone that enables the instrument to be used with other soft *(bas)* instruments of the time.

Crumhorn: Shown in sculpture and painting of earlier centuries, the crumhorn family of double reed instruments was well-established and in wide use by 1500. The most unusual feature is that the reed is capped, that is, the player blows into a wind chamber to activate the reed and hence has no control over volume or tonal effect. The Renaissance instruments had a range of only a ninth, with no overblowing possible, so that its buzzing tone gave a dronelike effect; modern replicas often have keys to reach the eleventh. Because of the cylindrical bore, only short lengths were needed for the tenor and bass sizes.

Rauschpfeife: Like the crumhorn, the rauschpfeife is a capped double-reed instrument. Its tone, however, is much more like a shawm's so that it belongs with the loud *(haut)* instruments of the Renaissance and was used for outdoor music. It, too, was made in several sizes; modern replicas, however, are so far limited to a soprano and an alto.

Rauschpfeife   (roush'-pfife')

Crumhorns   (krum'-hornz)

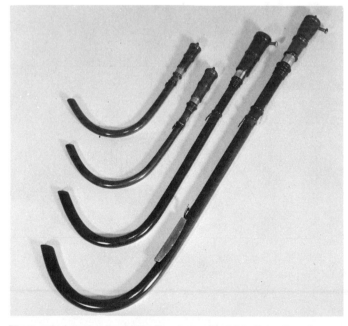

Photographs from the album, "The Renaissance Band," by Decca Records. Used by permission.

Transverse Flutes   (tranz-verse' floots)

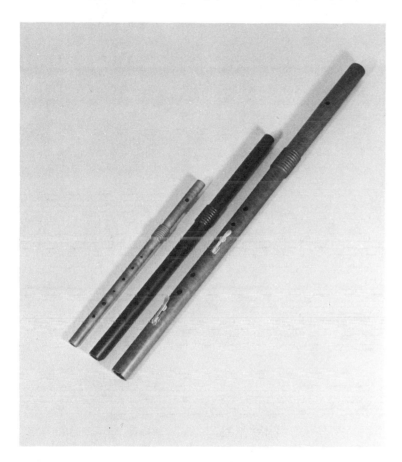

Recorder: The revival of interest in older instruments has been signaled by the widespread popularity of the recorder, the fipple flute. In the Renaissance the recorders were made in a family or consort in the sizes shown: the smallest, sopranino, then soprano, alto, tenor, and bass. However, in the Baroque only the alto survived and then as a solo instrument, consorts no longer being popular. The photograph shows the three small sizes in Baroque style, which have a conical bore, while the tenor and bass are Renaissance types with cylindrical bores and butterfly keys.

Recorders   (ree-kord'-erz)

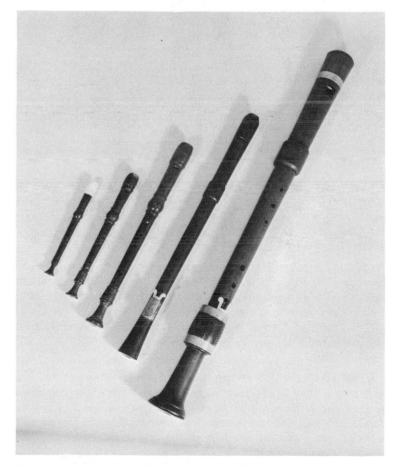

Transverse Flute: The Renaissance transverse flute family consisted of a descant, tenor, and bass, as shown. These instruments were cylindrically bored and made of one piece of wood, so that tuning by pulling out was not possible. The descant flute was developed in the Baroque to a conically bored instrument with a key; in the nineteenth century, the modern flute developed by Boehm reverted to a cylindrical bore. The Renaissance instrument, however, never sounds like a horn or a reed; its six holes are equidistant and its tones pure.

Photographs from the album, "The Renaissance Band," by Decca Records. Used by permission.

Sir Eglamore

Key: G   Starting Tone: G (1)
Autoharp Key: F   Starting Tone:
   F (1)
Autoharp chords not in Pupil's Book
Meter: $\frac{6}{8}$ $\left(\frac{2}{\downarrow.}\right)$
Piano accompaniment on page 243

*EXPRESSION: Because in ballad singing the words must be perfectly understood, approach the learning of "Sir Eglamore" as an experience in choral reading. Particular attention should be focused upon uniform pronunciation of words ("drag-on" not "drag-in"), on word endings ("valiant" not "valian"). In the beginning have the class over-pronounce all words. Assist the class to use inflection that results in expressive reading.

*RHYTHM: The basic patterns in $\frac{6}{8}$ meter are contained in this song. Ask the children to clap them and play them on percussion instruments. Then ask the class to clap or play the rhythm of the melody of the entire song.

As in "Sing a Merry Noel," ancient instruments are also appropriate to accompany this ancient song. On the first instrumental the cornett plays the first two measures and is answered by the rauschpfeife in the next two measures; then the viola da gamba plays two measures and is answered by the regal organ. Use these measures to help children identify the sounds of the four instruments.

LATER EXPRESSION: When children know the song well and you return to it later in the year, suggest that new verses be composed to tell more of the story as the children might imagine it. The song can be accompanied by a pantomime performed by the singers or a separate group of children. It might be dramatized by puppets the children make.

See pages 89a to 89d for a discussion of ancient instruments.

Sir Eglamore

Old English Ballad

In the recording of this song, you can hear four ancient instruments—a rauschpfeife, a cornett, a regal, and a viola da gamba.

The **ballad** is one of the oldest types of songs. The first ballads were probably sung by the **troubadours** nearly a thousand years ago! When you have learned this ballad and the one on the next page, make your own definition of a ballad. What is the difference between a ballad and other kinds of songs?

1. Sir Eg - la - more,— that val - iant knight, Fa   la
2. There starts a huge drag - on out of his den, Fa   la

lank - y down dil - ly, He took up   his sword and he
lank - y down dil - ly, Which had___ killed I know not

went for   to fight; Fa la   lank - y. down dil - ly,
how man - y   men; Fa la   lank - y. down dil - ly,

And   as   he   rode o'er hill   and dale, All
But when   he saw   Sir Eg - la - more, If

Record 4   Side B   Band 1.   VOICES: 2 baritones, 2 sopranos.
ACCOMPANIMENT: rauschpfeife, cornett, regal organ, viola da gamba.
FORM: Instrumental; Vocal, *vv. 1-4.*

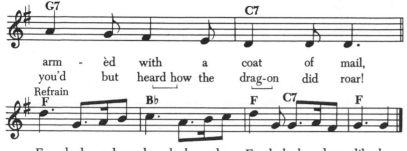

arm - èd with a coat of mail,
you'd but heard how the drag-on did roar!

Refrain

Fa lank - y down, la lank - y down, Fa la lank - y down dil - ly.

3. This dragon had a plaguey hard hide,
Fa la lanky down dilly,
Which could the strongest steel abide;
Fa la lanky down dilly,
But as the dragon yawning did fall,
He thrust his sword down hilt and all,
Fa lanky down, la lanky down.
Fa la lanky down dilly.

4. The dragon laid him down and roared,
Fa la lanky down dilly,
The knight was sorry for his sword;
Fa la lanky down dilly,
The sword it was a right good blade,
As ever Turk or Spaniard made,
Fa lanky down, la lanky down.
Fa la lanky down dilly.

In days before books people learned much by listening to tales of exciting events from far-away places as they were described in songs called ballads. Many of these song-stories told of valiant deeds, such as the ballad "Sir Eglamore." Other ballads tell of an unhappy love, such as "The Wraggle-Taggle Gypsies." Some ballads told humorous stories, such as "Little Fox."

In early times a king would appoint a musician to the court. The musician's duties were to make up songs praising the wars that had been fought, the victories won, and the generous rewards given brave warriors by their king. The word "ballad" originally referred to a dancing song. Singers sang and acted out the stories in dance while the listeners lustily joined in on the refrains between the verses. Some of these ballads, though centuries old and created in other lands, are so charming that we still sing them today.

There have been many kinds of accompaniment for folk ballads. The guitar is popular for this purpose at the present time. The concertina (small accordion), mouth organ, fiddle, banjo, zither, spoons, bones, reed organ, piano, small drums, tambourine, and recorders have all been popular at different times and places. As children study ballads and other folk songs, encourage originality in planning accompaniments. Since ballads are original songs of the singer, often improvised for an occasion, they are ideal for children's original additional verses. When some examples have been learned, encourage children to compose their own ballads about events of interest at the present time.

The Wraggle-Taggle Gypsies

Key: D minor Starting Tone: A (5)
Autoharp chords in Pupil's Book
Meter: $\frac{4}{4}$ ($\frac{4}{\downarrow}$)
Piano accompaniment on page 244

4. Come saddle to me my milk-white steed,
And go and seek my pony, O!
That I may ride and seek my bride,
Who is gone with the wraggle-taggle gypsies, O!

5. Then he rode high, and he rode low,
He rode through wood and copses too.
Until he came to an open field,
And there he espied his-a lady, O!

6. "What makes you leave your house and your land?
What makes you leave your money, O!
What makes you leave your new-wedded lord,
To go with the wraggle-taggle gypsies, O!"

7. "What care I for my house and my land?
And what care I for my money, O!
What care I for my new-wedded lord?
I'm off with the wraggle-taggle gypsies, O!"

8. "Last night you slept in a goose-feather bed
With the sheet turned down so bravely, O!
But tonight you sleep in a cold, open field
Along with the wraggle-taggle gypsies, O!"

9. "Oh, what care I for a goose-feather bed
With the sheet turned down so bravely, O!
For tonight I shall sleep in a cold, open field,
Along with the wraggle-taggle gypsies, O!"

*EXPRESSION: The story of this ballad is told by more than one person—the narrator (who might be a servant), the rich lord, and his newly-wedded wife who has decided to run off with the gypsies. WHICH VERSES ARE SUNG BY THE NARRATOR, WHICH BY THE LORD, AND WHICH BY THE LADY? (Verses 1, 2, 3, 5—narrator; verses 4, 6, 8—rich lord; verses 7 and 9—wife.) Divide each verse into two phrases. Take a breath only after the word "O!" to help the flow of the story. For an interesting performance, a verse might be spoken, some verses may be sung slowly, others in a fast tempo, some may be sung softly, others loudly. If instruments are used, establish the

The Wraggle-Taggle Gypsies

Old English Ballad

Many people have dreamed of running away to live the life of a gypsy. Perhaps that is the reason why this ballad has been enjoyed by so many generations of people. It was sung hundreds of years ago in England. It was brought to Virginia in Colonial times and has been popular in the United States ever since.

1. There were three gyp-sies a-come to my door,
2. Then she pulled off her silk fin-ished gown,
3. It was late last night when my lord came home,

And down-stairs ran this-a la - dy, O!
And put on hose of leath - er, O!
In - quir - ing for his la - dy, O!

The one sang high, and an-oth-er sang low,
The rag - ged rags a - bout our door,
The ser - vants said on ev - ery hand,

And the oth - er sang, "Bon - ny, bon - ny Bis - cay, O!"
And she's gone with the wrag-gle-tag-gle gyp-sies, O!
"She's gone with the wrag-gle-tag-gle gyp-sies, O!"

Record 4 Side B Band 2. VOICES: soprano, tenor, baritone.
ACCOMPANIMENT: violin, harpsichord.
FORM: Introduction, *2 meas.;* Vocal, *vv. 1-9.*

This song was written by a famous troubadour who lived a very long time ago, about the year 1200. When you know the melody, pretend that you are a troubadour and compose another verse.

Troubadour Song

Music by Colin Muset
Words by William S. Haynie

When cold is the wind, I look for a friend
And there I would stay, no mon-ey to pay,

To give a sing-er a room for the night.
And then be gone with the dawn's ear-ly light.

I'll play on my lute a ron-deau sweet,

If my host will give me food to eat.

Roast pheas-ant and quail, fat duck-ling and hens,

Rich cheese and mut-ton would make us good friends.

Record 4   Side B   Band 3. VOICE: baritone.
ACCOMPANIMENT: 2 crumhorns, viola da gamba, lute, drum, finger cymbals.
FORM: Introduction, *4 meas.;* Vocal; Interlude, *4 meas.;* Vocal.

tempo and mood by a short *introduction*. Separate the verses by short instrumental *interludes* and end the song with an instrumental *coda*.

On the recording the song is played by a violin and harpsichord. Listen to the special effects created by the two instruments.

HARMONY: Study the autoharp markings above the staff in the pupil's book. Notice that the chord markings include a small "m." Discuss the purpose of this. Listen to the song; ask children to decide whether the song is in major or minor. When they have concluded that it is minor, point out that the small "m" stands for minor. It tells us that we must play the D, G, and A minor chords rather than major chords.

Give children an opportunity to practice the autoharp accompaniment. Draw attention to the measures where the chords must be changed in the middle of the measure. Play with two strokes per measure.

Key: C   Starting Tone: G (5)
Meter: $\frac{6}{8}$ ($\frac{2}{J.}$)
No piano accompaniment

Troubadour Song

* EXPRESSION: On the recording listen for the crumhorns, viola da gamba, lute, drum, and finger cymbals. This song is a perfect example of music of long ago. Listen for percussion parts played by the finger cymbals and drum. Encourage children to become familiar with the percussion patterns on the recording and to learn to play them on percussion instruments.

When children know the song, they may enjoy composing another verse or verses. This might be the work of an individual, or the whole class.

In other projects children might work individually or in small groups to compose "troubadour songs," both words and music. The songs might convey some news, describe something of interest, or simply entertain the listeners. The autoharp might be plucked to simulate the sound of the lute. The recorder, song flute, or tambourine might be played in accompaniment. The singer might also dramatize his song, as did many troubadours.

See pages 89a to 89d for a discussion of ancient instruments.

The music on these two pages is secular, written for the purpose of entertainment and dancing. It is of historical significance because it tells us much about the tastes and daily activities of the people of the time.

Danse

ANONYMOUS (THIRTEENTH CENTURY)

This gay dance has an interesting arrangement of phrases. The music printed on the pupil's page shows the first two phrases of the three-phrase melody played at the beginning. The three phrases are repeated exactly. Then a kind of variation of the melody is heard. It is also in three phrases and is repeated. The design of the entire dance is A A B B C C, each letter representing a twelve-measure melody.

In response to the question in the children's book, help them to determine that the percussion instruments used are tambourine, finger cymbals, and rhythm sticks.

In composing a dance for the music, divide the class into three groups. Have one group invent movements suitable to the mood and design of the melody. Another group may invent movements to fit the rhythm of the tambourine: $\frac{3}{8}$ ♩ ♪ | ♩ ♪ |. The third group may move to the rhythm of the finger cymbals: $\frac{3}{8}$ ♩. | ♩. |.

Most of us like to read the tales of long ago when kings and nobles ruled and life centered around the great castles. We like to imagine how the people lived and worked and what they did for enjoyment.

Much of what we know about this long ago time we have learned from the stories and songs which have come down to us. Wandering musicians, or troubadours, traveled from castle to castle, giving the villagers and nobles the latest news in song. Sometimes the kings and noblemen themselves wrote poetry and music for the entertainment of their families and friends. Often the jongleurs or jugglers, entertainers who stayed at the castle, played instrumental music for dancing. In the time when there was no mechanical means of reproducing music, many people played and sang for their own enjoyment and for the enjoyment of their friends.

Danse

Anonymous (Thirteenth Century)

Listen to "Danse" by an unknown French composer. Here is the main melody. Notice the imaginative variations on the simple melody.

The melody is played on a **recorder,** which is a wooden flute with a sweet, pure sound. At this long ago time, music was written without harmony. Sometimes percussion accompaniments were played. What percussion instruments do you hear in "Danse"?

Record 9   Side B   Band 2.
The Manhattan Recorder Consort,
LaNoue Davenport, director.

As you listen to "Danse," imagine the people in the castles dancing while jongleurs played. Dances of this period were usually danced in a circle. The steps were often dignified and stately. Perhaps you can invent your own dance with the music.

Music for Instruments

by Heinrich Isaac

Compare the sound of the first recorder composition with the second. The second composition was written two hundred years later. Recorders were made in different sizes so that music which covered a wider range of notes could be played. There were soprano, alto, tenor, and bass recorders.

As you listen to "Music for Instruments," notice how the recorders imitate each other. One recorder announces a melody which is played by each of the others in turn. The melodies of the four recorders intertwine, sometimes imitating each other, sometimes answering with a new melody. The music never seems to stop from beginning to end.

Although recorders were played long ago, many people enjoy playing them today. If there is a group of recorder players in your community, invite them to come and play for you.

Record 9   Side B   Band 3.
The Manhattan Recorder Consort,
LaNoue Davenport, director.

Music for Instruments

BY HEINRICH ISAAC
BORN C. 1450   DIED 1517

In comparing the two compositions of this lesson, help children recognize that in "Danse," the melody is played by one instrument without a harmonic accompaniment. In "Music for Instruments," each of the four recorders is almost equally important. The harmony is not a chordal accompaniment. Even when an instrument does not have the main melody, it usually plays a pattern which has a melodic and rhythmic contour of its own.

Listen especially to the last section of the composition. Children should hear that although the highest recorder is playing the main melody, the other instruments have interesting parts to play. Guide children to hear the melody with this rhythm:

This short melody is exactly repeated and then heard again beginning one step lower. It is repeated at this pitch and then played one step lower. The repetition at this pitch is the last phrase of the composition. The use of sequences in this way is a very important feature of this style of music.

Follow Me

Key: F Starting Tone: F (1)
Meter: $\frac{2}{4}$ $\left(\frac{2}{\downarrow}\right)$
No piano accompaniment

ABOUT THE SONG: The term "canon" with the literal meaning of "law," is given to part songs in which the melody is sung in exact imitation.

HARMONY: The question and answer nature of the two vocal parts is an excellent introduction to part singing. The recording of this song will be very helpful in making the class aware of the two parts. After the introduction children sing the upper part and the clarinet plays the lower part. On the second vocal the clarinet plays the upper part and children sing the lower part. On the third vocal children and clarinets sing and play both parts.

Introduce the children to the double staff. DO YOU SEE ANYTHING IN THE WAY THIS SONG IS WRITTEN THAT IS DIFFERENT FROM OTHER SONGS YOU HAVE STUDIED? Help children notice that the two staffs are connected with a heavy black line. Guide them to realize that this means that both staffs are to be read simultaneously.

* RHYTHM: The quarter rest ₹ receives the same time value as the quarter note ♩ or two eighth notes ♫ . The eighth rest ʔ receives the same time value as the eighth note ♪ . The half rest ▬ receives the same time value as the half note ♩ . When children know the song and have

followed the instructions in their books to clap the rhythm of the melody against the steady beat, challenge them to try a rhythm canon. First, suggest that they chant the words as they clap. Later they may clap the rhythm in the two parts without words. At another time, suggest that class members play two different percussion instruments in the rhythm canon or that they play the melody on two sets of bells.

Follow Me

Traditional Carol

Study the rhythm of the first voice part of "Follow Me." Notice that the rhythm patterns include notes and rests. Compose dance movements for each section of the canon.

Clap these patterns while someone plays the beat on a drum. Be silent on every rest. Listen carefully for the beat so that you will know how long to be silent for each rest.

Pattern

Which note is the same length as each of these rests?
Give each rest the same name as the note.

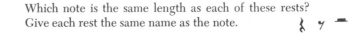

Come a - long,   Sing a   song,

Come a - long,   Sing a

Fol - low me;   It is eas - y, you can

song,   Fol - low me;   It is

Record 4   Side B   Band 4. VOICES: children's choir.
ACCOMPANIMENT: clarinet.
FORM: Introduction, *8 meas.;* Vocal (voices on upper part, clarinet on lower part); Vocal (clarinet on upper part, voices on lower part); Vocal (voices on two parts).

see. Ev - ery day, In this way,

eas - y, you can see. Ev - ery day, In this

Just re - peat 'Til the tunes com - plete.

way, Just re - peat, com - plete. _____

Can you find the home tone of this round? If you need help, turn to page 56.

Why Shouldn't My Goose?

Traditional Round

1. Why should-n't my goose Grow as fat as thy goose,

2.

3. When I paid for my goose Twice as much as thine?

4.

Key: F   Starting Tone: F (1)
Meter: $\frac{2}{4}$ $\left(\frac{2}{\text{♩}}\right)$
No piano accompaniment

Why Shouldn't My Goose?

* EXPRESSION: Four ancient instruments—two crumhorns, viola da gamba, regal organ—play in the recording of this round. Discuss why the unusual sounds of these instruments are appropriate for this round. The nasal quality of the instruments imitates the sound of a honking goose.

When the class knows the round, suggest that the children develop dance movements. Through experimentation and discussion, the children will no doubt discover appropriate steps of their own. The dance might be improvised and danced in a round as the song is sung. The dancers might sing or one group might sing while another group dances.

The dance will have more attractive style if dancers use their bodies and bend with the flow of the music, rather than letting it be a foot dance only. One dancer might play the rhythm on the tambourine. The dancers might sometimes dance the round dance without the song, using the tambourine for the rhythm.

* MELODY: Follow suggestions in the pupil's book and help the children locate the home tone. Conclude that the song is in F. When children know the song, sing it as a four-part round. One part may be played on the bells, or the bells might play one phrase over and over while the class sings the round as written.

See pages 89a to 89d for a discussion of ancient instruments.

Record 4   Side B   Band 5. VOICES: children's choir.
ACCOMPANIMENT: 2 crumhorns, viola da gamba, regal organ.
FORM: Vocal (unison); Vocal (4-part round); Instrumental.

The Riddle Song

Tonality: Pentatonic (G A B D E)
Starting Tone: D
Autoharp chords in Pupil's Book
Meter: 4/4 (♩)
Piano accompaniment on page 245

* MELODY: The pentatonic scale is made up of five tones that include no half steps. The scale consists of three whole steps and one interval of a step and a half. The tones of this melody are D E G A B. (Both low and high D and E are used in the melody.) "A Good Day in Japan," page 60, is also based on a pentatonic scale.

* HARMONY: Because of the nature of the pentatonic scale, any tone harmonizes pleasingly with any other. For this reason, the children may choose any of the tones for their accompaniment. Suggest they try the rhythm of the first measure of the song and repeat that throughout the song. Then they might try the rhythm of the second measure and, finally, different rhythms of their own. Each accompanist might have a different accompaniment for the song.

* EXPRESSION: The song should be sung in a rather straight tone with unaffected quality. Each phrase should be sung on one breath. Point out that "cryen" is used instead of the real word "crying." Folk songs often include words in the dialect of the people from which the song comes.

The Riddle Song

American Folk Song

One of the oldest scales is the pentatonic scale. For another song based on this scale, see pages 60-61.

| | | G | C | C | G |

1. I gave my love a cher-ry that has no stone;
2. How can there be a cher-ry that has no stone?
3. A cher-ry when it's bloom-ing, it has no stone;

I gave my love a chick-en that has no __ bone;
How can there be a chick-en that has no __ bone?
A chick-en when it's pip-ping, it has no __ bone;

I gave my love a ring __ that has no __ end;
How can there be a ring __ that has no __ end?
A ring __ when it's roll-ing, it has no __ end;

I gave my love a ba-by, there's no cry-en.
How can there be a ba-by, there's no cry-en?
A ba-by when it's sleep-ing, there's no cry-en.

Study the notes of the melody and name the tones which make up the pentatonic scale for this song. Choose two or three tones from this scale. Create a one-measure pattern to repeat throughout the song.

Play your accompaniment on the bells or piano, or pluck it on the autoharp.

Record 4   Side B   Band 6.   VOICE: soprano.
ACCOMPANIMENT: English horn, guitar.
FORM: Introduction, 2 meas.; Vocal, v. 1; Interlude, 2 meas.; Vocal, v. 2; Interlude, 2 meas.; Vocal, v. 3; Coda, 2 meas.

98

Sing this song with strong accents and full voices in the style of the sea chantey.

Bound for the Rio Grande

Sea Chantey

Key: F   Starting Tone: C (5)
Autoharp chords in Pupil's Book
Meter: 6/8 (2/♩.)
Piano accompaniment on page 246

Bound for the Rio Grande

ABOUT THE MUSIC: Although many assume that "Rio Grande" refers to the river along our Mexican border, most versions of the song show the Rio Grande to be a port or region of that name in southern Brazil. The sailors had a long sea voyage to reach the "Rio Grande." The words "flows down golden sand" refers to the shifting sand shoals which make the entrance to the Brazilian port extremely hazardous except at high tide.

This sea chantey was sung by sailors while hauling the anchor in preparation for leaving port. To raise the anchor, stout capstan bars were quickly fitted into the capstan head like spokes in a wheel. Sailors, pushing on the bars, tramped around the capstan as its pawls (teeth) gripped the anchor chain and slowly "broke out" the heavy anchor from the bottom of the harbor. Consequently, this type of chantey is often called a capstan chantey.

* EXPRESSION: Capstan chanteys were sung with a swing and a pulse suited to the pace of the work. Try singing the song unaccompanied in full voice, but without shouting. Alternate solos with answering choruses. Have a group of boys dramatize the chantey and the slow circling around the capstan head (stepping two to a measure on beats 1 and 4).

* RHYTHM: Study the two contrasting rhythmic patterns, even (♪♪♪) uneven (♪. ♪♪).

HARMONY: Most chanteys lend themselves well to improvised harmonization. Much of this chantey can be harmonized by singing a third below the melody. When children return to the song later in the year, encourage them to try such harmonization. Suggest that they harmonize the two-measure phrase beginning "Oh, Rio" and the two measures beginning "Way down Rio."

The Young Voyageur

Key: B♭   Starting Tone: F (5)
Autoharp Key: C   Starting Tone: G (5)
Autoharp chords not in Pupil's Book
Meter: 3/4 (3/♩)
Piano accompaniment on page 247

* **EXPRESSION:** Be sure that children sing each phrase of the song on one breath. Insist that they sing the dotted eighth and sixteenth notes crisply and accurately. The song should be sung in full voice with a tone quality that is free and flowing in the style of the song.

* **RHYTHM:** Study the rhythm of the song and notice that much of the charm of the melody lies in the alternating uneven and even rhythm. The continuing quarter and half notes might sound dull without the crisp dotted eighth and sixteenth pattern. The 3/4 meter is felt one pulse to a measure instead of three to a measure because of the tempo and the natural accent of the words. This also causes the music to have a strong feeling of movement.

HARMONY: When children know the melody of the song well, teach them the descant. If the class has had only little experience in singing in harmony, the descant might be played on the bells as the class sings. Some time later the more capable children might sing the descant.

The Young Voyageur

Canadian Folk Melody
Words by John Andrews

1. Oh, the voy - a - geur bold from the north-land so cold,
2. Oh, this voy - a - geur dreams of the for - est and streams;

See the wild game he takes from the riv - ers and lakes.
Rough the por - tage and long, but he still sings his song.

Refrain

Hap - py and free, dar - ing is he.

Hear the ech - o - ing call of the young voy - a - geur.

Some of the class may want to sing this descant with the refrain of the song.

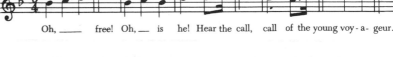

Oh, ____ free! Oh, ___ is he! Hear the call, call of the young voy - a - geur.

Record 4   Side B   Band 8.   VOICES: baritone, children's choir.
ACCOMPANIMENT: woodwind quintet.
FORM: Instrumental (Vocal Descant on refrain); Vocal, *vv. 1-2.*

Let's Explore Design

The **design** of a song is like a chain.
It is made up of many small parts linked together to form a complete composition.
Each part is essential to the whole.
Study the design of "The Young Voyageur."
Discover the links that form the complete design.

The smallest link is a **motive.**
The motive is a short pattern of rhythm or melody.
The first motive in the song has this rhythm:

Is this rhythmic motive repeated?
Is the melody of the motive repeated?
Find other motives in the song.

Motives are linked together to form a **phrase.**
In this song, two motives make up a phrase.
How many phrases are there in "The Young Voyageur"?

Phrases are grouped together to form a section or part of a song.
This song has a **two-part design.**
It has two sections.
Each section is made up of two phrases.

The design of a song can be written with letters.
The design of the phrases in this song would be written a b c a.
The design of the sections would be written A B.

Study "Bound for the Rio Grande" on page 99.
Can you find **motives, phrases,** and **sections** in this song?
Write the design of the phrases and of the sections with letters.

Let's Explore Design

Read each paragraph aloud and discuss the ideas presented.

Locate the rhythmic motives in "The Young Voyageur." Discuss the idea that a motive is the smallest possible musical unit that sounds complete in itself. To help children understand that such a brief pattern could be considered complete, ask them to tap and sing just the first three notes, then the first four, then the complete pattern. Help the children observe that the rhythm does not sound finished until the last time when the motive is complete. This rhythmic motive is repeated five times. (The third repetition, "from the rivers and lakes" is not exact in that it uses two eighth notes instead of a dotted eighth and a sixteenth.) The melody of the first rhythmic motive is repeated during the refrain. Another rhythmic motive occurs during the first two measures of the refrain. It is repeated during the third and fourth measures of the refrain.

There are four phrases in the song—two in each of the two sections. When children have analyzed the design of "The Young Voyageur," study "Bound for the Rio Grande" on page 99. The structure of this song is very similar to that of "The Young Voyageur." The first rhythmic motive is two measures long:

It is repeated, almost identically, during measures five and six and again during measures thirteen and fourteen. (In both cases the ending of the pattern is different from the original motive.) A second motive occurs during measures three-four:

Rhythmically, the first two and a half measures of the refrain make up a new motive: . Melodically, this is a variation of the melody at the beginning of the song. Another motive: ends the verse and the refrain.

Each phrase in this song is four measures long and consists of two melodic motives. The song is divided into two sections; each is made up of two phrases. The design of this song written in letters would be as follows: A: a b; B: a b.

As children continue to learn new songs, refer often to this page. Ask children to analyze the new songs. Help them to realize that awareness of the design of a song will help them learn the new music more quickly and more accurately.

Music of Your Own

Follow the suggestion in the pupil's book and review the *Violin Concerto in D Major* by Beethoven. Discuss its design. "Rondo" refers to a specific kind of design: A B A C A B A. Talk about the characteristics of the rondo. It is made up of seven sections; however, only three musical ideas are presented. Sections one, three, five, and seven are based on the A idea; sections two and six are contrasting and based on the B idea; the C idea is heard only once, in the fourth section.

Read the next three paragraphs with the children. They may discover their own pentatonic scale by beginning with any tone they choose and following this sequence of steps: whole-whole-whole and half-whole. (For example, C D E G A.) They may also improvise their melody on the black keys of the piano which automatically produces a pentatonic scale (G flat, A flat, B flat, D flat, E flat).

When children are sure of the procedure they are to follow, divide the class into groups of three. Give each group time to work with the bells, piano, and any other pitched instrument which the children can play, such as the song-flute. When they have had an opportunity to create and practice their rondos, ask them to perform for the class. Discuss whether or not they have followed the design correctly. DO YOU HAVE THREE SEPARATE MUSICAL IDEAS? DO THEY PROVIDE INTERESTING CONTRAST? ARE YOU PLAYING THEM IN THE PROPER SEQUENCE? Choose those which the class likes best and help the children to notate the composition.

Since the pentatonic scale lends itself easily to harmony, some of the groups may wish to add a harmonizing part for each section. As one child plays the main melody, suggest that a second child improvise an accompaniment which moves in contrasting rhythm and melody from the main theme.

Invite individuals to choose one of the other activities suggested in their book and create a dance, a poem, or a picture based on a rondo design. When all activities are completed, the class may wish to select the ones they like best and plan a "Rondo Program." Present it for another class or for the children's parents.

At another time, review the design of "Carillon," page 68, and invite children to create compositions based on the A B A form.

Music of Your Own

Listen again to the *Violin Concerto in D Major* by Beethoven, discussed on page 72. Review the meaning of the term "rondo." What is the design of a rondo?

Compose a rondo of your own for bells or piano. Use a pentatonic scale as the basis for your melody.

Work in groups of three. Let one person compose the main melody — A. Compose this melody first. Another person may compose the B section. The third person may compose the C section. Practice your rondo until you can play it correctly. Then each group can perform it for the rest of the class.

Experiment with rondo design in other ways. Create a dance in rondo form which can be performed with your music.

Write a poem that imitates the design of the rondo. How many verses will there be in your poem? Which verses will be the same? Which will be different?

Sketch a design or draw a picture that is like a rondo. How many different figures will you use in your design? How many times will you repeat the main section?

Read and discuss the poem "Sweet and Low." It was written by Alfred Tennyson, an important English poet of the nineteenth century.

Sweet and Low

Music by Joseph Barnby
Words by Alfred Tennyson

Sweet and low, sweet and low, Wind of the west - ern sea, ___

Low, low, breathe and blow, Wind of the west - ern sea, ___

O - ver the roll - ing wa - ters go, Come from the dy - ing

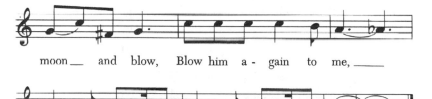

moon ___ and blow, Blow him a - gain to me, ___

While my lit - tle one, While my pret - ty one sleeps. ___

After you know the song well, you might want to add this harmonizing part to the last phrase:

While my lit - tle one, while my pret - ty one sleeps. ___

Record 5   Side A   Band 1. VOICE: soprano.
ACCOMPANIMENT: string quartet.
FORM: Instrumental; Vocal; Instrumental (vocal on last 4 meas.).

* EXPRESSION: As children follow the suggestion in their books to study the Tennyson poem, discuss with them the mood and meaning of the text. Discuss the vowel sounds that are prolonged, such as the "ee" sound in "sea," "me," "sleeps," the "o" in "blow" and "low," the "oo" in "soon" and "moon." Help the class to read the poem with expression, holding the vowel sounds. Ask children to speak in their natural voices and to listen to the interesting "class tone" which is made up of the different tones of the individual voices. This is a more interesting sound in speech than one which is a unison sound copied from one voice.

In discussion of what they hear in the recording, the children should notice that the long vowels in the words are given long notes by the composer. The gentle rolling rhythm of the words is kept in the 6/8 meter with many patterns of "even" rhythm, as in measures 9, 10, 11, and 12.

As children sing the song, insist that vowel sounds be held for the full value of the note or notes, that consonants be sung clearly, and that breath be taken in places that will not break the flow of the rhythm (at each comma and semicolon except in the last four measures which are better sung as one phrase).

The song is played by a string quartet on the recording. Help the children identify the cello as the melody instrument on the second instrumental. Suggest that they refer to page 172 for pictures of the string instruments.

This song is also scored for instruments and the arrangement can be found in the "Exploring Music Instrumental Supplement."

HARMONY: The simple harmonizing part on the last phrase which appears in the pupil's book can be used to develop initial experiences in part singing. Guide the children to learn the part by listening to it in relationship to the melody, not as an isolated "second melody."

 Scored for instruments.
See "Exploring Music Instrumental Supplement."

Old Folks at Home

Key: C Starting Tone: E (3)
Autoharp chords in Pupil's Book
Meter: $\frac{4}{4}$ $\left(\frac{4}{\downarrow}\right)$
Piano accompaniment on page 249

* MELODY: Challenge the class to learn the melody of the song by reading the notes. Write the C scale on a staff on the board and ask the class to assist you in writing numbers and letter names for the notes. Include the D above high C because it appears in the song.

```
1 2 3 4 5 6 7 8 2
C D E F G A B C D
```

Practice singing the scale with letters and numbers. Ask children to look at the song and discover melody patterns that appear more than once. Make a list of the patterns with numbers:

pattern 1. 3-2-1	pattern 3. 5-3-1-2
pattern 2. 1-8-6-8	pattern 4. 5-3-1-2-2-1

Ask the class to practice singing the patterns with numbers and then with letters as you point to the notes of the scale.

Ask the class to look at the notation in their books and to discover the phrases and repetition of phrases in which the patterns appear. Measures 1, 2, 3 and 4 are phrase one and use patterns number 1, 2 and 3; in phrase two this is repeated except for the ending, which is different, and uses pattern 4 instead of pattern 3. The last phrase of the refrain is like phrase two with the exception of the ending. The first phrase of the refrain is different from all other phrases. Sing this phrase with numbers and letters. (Since this is more difficult, it may be best to sing it for the class rather than ask children to read it.)

Ask children to help you write the design of the song on the board with letters to designate phrases: a, a′, b, a′ (a prime sign designates a slight change in phrase a).

In the next lesson, study the rhythm—clapping, tapping, and playing it on percussion instruments. Chant the words in rhythm. Review the melody patterns. Sing the song with numbers, letters, and words.

Old Folks at Home

by Stephen Foster

Sometimes we sing songs written by composers so often that they seem as much a part of the music of the people as any folk song. "Old Folks at Home" is such a song.

1. Way down up-on the Swa-nee Riv-er,
2. All up and down the whole cre-a-tion,

Far, far a-way,
Sad-ly I roam,

There's where my heart is turn-ing ev-er,
Still long-ing for the old plan-ta-tion,

There's where the old folks stay.
And for the old folks at home.

Refrain
All the world is sad and drea-ry

Ev-ery-where I roam;

Record 5   Side A   Band 2. VOICE: baritone.
ACCOMPANIMENT: piano.
FORM: Introduction, *2 meas.;* Vocal, *vv. 1-2.*

O loved ones, how my heart grows wea-ry,

Far from the old folks at home.

Lovely Evening

Traditional Round

1. Oh, how love-ly is the eve-ning, is the eve-ning,

2. When the bells are sweet-ly ring-ing, sweet-ly ring-ing

3. Ding, dong, ding, dong, ding, dong.

Sing "Lovely Evening" as a three-part round and listen to the harmony. When you sing phrases one and two of the song at the same time, your voices sound in **thirds**.

Here are the two phrases written on one staff. Notice that the notes for the two voices are always three steps apart.

Record 5 Side A Band 3. VOICES: boy choir.
ACCOMPANIMENT: chimes.
FORM: Introduction, *4 meas.;* Vocal; Interlude, *4 meas.;*
Vocal (3-part round); Coda, *4 meas.*

Key: F   Starting Tone: F (1)
Autoharp chords in Pupil's Book
Meter: $\frac{3}{4}$ $\left(\frac{3}{\downarrow}\right)$
No piano accompaniment

Lovely Evening

* HARMONY: When children know the song well, help them to understand the meaning of "thirds." Use the resonator bells to demonstrate the three steps which are the basis for the term "third." Ask two children to play the song as a round on the bells. Have the class listen to the combination of tones "in thirds." Then ask the children to sing the round on the syllable "loo" as they listen again to the harmony in thirds.

In the same lesson or on the next day, you might return to "Bound for the Rio Grande," page 99, and help the class develop the harmony in thirds as suggested in that lesson.

Polly Wolly Doodle

Key: F   Starting Tone: F (1)
Autoharp chords in Pupil's Book
Meter: C $\left(\begin{smallmatrix}4\\ \downarrow\end{smallmatrix}\right)$
Piano accompaniment on page 250

* EXPRESSION: This song is a truly American folk song and one of the best known in our country. It is a nonsense song and should be sung in bright tempo and in the spirit of fun. The words should be enunciated clearly in the front of the mouth. The singing can be varied in many ways since each four-measure phrase can be sung as a solo and as an answering chorus. Suggest ways of singing the song and ask the class to invent others. Some possibilities would be: boys and girls sing alternately, one voice and the chorus sing alternately, percussion instruments accompany voices in answer measures, and so on.

* HARMONY: After the children have studied "Let's Explore Harmony" on page 108, return to the study material on page 107.

In the key of F, the tones of the I or F chord are F-A-C. In the song, measures 1, 2, and 8 of the verse and measure 8 of the refrain are made up of some of these tones. Measure 3 of the verse and measures 1, 2, and 3 of the refrain are made up mostly of these tones and are also harmonized with the I or F chord. (The B flat and G are **passing tones** between two tones of the chord.) The tones of the V7 (C7) chord are C-E-G-B flat. Measures 4, 5, 6, and 7 of the verse and measures 4, 5, 6, and 7 of the refrain include these tones and are harmonized by the V7 chord. (The chord changes on the last measure of each phrase.)

Assist the class to complete the chart of the chords for the song, writing the name of one chord for each measure. Encourage many children to learn to accompany the song on the autoharp. Some children may learn to play the chords on the piano. Play this measure when the F chord is used:

Polly Wolly Doodle

American Folk Song

1. Oh, I went down South to see my Sal,
2. Oh, my Sal - ly is a maid - en fair,
3. Be - hind the barn, down on my knees,
4. He ___ sneezed so hard with whoop - ing cough,

Sing Pol - ly wol - ly doo - dle all the day;

My ___ Sal - ly is a spunk - y gal,
With ___ curl - y eyes and laugh - ing hair,
I ___ thought I heard a chick - en sneeze,
He ___ sneezed his head and tail right off,

Sing Pol - ly wol - ly doo - dle all the day.

Refrain
Fare thee well, fare thee well, Fare thee

well, my fair - y fay, For I'm

Record 5   Side A   Band 4.   VOICE: baritone.
ACCOMPANIMENT: accordion, banjo, double bass.
FORM: Introduction, *2 meas.;* Vocal, *vv. 1-2;* Instrumental; Vocal, *vv. 3-4.*

106

going to Loui - si - an - a,   for to   see my Su - sy - an - na,

Sing Pol - ly wol - ly doo - dle all the day.

In what key is this song? Which tones make up the I chord in this key? Which tones make up the V7 chord? Look at the music. Find measures of melody made up of notes of the I chord. Find measures which include notes of the V7 chord.

Use only the I and V7 chords and play an autoharp accompaniment with the song. Play the I chord when the melody is made up of tones of that chord. Play the V7 chord when the melody is made up of those tones.

Make a chart of the chords which you will play. Write the name of the chord for each measure. The chart for the first phrase will look like this:

F	F	F	C7
I	I	I	V7

When you know the song and can play the autoharp accompaniment, learn to sing a harmony part. First sing the chord name as the autoharp is played. You are singing the **root** of the chord. Some people can sing the root of the chord with the autoharp while others sing the melody.

Play this measure when the C7 chord is used:

The plan of harmonizing with the singing voice is a valuable one because it helps children to understand harmonic structure and prepares them for more advanced part singing.

Help children follow the directions in their books to sing the chord root. They should first practice singing the chord names, "F" or "I," "C7" or "V7," at the beginning of each measure as the autoharp is played. (They may sing these or middle C or the fourth space C or both.) Suggest that children sing "loo" on the first beat of each measure as the autoharp is played. Then have them hold one tone until the change of chord. As the children are practicing this with the autoharp player, you might sing or say the words of the song to help them keep their places.

Later in the year when you return to this song, some members of the class may be capable of singing three chord tones against the melody. Write this arrangement of the chord tones on the board. Point out to the children that tones of a chord may be placed in various positions. Some children will sing the lowest tones, some the middle, others the high tones on the syllable "loo."

F   C   F

Gladness

Key: F   Starting Tone: C (5)
Meter: $\frac{4}{4}$ ($\frac{4}{\downarrow}$)

No piano accompaniment

*MELODY: Locate the bells of the F scale; establish tonality by playing and singing 1-3-5-3-1. Sing it with numbers; play it on bells.

Let's Explore Harmony

Sing "Gladness" as a four-part round. Sing slowly, sustaining each beat so that the children can hear the chord created by the four tones.

Discuss the fact that when sung as a four-part round all four measures of the melody are sounded simultaneously. Identify by letter the tones that are heard on the first beat of each measure. As they are named, place them on a staff on the chalkboard. Do the same thing for the second beat of each measure. (Notice that the C in the first measure is a dotted quarter and is sustained into the second beat, creating a full V7 chord on this beat.) Follow the same process for the other beats. Sing the chords on "loo"; play them on bells.

Help children answer the questions in their book. The notes used in each chord are: V: C-E-G; V7: C-E-G-Bb; I: F-A-C. The chords are named for the lowest tone in each chord. C7 is named thus because the fourth tone in the chord is seven steps above C. Chords may also be named by the number of the lowest scale step in the chord. C is the lowest scale step of the chord and the fifth step of the scale of F; therefore the C chord is called V. We identify chords by Roman numerals to distinguish them from scale steps in Arabic numerals.

The steps of the scale which are included in each chord are: C: 5-7-2; C7: 5-7-2-4; F: 1-3-5. Each tone in a chord is a third from its neighbor or a third apart. Review thirds on page 105.

Apply the information learned about building chords and build a IV chord in F. It must start on the fourth step of the scale of F-B flat. The three tones must be a third apart: B flat, D, F (4-6-8).

Help children build the I, IV, V, and V7 chords in the key of G. Play the chords on the bells. Review "Echo Yodel" on page 54. Examine the melodic notation and discover measures of melody that include tones from the I chord (measures 1, 2, 3, 8, 9, 10, 11) and tones from the V chord (measures 4, 5, 6, 7). Play the chords on the bells as the class sings. Emphasize the fact that one chooses chords as an accompaniment in relation to the tones included in the melody.

Gladness

Swedish-German Round
Words by Max Exner

Glad - ness costs you not a thing,

And he who's hap - py is a king.

Let's Explore Harmony

You are creating **harmony** when you accompany a song on the autoharp, play a descant for a song, or sing a round.

Sing "Gladness" as a four-part round and listen carefully to the harmony. Notice that each group is singing a different pitch. When several tones or pitches are sounded together, we hear a **chord.**

When you sang the round, you sang these chords:

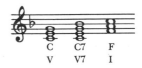

Play the chords on the autoharp. Play them on the bells. Study the chords and answer these questions:
- Which notes are used in each chord?
- Why are the chords named C, C7, F?
- Why are they also named V, V7, I?
- Which steps of the scale are used in each chord?
- How many steps apart are the notes of each chord?

Record 5   Side A   Band 5.   VOICES: children's choir.
ACCOMPANIMENT: brass quartet, percussion.
FORM: Vocal (unison); Vocal (4-part round); Instrumental (4-part round).

Chords can be built on any step of the scale. Use the bells or the piano. Build an IV chord in the key of F. Which three notes will you play?

Build the I, IV, and V chords in the key of G. Play the chords on the autoharp, bells, or piano.

Virginia Reel

Early American Folk Dance

The **reel** was originally danced in England to the music of an Irish jig. It was brought to our country by the early settlers and was a popular dance of pioneer Americans.

The reel was danced to many different tunes. "Turkey in the Straw," the tune played on your recording, was one of the favorites. Listen to the dance tune played on the violin, clarinet, accordion, banjo, and double bass. Listen to the music to discover when to begin the dance again with a new head couple.

You will dance these patterns used in many other early American dances:

Forward and back
Right hand around
Left hand around
Both hands around
Do-si-do
Sashay down and back
Reel the set and sashay back

Cast off to the foot
Form an arch
Form a new set

Virginia Reel

Play the recording of the dance music and allow the class to discuss the instrumental sounds and the "signal" that indicates when the dancers should form a new set and be ready to begin the dance again. (The signal is a new tune.)

The formation for the dance is two lines of four, six, or eight couples, facing. The couples are designated numerically with the first couple as the head couple and the last couple as the foot couple. The music is in four-measure phrases (4 meter, 16 beats to the phrase). Each
                                          4
phrase is used for a dance figure. The head lady and foot man dance each of the first five figures, alternating with the head man and foot lady.

phrase 1: Forward and Back—Walk forward 3 steps and bow, walk backward 4 steps to place.
phrase 2: Right Hand Around—Couple meets, joins right hands, circles and returns.
phrase 3: Left Hand Around—Same, joining left hands.
phrase 4: Both Hands Around—Same, joining both hands.
phrase 5: Do-si-do—Couple meets, walks around each other back to back and returns to place.
phrase 6: Sashay Down and Back—Head couple joins both hands and moves down center of line with 8 sliding steps and back in same way.
phrase 7: Reel the Set and Sashay Back—Head couple links right elbows, turns once and a half around; head lady goes to second man, head man to second lady, linking left elbows, turns once around; on to third man and lady, then to fourth with right to the partner and left to the side. Couple sashays back to place. (Phrase 7 contains six measures to allow time for completion of pattern.)
New melody: Lines walk, men lead by head man to left, ladies by head lady to right. Head couple at foot of set forms arch and others go through to places with second couple now in head place.

The dance is repeated until all couples have been at head place or as many times as desired.

Dakota Hymn

Key: D minor   Starting Tone: D (1)
Meter: $\frac{4}{4}$ ($\frac{4}{\text{♩}}$)
No piano accompaniment

ABOUT THE MUSIC: The Dakotas, one of the largest Indian tribes, have always believed in a universal power that shows itself in nature—in rivers and lakes, trees and flowers, rain, lightning and fire. They have also believed in a life dedicated to giving. Notice the numerous references to nature in the dignified prayer. Discuss these ideas with the children in the first lesson when they hear the recording and study the text.

* EXPRESSION: Follow the suggestion in the pupil's book and have the children compare this song with "Beautiful Savior" on page 139. They are both songs of worship. They both express the idea of a divine being creating the earth. They are both prayers. In sound, one is major ("Beautiful Savior") and one is minor ("Dakota Hymn").

FORM: Play the recording of the song and ask the children to identify the song form (A B A). The first and last phrases are seven measures in length; the second phrase, eight measures.

* MELODY: Discuss the contour of the melody of the three phrases, noting that each phrase ascends to its highest note in the second measure, but in the second phrase the melody skips an octave to the highest note in the song. The melody of the song can be easily played on the bells. Learning to do this may be given as an assignment to individual children at times when they can work apart from the class.

Dakota Hymn

American Indian Melody
Words Paraphrased
by William Frazier

Ever since early times, men have sung songs of worship. Compare the ideas expressed in this song and those in the song on page 139. Compare the sound of the two songs.

Accompany the song by playing the drum with a soft mallet. Play a steady four-beat pattern with the accent on the first beat.

1. Man-y and great, O God, are thy things,
2. Grant un-to us com-mun-ion with thee,

Mak-er of earth and sky.   Thy hands have set the
Thou star-a-bid-ing one;   Come un-to us and

heav-ens with stars,   Thy fin-gers spread the
dwell with ___ us;   With thee are found the

moun-tains and plains.   Lo, at thy word the
gifts of ___ life.   Bless us with life that

wa-ters were formed;   Deep seas o-bey thy voice.
has no ___ end,   E-ter-nal life with thee.

Record 5 Side A Band 6. VOICES: men's ensemble.
ACCOMPANIMENT: drum.
FORM: Introduction, *1 meas.*; Vocal, *vv. 1-2.*

String Quartet No. 10 in C Major

First Movement

by Wolfgang Amadeus Mozart

Listen to this music for string quartet written by Mozart. A string quartet is made up of two violins, a viola, and a cello. The first violin plays the main melody. Notice times when the other instruments have important parts.

Mozart is remembered for his beautiful melodies. Listen to the melody which is the theme of this quartet. It is in two parts, A repeated, B repeated. Listen for the surprise toward the end of the second part.

Listen to the different ways Mozart treats this melody. Each new way is called a variation. In the first variation, the composer has used ornamentation. He has added tones to the original theme. Can you hear the original notes of the theme in the first variation?

In the second variation, the violin plays the melody an octave higher while the other instruments play a new accompaniment. Listen for the solo played by the viola.

In the next variation, Mozart alters the rhythm pattern.

In the fourth variation, the composer has added new material to the theme. While the violin continues to play the familiar theme, the other instruments play the new material in octaves.

Listen to the complete composition. Notice that it ends with a statement of the original version of the theme played without repeats.

Record 9   Side B   Band 5.
Barchet Quartet.

String Quartet No. 10 in C Major
First Movement

WOLFGANG AMADEUS MOZART (moh'-tsart)
BORN 1756   DIED 1791

Ask children to locate pictures of the instruments mentioned in their book (page 172). It was during Mozart's time that the string quartet became popular; many of Mozart's contemporaries, such as Haydn and Beethoven, began to write for this type of ensemble.

Discuss the meaning of the words "theme" and "variation." Before children listen to the music, ask them to think of ways that a composer might create variations on a theme.

Listen to the main theme; identify the two parts. The surprise is the rest which occurs on the first beat of measure seven of part B. Play the theme several times and discuss the contour so that children can recognize it when they listen to variations. Play the remainder of the composition; discuss each variation. Note that the two parts of the theme are not repeated during these sections.
◉

In Variation I, discuss the meaning of "ornamentation." One ornaments a dress by adding something to make it more interesting and pleasing. Mozart added new notes to make his original simple melody more interesting. WHAT HAS HAPPENED TO THE SURPRISE? (The violin plays a descending arpeggio.)
◉

During Variation II the accompaniment sounds in triplets:

Children may softly tap the rhythm as they listen to help sense the difference. Notice also that the melody has been slightly altered. The viola plays a brief solo during the surprise section.
◉

Notice the changes in rhythm during Variation III. WHAT OTHER DIFFERENCES DO YOU NOTICE? (The melody has been altered and ornamented.) Children may also be able to hear that the second violin plays the same melody as the first violin, an octave lower. Notice that the first violin plays a rising arpeggio during the surprise section.
◉

The new material in Variation IV consists of a thirty-second note pattern inserted at the end of each short motive of the theme.

Also, in the fifth measure, the second violin plays the original descending melody, while the first violin above it plays a new pattern which moves up. The A part is repeated and the B part omitted.

The Galway Piper

Key: E♭   Starting Tone: E♭ (1)
Autoharp Key: F   Starting Tone:
  F (1)
Autoharp chords not in Pupil's Book
Meter: $\frac{4}{4}$ $\left(\frac{4}{\downarrow}\right)$
Piano accompaniment on page 251

* EXPRESSION: Several components seem to contribute to the charm of this song—the bouncing quality of the rhythm in an even division of the beat into two, four, or three parts, and the melody moving up and down by close intervals or scale steps. The resulting jig melody is typically Irish.

The words should be sung lightly and crisply, especially on the sixteenth note patterns. Special care should be taken that the rhythm and melodic intervals are sung without undue slurring or blurring.

* RHYTHM: Study the rhythmic notation. On the board write the patterns which are made up entirely of notes that sound with the beat or in an even division of the beat. Have the class practice the patterns by clapping, playing percussion instruments, or chanting the words of the song. When the children have clapped or played each pattern several times in succession, ask them to clap or play the patterns consecutively as you point. Divide the children into groups and challenge the class to clap or play the patterns simultaneously, each group coming in when you point to the next pattern.

Beat
Patterns

* MELODY: Challenge the children to take turns and sing the melody with numbers, letters, or "loo." Have each child sing two measures. The class should note that the melody tones follow the scale or the interval of a third. Practice some of the patterns. Then challenge each child to sing in accurate rhythm and without changing tempo.

HARMONY: When you play the accompaniment in the pupil's book, the song is sung in the key of D. When you play the autoharp accompaniment in the teacher's edition, the song is in the key of F.

The Galway Piper

Irish Folk Song

Listen to the recording of this old Irish song. Study the interesting words. Listen again and study the notes of the melody. Discuss the special features that give charm to this song. Give reasons why people continue to enjoy singing it.

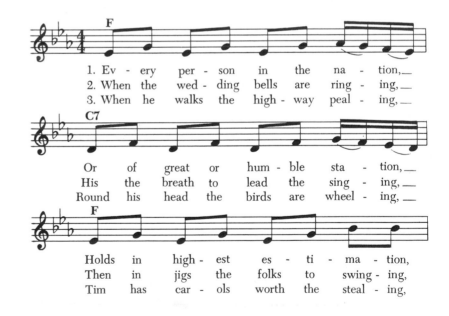

1. Ev - ery per - son in the na - tion,___
2. When the wed - ding bells are ring - ing,___
3. When he walks the high - way peal - ing,___

Or of great or hum - ble sta - tion,___
His the breath to lead the sing - ing,___
Round his head the birds are wheel - ing,___

Holds in high - est es - ti - ma - tion,
Then in jigs the folks to swing - ing,
Tim has car - ols worth the steal - ing,

Record 5   Side A   Band 7. VOICE: baritone.
ACCOMPANIMENT: recorder, percussion.
FORM: Introduction, *4 meas.;* Vocal, *v. 1;* Interlude, *1 meas.;*
Vocal, *v. 2;* Interlude, *1 meas.;* Vocal, *v. 3;* Coda, *1 meas.*

Pip - ing __ Tim __ of __ Gal - way.
What __ a __ splen - did __ pip - er!
Pip - ing __ Tim __ of __ Gal - way.

Loud - ly __ he can play or low;
He will __ blow from eve to morn,
Thrush and __ lin - net, finch and lark,

He can __ move you fast or slow,
Count - ing __ sleep a thing of scorn,
To each __ oth - er twit - ter, "Hark!"

Touch your __ heart or stir your toe,
Old he __ is but not worn out.
Soon they sing from light to dark,

Pip - ing __ Tim of Gal - way.
Know __ you __ such a pip - er?
Pip - ings __ learned in Gal - way.

You may add an interesting autoharp accompaniment to this song. Press down the D minor and the D7 chord buttons at the same time. Strum on the lower strings of the autoharp on the accented beat of each measure.

Review of Concepts of Design

Some of the following activities may be helpful in evaluating the children's progress as they develop concepts of design.

. . . Recognition of the phrase is basic to the understanding of all musical design, yet some fourth-grade children may still have trouble identifying the beginnings and endings of phrases. Help children learn to listen carefully for this small unit of music. Have each child make several cards; on each card, picture a different number of phrases.

. . . Play or sing a section of a song; ask the children to hold up the card which shows the correct number of phrases that they heard. On other days, choose individuals to sing a song or a section of a song while the class listens and holds up the card that shows the correct phrasing. The child who is singing must decide if the children's answers are correct.

. . . To evaluate the children's recognition of phrases, have them form a circle around the room. Play a recording of a familiar song. As children walk around the room in time to the music, they must turn at the beginning of each new phrase. Fourth-graders enjoy making this a game. The child who forgets to turn at the proper time must take his seat. Continue until only a few are left in the circle.

. . . Evaluate children's recognition of phrases as **same** or **different**. Divide the class into several small groups. Give each group the name of a familiar song. Ask them to plan movements which reflect the design of a song. Allow the groups to perform for each other. Ask the class to decide if the movements were appropriate for the song design.

. . . Cut interesting shapes from colored construction paper or from felt. Play a song or instrumental composition. Allow children to take turns arranging the shapes into a design which matches the musical design of a song.

. . . Give children an opportunity to draw or paint the design of a song as they listen. After the pictures are completed, hold a class discussion. Decide which pictures best reflect the design of the music. Point out that unity and variety in pictures may come from the use of color, line, and shape.

Pictures at an Exhibition

BY MODEST MUSSORGSKY
BORN 1839   DIED 1881

This suite of compositions was inspired by and named for paintings and drawings in a memorial exhibition of the works of Victor Hartmann held in St. Petersburg in 1874. Hartmann was primarily an architect but was also a designer in metal and wood, a designer of stage settings and costumes for the theater, and a painter in watercolor. The Russian composer Mussorgsky was much moved by the death of his close friend who had lived to be only thirty-nine. Mussorgsky wrote the music for piano in 1874 and it was later orchestrated by the French composer Maurice Ravel. In the latter form, the suite is popular in orchestral concerts. Mussorgsky is well known for his opera "Boris Godunov" and many delightful songs.

The suite holds particular interest for children and it is especially suitable for interpretation in movement and in children's painting and drawing. Many pianists play the composition, and you might invite someone to play for the class as a culmination of the study from the recording. You might also procure the recording of the orchestral version and play that for the class following their study of the original composition. There are ten parts in the complete suite, each with its own title. The parts not on this record would be of interest if you should later wish to teach additional sections.

Promenade

This music serves as an introduction to the suite and also as a connecting passage between the musical sketches. According to photographs, Mussorgsky was a portly man, and the rhythm of the music possibly indicates this. In addition, there are impressions, as the promenade is faster or slower, that the composer's attention was attracted to a picture, that he thinks sadly of his friend, and so on. The rhythm alternates between $\frac{5}{4}$ and $\frac{6}{4}$ (occasionally $\frac{3}{2}$) meter.

The Tuileries

The musical sketch of children playing and quarreling in the French garden is characterized by a song-like refrain and running scale passages. Children can learn the music very well as they move in their

Pictures at an Exhibition

by Modest Mussorgsky

The Russian composer wrote this music to honor a friend who had been an architect and painter. The composer attended an exhibit of his sketches and paintings. Certain works of the artist became the subjects of the composer's musical "pictures."

Promenade

First the composer placed himself inside the gallery. As you listen to "Promenade," you will be able to imagine his walk through the art gallery. From the music, can you imagine what the composer looked like? The Promenade Theme is heard again before the musical description of several of the pictures.

The Tuileries

The gardens called the Tuileries in Paris are a favorite playground for children. The artist's picture represented a path in the garden with a group of children and nursemaids. The composer added his own title for the musical picture: "Dispute of the Children after Play." What musical ideas did the composer use to "paint" the picture in music?

Record 10   Side A   Band 1.
Gary Graffman, pianist.

Ballet of the Unhatched Chicks

The picture was a sketch for a child's ballet costume. The costume was supposed to make the dancer look like a chicken coming out of the egg. The composer looked at the costume sketch and imagined the child's dance. What description of the dance and of the "unhatched chicks" do you hear in the music?

The Great Gate of Kiev

The architect's sketch was of a huge arched gate to be built in the city of Kiev. As the composer studied the sketch, he imagined a great procession. You will hear music describing military pageantry, the chanting of priests, and the triumphant ringing of bells. What sounds of the piano are used in the processional description? By what means did the composer relate this picture to the others and make it the **grand finale** for the entire work?

As you study the music on different days, discuss all the ways in which the Promenade Theme is played. Discuss the different sounds of the **piano** which give the composition variety. Discuss the composer's use of rhythm in the various pictures.

When you know the music, develop a dance with each composition. You might connect the dances to make a complete dance drama. You might enjoy sketching or painting your impression of how the pictures might have looked.

own interpretations. Two children might work together to dramatize the ideas inspired by the music.

Ballet of the Unhatched Chicks

The promenade theme in minor key precedes this section of the suite. Again in $\frac{2}{4}$ meter, but in quick tempo, the piece is composed of quick alternating notes of right and left hands, chromatic scale runs, cluster chords, and trills. It is easy to imagine the picking on the egg shell, the rustle inside, and for that matter, the dance of the "prematurely-hatched" ballet dancer, a bit of humor to be reserved for adult listeners. The music is in A B A design. Children will enjoy developing individual dances in their own "ballet."

The Great Gate of Kiev

In $\frac{4}{4}$ meter, and in tempo suggesting the majestic, the music presents a new version of the promenade theme. Mussorgsky then introduces an ancient hymn tune.

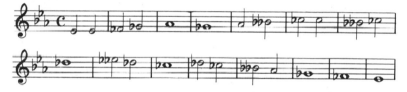

The grandiose composition is in G minor. There is great variety in the sounds of the piano in the heavy chords, scale tones played in octaves, the hymn melody with their harmonization in middle piano, the alternate left and right hand notes suggesting bell sounds, and the tremolo chords at the close of the music. The promenade theme is used to relate this musical picture to the others. Hartmann's picture was a fantastic sketch for a huge gate of carved stone, wrought iron, tile, and stained glass resting on columns sunk deep in the ground. The whole thing was topped by a cupola in the form of a helmet. The gate was never erected, but the sketch caught Mussorgsky's imagination, resulting in the musical picture of a gigantic procession through the gate.

Music and Other Arts
Painting and Sculpture

Time, place, circumstances, and materials at hand help to determine the nature of any work of art. The great artist—whether sculptor, painter, or composer—starts with what he has learned from the past. He builds on the past and, in doing so, affects the artistic thinking of those who follow him. Part of the style in which he works is of his own making, and part is a product of his age.

Michelangelo Buonarroti (1475-1564) lived in Italy at a time when princes of church and state wanted to sponsor great monuments. They often engaged in a kind of competition to commission great artists to create impressive monuments. They wanted realistic statues of heroic figures, designed with great attention to detail.

In 1505, Pope Julius commissioned Michelangelo to do a tomb with 40 figures illustrating the history of Christianity and the Church. Michelangelo first had to complete the ceiling of the Sistine Chapel. The Pope died in 1513, shortly after work on the tomb had begun. Money ran out, and the original plan was reduced. Only *Moses* and two other figures were actually completed for the tomb.

Moses has become one of Michelangelo's most famous and impressive works. Although the figure is seated, the exaggeration of the musculature and other physical elements gives the work an amazing aura of energy and strength. The textural contrasts add to the visual interest both in minute detail and in the entirety.

Moses is carved out of marble. Marble is hard and must be carved with chisels and a mallet. If finished properly, it has good highlights and shadows. It can show smooth surfaces as well as textures and can endure for centuries. When a sculptor works in marble, he works in a material that has a tradition of heroic themes designed to endure.

Henry Moore (born 1898) creates his works in an age when most sculpture is exhibited in public museums or kept in private homes. Today people rarely commission art works, but buy them after completion. The artist works to express his own personal ideas and emotions. Moore likes to bring out qualities of the material itself. He has often said that the material he uses helps determine the finished piece. He often uses wood. It is softer and less brittle than marble. Generally, it is carved with gouges and a mallet. Many sculptors try to incorporate the grain of the wood in their designs. Wood is not as durable as marble. It is not usually used for heroic themes.

Music and Other Arts

Painting and Sculpture

Like music, paintings and sculpture trace the story of man. Each period of time produces works of art which have their own style. Each artist has his own ideas and ways of expressing them.

The artist shows us the object or idea as it appears to him. Some works of art are realistic. Others give only an impression of a scene. Some paintings and sculpture include a great deal of detail. Others express through simple forms.

Study these photographs of sculpture. Notice the materials with which the artists worked. Discuss the differences in kinds of expression. What can you tell about the time when each artist lived and worked?

Study the photographs of great paintings opposite page 1 and on pages 23, 30, 120, 153, and 156.

MOORE, Henry, *Two Forms* (1934), Pynkado wood, 11" high, Collection, The Museum of Modern Art, New York, Gift of Sir Michael Sadler

Old man with pipe, Africa, Dahomey cast bronze, Courtesy of the AMERICAN MUSEUM OF NATURAL HISTORY

Michelangelo, *Moses*, Alinari—Art Reference Bureau

In this century simplicity of design is important. Strict realism is valued less than good design. The artist wants to *create* new forms. In *Two Forms* Moore has created two shapes that complement each other. Together they make a strong design. If we could walk around this piece, we would see that the changing negative space in and around the forms is as much a part of the design as the solid wood. The negative space itself becomes a form.

Dahomey is a small country in eastern Africa on the Gulf of Guinea. Since the *Old man with pipe* was probably made around the turn of this century, it is likely that the craftsman who made it was familiar with Western art and technology.

Pieces of this type were usually made by craftsmen for noblemen to give as presents. They were not designed to be heroic monuments nor experiments with artistic forms. They are stylized figures, simplified and exaggerated like caricatures.

The figure is of bronze, a medium requiring a method of working different from that used in stone or wood. The artist first created his figure in clay or wax. Instead of carving, he builds the figure up. Designs or textures, such as the patterns on the cloak and skirt are drawn on the soft surface. When the figure is completed, a mold is made and filled with molten bronze. The finished bronze is a duplicate of the clay figure and retains some feeling of the clay.

Modern artists of all countries have studied ancient and modern work of the rest of the world. For this reason, modern art is influenced by the art of the entire world, not just that of a particular area. Modern musicians also study the music of other countries and other times. In fact, if there is one element common to all modern art, it is the multiplicity of the past from which it borrows.

Like the sculptor, the musician must consider his materials: human voices, traditional musical instruments, and electronic media such as tape recorders and sound synthesizers. Each medium contributes a different sound quality. Each has its strengths and its limitations. The composer also considers how he will use his materials. His work may be intricate with sharp contrasts, like *Moses,* or it may be stylized with repeating patterns, like the *Old man with pipe,* or it may be broad and simple, like *Two Forms.*

Music may be light and humorous or grand and heroic. Or its main interest may be exploration of form. Pauses may give it shape. Like art, music is an expression of the character of a particular time, a particular place, and a particular man.

Little Fox

Key: F Starting Tone: C (5)
Autoharp chords in Pupil's Book
Meter: $\frac{4}{4}$ $\left(\frac{4}{\quarternote}\right)$
Piano accompaniment on page 252

* RHYTHM: The reading of the song may be completed in one or two lessons, depending upon the earlier experience of the class. Review the meter signature and its meaning (see page 34) and conduct the rhythm study as suggested in the children's book. Ask the class to locate the patterns of rhythm in the song. Each pattern might be practiced by repeating it four times. It may be best to write the patterns on the board. Tap the beat as the children are practicing. When children can clap and play the patterns, they should be able to clap easily or play the rhythm of the melody from the book. Then have the children chant the words in the correct rhythm.

* MELODY: Establish tonality by playing the scale and the chord tones F-A-C-A-F. Ask children to practice each pattern of melody by repeating it four times, first with numbers and then with letters. Then have the class locate the melody patterns in the song. When they can sing the patterns, they should be able to sing the melody from the book with letters and with "loo" as directed.

When children have sung the song once with words, play the recording and ask the class to listen and look at the notation in their books to discover whether they have read the song correctly.

Teach the rest of the verses. Explain to the class that the bracket under the words "to the" indicates that two syllables are sung to the quarter note above. In this case the quarter note is actually replaced by two eighth notes. In some songs a line is used after a word to indicate that the syllable is held through two notes. Write a few examples of this on the board. ("The Galway Piper," page 112, "Polly Wolly Doodle," page 106, or "Bound for the Rio Grande," page 99.)

Little Fox

English Folk Song

1. Lit - tle fox went out on a chil - ly night;
2. So the fox he ran till he came to the pen;

He prayed to the moon to give him light.
The ducks and the geese were put there - in.

He'd man - y a mile to go that night
"A cou - ple of you will grease my chin

Be - fore he'd reach the town - o, town - o, town - o,
Be - fore I leave this town - o, town - o, town - o,

He'd man - y a mile to go that night
A cou - ple of you will grease my chin

Be - fore he'd reach the town - o.
Be - fore I leave this town - o."

Record 5   Side B   Band 1.   VOICE: tenor.
ACCOMPANIMENT: lute.
FORM: Introduction, *4 meas.;* Vocal, *vv. 1-5;* Coda, *2 meas.*

3. Well he grabbed a grey goose by the neck;
   He flung it up across his back.
   He didn't mind the quack, quack, quack, } 2 times
   And the legs all dangling down-o

4. Now old Missus Flipperflopper jumped out of bed;
   And up to the window she cocked her head.
   She cried, "John, O John, the grey goose is gone, } 2 times
   And the fox is on the town-o."

5. Little fox he ran till he came to his den;
   And there were his little ones, eight, nine, ten.
   They said, "Daddy, you'd better go back again, } 2 times
   It must be a mighty fine town-o."

The following patterns of rhythm are in the song but not in this order. Practice the patterns. Clap them and play them on instruments. Practice each measure separately and then play the patterns straight through.

Look at the notes in your book. Clap the rhythm. Chant the words in rhythm.

The following patterns of melody are in the song but not in this order. Practice the patterns. Sing them with numbers and with letters. Then find the patterns in the song.

Look at the notes in your book. Sing the melody of the song with letters as you tap on the beat. Sing the melody with "loo."

Improvisation in Rhythm

As suggested on page xvi of this book, children can gain understanding of rhythm as they enjoy games of experimentation and improvisation. They may chant a word pattern and determine the notation of the rhythm. They may accompany their chants with percussion instruments and later play the patterns of rhythm without the chant.

Go tell Aunt Rho - - die

John Brown had a lit -tle In - dian

Suggest that a child make up an original chant. As he continues his chant, another child may chant other words in the same rhythm but in a different pattern.

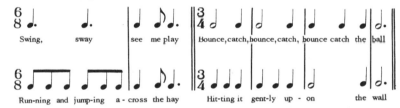

Swing, sway see me play | Bounce, catch, bounce, catch, bounce catch the ball

Run-ning and jump-ing a - cross the hay | Hit-ting it gent-ly up - on the wall

When the children have become fluent in speaking and notating original chants, suggest that they compose a "rhythm rondo." They may agree upon one chant as the main theme or A section of the rondo which the class will chant. One class member may add a different rhythm but with the same number of beats and call it the B section after which the A section is chanted again. Section C is added by another child and so on until the rondo has five or six different sections. The same game can be played with children playing rhythms on percussion instruments instead of speaking in chants.

Another rhythm game might be a cumulative one. The first child plays a rhythm, the next child plays the first rhythm and adds a new one, the third child remembers and repeats the first two rhythms and adds a new one. The game continues until everyone in the circle or line has "missed" by being unable to repeat the entire set of rhythms.

Three Musicians

BY PABLO PICASSO
BORN 1881

Musicians and artists of our time have studied music and art of long ago as well as the music and art of far away. Using what they learned and adding their own ideas and imaginations, they have created new styles that are very clearly of our own time.

In art, one of the men who has been part of almost every great movement, who has experimented with his own ideas, and who has learned from other artists, is Pablo Picasso. Many people consider him to be the greatest of modern artists. In his work we see an emphasis on the formal aspects of painting: shapes, colors, arrangement. We can contrast this with the romantic themes of the nineteenth century in which the emphasis was on love of nature and a heroic image of man.

Three Musicians captures much of the spirit of modern music as well as modern art. Picasso incorporates the modern style of echoed tones and contours in place of strict repetition of form. He also indicates a very modern sense of humor in such details as the mustache on the figure at the left and the almost hidden dog with his ears at the left and his tail wagging under the table. The costumes on the three figures suggest some borrowing from classical stage figures of the past. But the subject matter is less important than the creation of an abstract composition in which colors play against each other to give life to the work. Notice how the white stands out against the browns and blue, but recedes next to the harlequin pattern. Other colors likewise recede or stand out according to the neighboring color. The angularity of the entire composition not only unifies the work, but is a major theme.

Have the class return to this as they listen to such contemporary pieces as *Imitations* by Milton Babbitt (page 124) and *Ionisation* by Edgar Varese (page 126). Discuss the modern interest in form and experimentation.

PICASSO, Pablo, *Three Musicians* 1921 (summer), Oil on canvas, 6'7" x 7'3¾", Collection, The Museum of Modern Art, New York, Mrs. Simon Guggenheim Fund

Music Here and Now

Today we can enjoy music from far away, music of long ago, and music of here and now. We like to sing songs from other countries and of many years ago. We enjoy the old and new songs of our own country. We enjoy music composed by artists of our time. We can hear great music from all over the world on recordings and at concerts.

Music is important to each of us. We can express our thoughts and feelings in music. We can make music by ourselves or with other people. We like to explore different ways of making music.

Enjoy the music that you know at different times and in many places. Join in the music of worship. Sing, play, or dance for recreation at camp or with your friends at home. Your school day will be happier and more interesting if you study music.

You can develop some special skills in music. Discover music that you especially like and learn it well. It will be with you wherever you are. Listen for new sounds in music of today. Learn to make new music of your own as you explore music here and now.

Read the page aloud together and discuss each idea. As children read the first paragraph, ask them to recall songs they have learned from far away. What songs of long ago have they learned which they enjoyed? Look through the songs in this section to find music composed by artists of our time. Discuss reasons why songs such as "Old Texas" and "Weggis Dance" are included in Music Here and Now. Suggest that it might be because we can enjoy today songs that were composed long ago and far away.

Read the second paragraph. Ask children to recall the different ways one can make music. The children might suggest playing instruments, singing, composing individual compositions, or dancing. Give each child an opportunity to talk about the way he likes best.

The third paragraph describes some of the different times and places in which to enjoy music. Ask children to tell of times they have participated in music as suggested in this paragraph. Have they sung at church? Have they joined in singing at camp? Are there other times and places that they have joined in musical activities which are not mentioned on this page?

It's Quiet on the Moon

Key: F   Starting Tone: C (5)
Meter: $\frac{4}{4}$ $\left(\frac{4}{\text{♩}}\right)$
Piano accompaniment on page 254

EXPRESSION: Read the first paragraph in the pupil's book. Invite the children to offer their ideas about life on the moon and other planets. When the children have learned the melody, follow the suggestions in their book and write a second verse about life on another planet.

* HARMONY: Help children to answer the question in their book. The two voices are a **third** apart in the first measure. To determine the **interval** between two notes, call the lowest note "1." Count each line and space to the highest note:

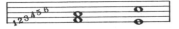

Practice singing up and down the scale in thirds, then in sixths. Listen carefully to be sure your voices are in tune!

Scan the notation of the first section of the song (lines one and two). Find places where the voices move by steps, by skips. WHEN DO THE TWO VOICES MOVE IN THE SAME DIRECTION? (The measures where they sing in thirds.) CAN YOU FIND PLACES WHERE THE MELODIES MOVE IN OPPOSITE DIRECTIONS? (Measures 2 and 6.)

Divide the class in two groups. Establish tonality and encourage children to sing the two parts at the same time. Sing on "loo." Listen to the recording and help children correct their errors. Work on both parts at the same time so that children will begin to develop the correct habits of part singing.

Ask two children to play the song on the bells as a duet. They may take turns playing the unison section.

FORM: Be sure children understand the explanation of *"D.C. al Fine"* given in their books. Listen to the song and determine the design: A B A. Notice that each section is made up of two phrases. In the A section the two phrases are the same. The B section is made up of two contrasting phrases.

It's Quiet on the Moon

Words and Music
by Ruth De Cesare

Music often expresses the ideas and interests of the time in which we live. Today we are interested in the exploration of space. The words of this song are one person's ideas about the moon.

It's   qui-et   on   the shin-ing moon to - night;___
Per - haps we'll reach the shin-ing moon to - night;___

We've   seen   its   pic - ture from our sat - el - lite.___

Fine

Now   all   the   stars are wink- ing, bright-en - ing the sky;

D.C. al Fine

Lone - ly plan - ets blink - ing   show it's time to   try.

When you know the melody, write a verse about another planet.

The first section of this song is to be sung in two-part harmony. Look at the first measure. How far apart are the voices? At the end of the second measure, the voices are a **sixth** apart.

Notice the sign *"D. C. al Fine."* It means to return to the beginning and sing to the end marked *"Fine."* How does this affect the design?

Record 5   Side B   Band 2.   VOICES: children's choir.
ACCOMPANIMENT: 2 saxophones, contra bassoon, celesta, timpani.
FORM: Instrumental fade-in; Vocal; Instrumental (vocal beginning on 3rd line); Instrumental fade-out.

A Timely Rhyme

Music by Jean Moe
Words Anonymous

The music for "A Timely Rhyme" was composed by a present-day composer. Listen to the recording. Compare this composed song with "Old Folks at Home" on page 104. Discuss the differences which help you to know that "A Timely Rhyme" was composed a hundred years after "Old Folks at Home."

The time of day I do not tell as some do by the clock,

Or by the dis-tant chim-ing bell set on some stee-pled rock;

But by the pro-gress that I see in what I have to do,

It's ei-ther "done o'-clock" for me, or on-ly "half-past through."

Record 5 Side B Band 3. VOICES: children's choir.
ACCOMPANIMENT: piano.
FORM: Introduction, *3 meas.*; Vocal; Coda, *3 meas.*

Key: F Starting Tone: C (5)
Meter: $\frac{2}{4}$ $\left(\frac{2}{\text{♩}}\right)$
Piano accompaniment on page 255

A Timely Rhyme

* COMPOSER'S STYLE: Read the paragraph in the pupil's book. Listen to the recording of "A Timely Rhyme" and of "Old Folks at Home," page 104. Discuss the differences in the sound. The melody of "Old Folks at Home" has much repetition and a strong feeling of home tone. The melody for "A Timely Rhyme" often moves in an unexpected manner to tones that do not belong to the key. There is little repetition. Some children may be able to sense the lack of a strong home tone in the middle section of the song.

Compare the accompaniments of the two songs. Foster's accompaniment follows the melodic line and is primarily choral. The accompaniment for "A Timely Rhyme" often moves in contrasting directions and rhythms. The chords are more complex than those of "Old Folks at Home."

* MELODY: Ask children to determine the key. Sing up and down the F scale. Write the scale on the chalkboard. Listen to the recording. DOES THE MELODY ALWAYS SOUND AS THOUGH IT WERE USING THE TONES OF THIS SCALE? Help children discover as they listen that the end of the second phrase (measures seven and eight) and the entire third phrase do not sound as though they were in F. Look at the notation and draw attention to the **accidentals.** SOMETIMES A COMPOSER WISHES TO ADD INTEREST TO HIS MELODY BY USING TONES OTHER THAN THOSE IN THE SCALE ON WHICH THE SONG IS BASED. HE TELLS US THE NEW TONES BY ADDING SHARPS OR FLATS IN FRONT OF THE NOTE. THE ACCIDENTALS INDICATE THAT THE TONE SHOULD BE RAISED (SHARPS) OR LOWERED (FLATS). To help children understand the function of the accidental, play the melody of measures 7-12 omitting all accidentals.

The melody now remains in F and we can identify the home tone. It is still an acceptable melody, but it is not as interesting or as appropriate to the mood of the words.

Imitations
for two instruments

BY MILTON BABBITT
BORN 1916

The title refers to the seven sections of the composition, each of which can be considered a specific kind of imitation of the twelve-tone set which is the basis of the composition. Each of the seven sections is begun by the lower voice, and in the reduction of the pupil's page they are marked with bracketed numbers.

Within each section, each voice states a form of the twelve-tone set. In addition, the total progression of the two voices is always in twelve-note units. Following is a reduction of the first section without the music values showing that the notes progress both vertically and horizontally in twelve-note units.

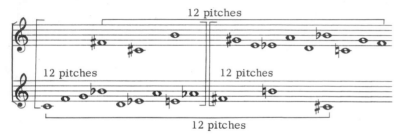

The phrase marks (slurs) divide the twelve pitches into groupings of three, four, and five notes. These groupings indicate the collections of notes (not necessarily in the same order but the same pitches) which are shared (or imitated) between the two voices in a particular section. For example, below is an analysis of the phrase groups in section three.

Notice that the second voice begins one note later in each successive section, so that in section one the second voice begins after three notes, in section two after four notes, in section three after five notes, and so on.

Imitations
for two instruments

by Milton Babbitt

Milton Babbitt, a well-known American composer, wrote this composition especially for this book.

Record 10   Side A   Band 2.

124

Children may be helped to discover some other manifestations of the technique. For example, have half of the class read aloud only the pitch names of the lower voice at the beginning of section seven (starting with the pitch C), while the other half reads silently the pitches of the upper voice in section six starting with the *last* note and going backwards. They will discover that the sequence of pitches is the same. When the pitches of a twelve-tone set are imitated by progressing backwards pitch 12 to pitch 1, it is called a **retrograde.**

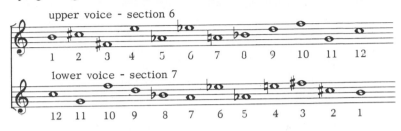

Section two is an example of imitation by **inversion.** The upper voice imitates all the pitch intervals in a mirror-like fashion. In other words, if the first voice moves down a whole step and then *down* a perfect fourth, the second voice will imitate by moving up a whole step and then *up* a perfect fourth. In the illustration below, the lines indicate the general contour of the two parts, the second part being a mirror image of the first.

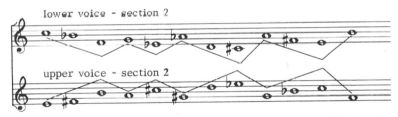

In the recording of "Imitations," listen for each section to begin with a clarinet solo, which is soon "imitated" by the oboe. Notice that the entire piece is in $\frac{3}{4}$ meter except for section four, the very middle of the piece, which is in $\frac{4}{4}$ with slow triplets.

Remind children that just as it is not necessary to be aware of all the compositional techniques while listening to traditional music, they do not need to hear every twelve-tone device in "Imitations." It should be played several times during the year until children become familiar with its sound and structure.

Ionisation

BY EDGAR VARESE (va-rezź)
BORN 1883   DIED 1965

Play the recording before the children have read the discussion in their books. Present it without comment, then ask children to give their reactions to what they heard. DOES THIS SOUND LIKE OTHER MUSIC YOU HAVE HEARD? IN WHAT WAYS IS IT DIFFERENT? IN WHAT WAYS IS IT SIMILAR? Children may suggest that it is different because they can hear no melody or harmony. It is similar in that some of the instruments are familiar, and it contains many interesting rhythms. Some may suggest that it sounds like primitive music.

Read the first paragraph aloud with the children. Discuss the first sentence. WHY WOULD YOU KNOW THAT THIS WAS WRITTEN BY A COMPOSER OF TODAY? Help children conclude that this type of music, in which tone color and rhythm are emphasized instead of melody and harmony, is a recent musical development. It is one of the many kinds of music which have resulted from the search of modern composers for new musical sounds.

Listen again and ask children to identify as many percussion instruments as possible. Following is a complete list: gongs of high and low pitches (called tam-tams); cymbals; three sizes of bass drums (which sound at different pitches); bongo drums; snare drums; quiros; Chinese temple blocks; claves; triangle; maracas; castanets; tambourine; chimes; celesta; and piano. The last three instruments are heard only at the end of the composition. The music on this recording is an excerpt from the complete composition and does not include these instruments.

In addition, instruments which may be heard that are not usually considered musical instruments include two sirens of different pitches, anvils in two registers, sleighbells, and slapsticks.

Discuss ways the composer builds a climax: he adds instruments, creates more complex rhythms, makes sudden contrasts of tone colors.

In discussing the title, suggest that Varese may have treated his composition by a method similar to ionization. He adds and subtracts sounds, as one adds and subtracts electrons. He may also have chosen the title to help people know that this is a contemporary composition because the process of ionization was developed during this century.

Ionisation

by Edgar Varese

When you listen to "Ionisation," you will know that it was written by a composer of today. Varese combined interesting sounds in his compositions. He explored different qualities, colors, and textures of sounds. Other composers create a composition by combining sounds of different pitches in an interesting way. Varese created his composition by arranging sounds of different quality in an interesting sequence.

Varese used many common percussion instruments in "Ionisation." He also introduced some sound-makers which are not usually considered musical instruments. What do you think Varese used to produce the wailing sound in this composition? As you listen to "Ionisation," try to identify other sound-makers and percussion instruments.

Notice how sounds of contrasting quality and texture are heard one after the other. Booming, ringing, swishing, and rattling sounds follow one another quickly. High-pitched sounds follow low-pitched ones. Loud sections contrast with calm, quiet sections. In what way does the composer build a climax?

Ionization is a scientific word which means "the adding or subtracting of one or more electrons to an atom, giving it an electrical charge." Why do you think Varese chose this title for his musical composition?

Record 10   Side A   Band 3.
Ensemble; Robert Craft, conductor.

Search for sounds that you think would be interesting to use in a musical composition.

Play each of your percussion instruments. Group them by the sounds they make: booming, ringing, rattling, swishing, and so on. Explore different ways of playing on these instruments. Find other sound-makers in your classroom or at home. Add them to your list.

Work in groups of three or four and plan a composition. Choose sounds of contrasting quality. Play a different rhythm on each instrument. Decide when each sound pattern should begin and end.

You may wish to repeat some of your patterns. You might repeat the pattern exactly. You might play only part of it. You might extend the pattern by creating a variation.

Practice your composition until you are satisfied with the sequence of sounds. Play your composition for the class.

When children have studied "Ionisation," read the suggestions on this page in the pupil's book. Give the class the opportunity to experiment with each percussion instrument and to explore different ways of playing each instrument. Encourage the children to create different and unusual sounds. For example, tap the drum with different types of mallets; play in different places on the drumhead and on the sides of the drum. Discover the differences in the sound of a tambourine when it is shaken, when it is tapped with the tips of the fingers, and when it is played with a soft beater. Lay the tambourine on a desk and tap it to discover another sound. Group the instruments in various categories as suggested in the pupil's book.

Invite children to bring "sound-makers" from home. Explore the sound possibilities of each of these "instruments." Group them according to type of sound. The children may have to add new titles to the categories suggested in their book in order to include all the different kinds of sounds they have discovered.

When the class has completed the exploration of sounds, divide the children into small groups to develop original compositions. Before they begin to work, discuss the suggestions in the pupil's book. Each group might choose one or two instruments from each of the sound categories. Encourage the children to experiment with different rhythm patterns to make their compositions as varied as possible.

Review the discussion on design on page 101. Talk about developing rhythmic motives, melodic phrases, and sections for their compositions. Recall three-part form and the rondo. Children may wish to base their composition on one of these designs. Remind them that interesting compositions must have variety. Talk about the ways they can create variety. Refer again to "Ionisation" and examine the ways Varese created variety in his composition. Discuss ways of creating a climax in their music. Talk about the necessity of repetition of instrumentation and musical ideas to create unity.

When children have had the opportunity to improvise their compositions and to practice them, have a class program. Each group may play its composition for the class. Discuss each composition in terms of its use of tone color, rhythms, and design.

Psalm 100

Key: D   Starting Tone: A (5)

Meter: $\frac{4}{4}$ ($\frac{4}{\downarrow}$)

Piano accompaniment on page 256

* EXPRESSION: Discuss the fact that much of the music of worship which we sing today was actually written long ago. Many present-day composers have written music using scripture from the Bible. Such is the case with this song. Ask children to recall other songs of worship which they have learned which were first sung long ago but which we still enjoy today.

Locate the various marks of expression on the song page. These were introduced on page 75. Review the meaning of each: *"mf"* means "moderately loud"; *"f"* means "loud"; *"ff"* means "very loud." Notice the crescendo mark near the end of the song. Discuss the importance of singing according to marks of expression, but remind children that they must also sing with a pleasing quality. DO NOT SING SO LOUDLY IN THE SECTIONS MARKED "FF" THAT THE SOUND OF YOUR VOICE BECOMES HARSH!

* FORM: Listen to the song. Study the notation and write the design in letters. Discuss the unusual characteristics of this design in comparison to most songs that the children know. The phrases are of different lengths and there is little melodic repetition. A (4 measures) B (5 measures) C (8 measures) A′ (10 measures, extended to include a coda).

MELODY: When children have studied the design, observe the contour of the melody. Notice that it moves primarily by steps. Practice the skip from 5 down to 2 (end of first phrase, beginning of third phrase). Establish tonality, ask children to sing the song with numbers. Listen to the recording to correct any reading errors. Then sing the song with words, observing the marks of expression.

Psalm 100

Music by Jane M. Marshall

The words of this song are ancient. The music was written by a composer of today. Study the design. How many phrases are in the song? Write the design of the phrases with letters.

Gaily

Make a joy - ful noise un - to_ the Lord, all ye lands.

Serve the Lord_with glad - ness: come be - fore_ his pres - ence with

sing - ing. En - ter his gates_ with thanks-giv - ing, _

_ and his courts, his courts with praise: _

Make a joy - ful noise un - to_ the Lord, _

all ye lands. _____

Record 5   Side B   Band 4.   VOICES: children's choir.
ACCOMPANIMENT: piano.
FORM: Introduction, *4 meas.;* Vocal.

People take the music of other lands and make it their own. In Israel, this is a work song. In the United States, we sing it for recreation.

Zum Gali Gali

Israeli Work Song

```
(Melody) Gm                    C        Gm

1. He - cha - lutz      l' - maan a - vo - dah; _____
2. A - vo - dah         l' - maan he - cha - lutz; _____
3. He - cha - lutz      l' - maan ha - b'tu - lah; _____
4. Ha - sha - lom       l' - maan ha - 'a - mim; _____

Chant

Zum ga - li ga - li ga - li, Zum ga - li ga - li,

Gm                             C        Gm

___ A - vo - dah       l' - maan he - cha - lutz.
___ He - cha - lutz    l' - maan a - vo - dah.
___ Ha - b'tu - lah    l' - maan he - cha - lutz.
___ Ha - 'a - mim      l' - maan ha - sha - lom.

Zum ga - li ga - li ga - li, Zum ga - li ga - li.
```

Listen to the recording to learn to pronounce the words.

Sing the chant softly as an **introduction** to the song. At the end of the fourth verse, repeat the chant several times as a **coda.** Let your voices grow gradually softer in a **diminuendo.** Gradually sing more slowly during the last repetition in a **ritard.**

Record 5 Side B Band 5. VOICES: baritone, children's choir.
ACCOMPANIMENT: tambourine.
FORM: Introduction, *4 meas.;* Vocal, *vv. 1-4;* Vocal fade-out.

Key: F minor   Starting Tone: F (1)
Autoharp Key: G minor
  Starting Tone: G (1)
Autoharp chords not in Pupil's Book
Meter: 2/4 (♩)
No piano accompaniment

* EXPRESSION: Discuss the first paragraph in the pupil's book. Review some of the other work songs that the children have learned this year such as "Donkey Riding," page 36, and "The Railroad Corral," page 4. Discuss the fact that these songs are also work songs which we can enjoy singing for recreation. Listen to "Zum Gali Gali." WHY IS THIS A GOOD WORK SONG? (The steady tempo and strong accents provide a good rhythm for work.)

* HARMONY: Study the song page; discover that this is a song to be sung in harmony. The low part is a **chant,** that is, the same melody is repeated over and over. The high part is the main melody. Notice that it is also repetitious.

* MELODY: WHAT IS THE HOME TONE IN THIS SONG? Remind children that they must not only look at the key signature to determine the home tone but must also scan the melody line. Notice that the song centers around F Ab and C, the first, third, and fifth steps of F minor. If the song were in F major, it would center around F A and C.

Sing up and down the F Minor Scale:

Scan the notation of the chant. Notice that it moves by steps, except for the skip down to low 5 in measures two and four. Challenge children to sing the chant without assistance.

Study the notation of the melody. It also moves by steps. Divide the class into two groups. While one group repeats the chant, encourage the other group to sing the melody at sight on a neutral syllable. Listen to the recording to learn the Hebrew words.

When the song is learned, follow the suggestions in the pupil's book and add an introduction and coda. Discuss the meaning of the words *diminuendo* and *ritard.*

The Hebrew words mean: (1) The pioneer's purpose is labor, (2) Labor is for the pioneer. (3) The pioneer works with his girl. (4) Peace for all nations.

Banana Boat Loader's Song

Key: G   Starting Tone: G (1)
Meter: $\frac{4}{4}$ (𝅘𝅥)
Piano accompaniment on page 259

* FOLK STYLE: Read the paragraph on page 130 in the pupil's book. Locate the West Indies on a world map. Listen to the recording and discuss the characteristics of calypso music. Some of the unique features which children may observe include the shifting of word accents to accommodate the rhythm of the melody, the many interesting rhythmic patterns which are heard simultaneously in melody and accompaniment, and the wide variety of percussion instruments.

As children study the melody, draw attention to another characteristic—the melody is based primarily on tones of the I and V7 chords. This is also true of music from other parts of Latin America. Compare the sound of this song with "La Jesucita," page 179, and "San Serení," page 178.

EXPRESSION: Calypso songs often tell of daily activities. The first calypso songs came from the plantations in the West Indies. The leader of the work gang would sing to keep his workers happy as they labored. This song may have originated on a banana plantation or at the docks where the bananas were loaded to be shipped to the United States. The calypso singer often made up words and music as he sang. The songs are sometimes sung in question and answer form similar to the style of the Negro work songs of this country. When children know the song well, they will enjoy singing it in this style. Choose a leader to sing the verse sections; the class may join in on the repetitive refrains. Suggest to the leader that he might make up new words to keep his workers interested!

On the recording, notice how the last phrase is repeated over and over, growing softer and softer, until it fades out.

Banana Boat Loader's Song

Jamaican Folk Song

This song from the West Indies is a **calypso** work song. Find the West Indies on a map. Calypso songs are popular in the United States.

Day oh! Day_ oh! Day is break - ing,_ I wan' go home._

1. Come, Mis - ter Tal - ly - man, come tal - ly my ba - nan - as.
2. Came here for work, I did - n't come here for to i - dle.

Day is break - ing,_ I wan' go home._

3. Three han', four han', five han', Bunch!

Six han' seven han' eight han', Bunch!

Day is break - ing,_ I wan' go home._

Record 5   Side B   Band 6.   VOICES: baritone, children's choir.
ACCOMPANIMENT: cowbells, guitar, claves, bongo drums.
FORM: Introduction, *9 meas.;* Vocal, *vv. 1-6.* Instrumental and vocal fade-out.

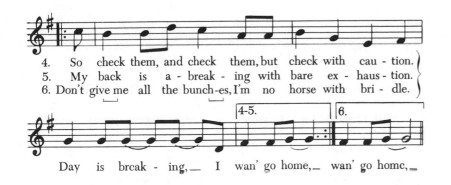

4. So check them, and check them, but check with cau - tion.
5. My back is a - break - ing with bare ex - haus - tion.
6. Don't give me all the bunch-es, I'm no horse with bri - dle.

Day is break - ing, — I wan' go home, — wan' go home, —

People from the West Indies often improvise percussion accompaniments for their songs. They use deep-pitched **conga drums,** two-headed **bongo drums,** and **cowbells.** They also play **maracas,** which are gourds filled with dried seeds. **Claves,** sticks made of hardwood, always have an important part in accompaniments from the West Indies.

Find these patterns in the song. Practice each pattern until you can play it correctly. When the class knows all the patterns, choose the ones that you like best to accompany the song.

* RHYTHM: As children listen to the recording, draw attention to the interesting rhythm on "Day is breaking, I wan' go home." It is created by shifting accents to the unimportant part of the beat. This type of rhythm is called **syncopation.** To help children feel the syncopated rhythm, ask them to clap and chant this pattern as one child taps the beat:

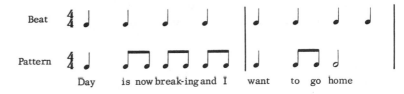

Now tap and chant the pattern from the song. Discuss the difference. Notice that in the second pattern they are tapping and chanting just ahead of the beat instead of with it. This causes a shift in the accent to the unimportant part of the beat and creates an uneven pulsation.

Listen to the recording again. Sing softly with the recording on this repetitive chant. When children can sing it accurately, suggest that they also join in on the verse sections. Notice the difference in rhythm. The patterns in these sections are even and regular, and sound with the beat.

HARMONY: Follow the instructions in the pupil's book and play a calypso accompaniment. See the article, "Latin-American Instruments" on page 17 for additional suggestions.

Old Texas

Key: F   Starting Tone: C (5)
Autoharp chords in Pupil's Book
Meter: $\frac{2}{4}$ $\left(\frac{2}{\downarrow}\right)$
Piano accompaniment on page 260

EXPRESSION: Ask children to recall other work songs of long ago and far away which they have learned this year. Review some of these such as "Donkey Riding" on page 36 and "The Railroad Corral" on page 4.

MELODY: Scan the notation. Notice that most of the melody is made up of 1-3-5. Establish tonality. Divide the class into two groups and sing the song in two parts as suggested in the pupil's book. Then listen to the recording to see if the class sang the song correctly.

MUSICAL SYMBOLS AND TERMS: Draw attention to the curved lines above the words "leave" and "old." Help the children learn the difference in their meaning. The first curve, above "leave" connects two notes on the same space and is called a **tie**. It tells us to hold the word through the time value for both notes (two and a quarter beats). The second curve, above "old" connects notes on different lines and spaces. It is called a **slur**. It tells us to sing the one word on two notes.

Doney Gal

Key: G   Starting Tone: D (5)
Autoharp chords in Pupil's Book
Meter: $\frac{3}{4}$ $\left(\frac{3}{\downarrow}\right)$
Piano accompaniment on page 260

* **RHYTHM:** Ask one child to study the meter signature and establish the beat. Ask the class to decide if he has established it correctly. Discuss the importance of tapping a steady beat and clearly accenting the first beat in each group of three.

Study the rhythmic notation of the refrain. Help children realize that the rhythm of the melody begins on the third beat of the measure.

Old Texas

Cowboy Song

"Old Texas" and "Doney Gal" are work songs of long ago. They are still enjoyed today.

This is an "echo" song. Group one sings the first phrase, "I'm goin' to leave old Texas now." While they hold the last word of this phrase, group two echoes the melody. Sing the complete song in this manner.

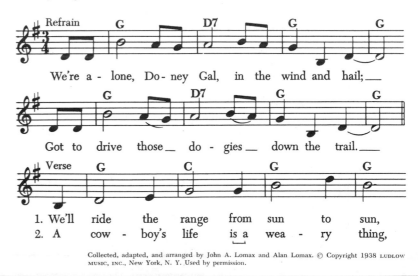

Doney Gal

Cowboy Song

Collected, adapted, and arranged by John A. Lomax and Alan Lomax. © Copyright 1938 LUDLOW MUSIC, INC., New York, N. Y. Used by permission.

Record 5   Side B   Band 7.   VOICE: baritone.
ACCOMPANIMENT: 2 guitars, double bass.
FORM: Introduction, *2 meas.;* Vocal; Instrumental; Vocal; Instrumental (voice on hum); Vocal; Instrumental fade-out.

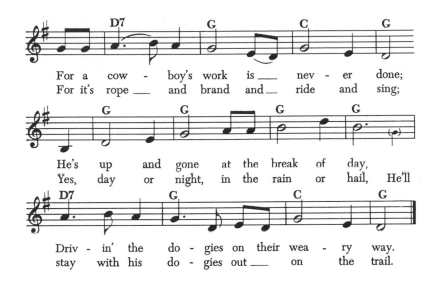

For a cow - boy's work is ___ nev - er done;
For it's rope ___ and brand and ___ ride and sing;

He's up and gone at the break of day,
Yes, day or night, in the rain or hail, He'll

Driv - in' the do - gies on their wea - ry way.
stay with his do - gies out ___ on the trail.

Accompaniments to cowboy songs often suggest an "on the trail" feeling. On the recording this feeling is provided by the guitar and temple blocks. Listen to the recording and develop a similar accompaniment of your own.

Play, on the piano, the same basic pattern played by the guitar.

Sometimes you will have to change one note in the pattern to create better harmony with the melody.

Decide where in the song you play pattern A and where you play pattern B.

Record 5   Side B   Band 8.   VOICE: baritone.
ACCOMPANIMENT: harmonica, guitar, double bass, percussion.
FORM: Introduction, *8 meas.;* Vocal, *v. 1;* Interlude, *8 meas.;*
Vocal, *v. 2;* Instrumental fade-out.

WE SAY IT BEGINS ON THE UP-BEAT. Notice the repetitious rhythm in the first phrase. Compare it with the rhythm of phrase two. WHAT DO YOU NOTICE ABOUT THE TWO PHRASES? (They are exactly the same.) THE RHYTHM OF THE VERSE IS EVEN EXCEPT FOR THREE MEASURES. CAN YOU FIND THEM? (Measures 5, 13, and 14.)

* MELODY: Study the key signature; determine that the song is in G. Ask one child to establish tonality by playing D-G(low)-B-D-G(high). Notice that the song begins with a skip from low 5 to 3. Practice this interval. Sing the melody with numbers, then with words.

HARMONY: Follow the suggestions in the pupil's book and add an accompaniment. Help the children decide that they will need to play the B pattern in measures 2, 6, 13, and 21. The patterns can be played in any octave. When the children can play the patterns in the treble clef, write them on the board in the bass clef. Draw attention to the new clef sign (𝄢). THIS IS CALLED A BASS CLEF. IT IS USED FOR MELODIES THAT ARE MADE UP OF TONES TOO LOW TO BE PLACED ON THE TREBLE STAFF (𝄞), the staff which is used for all of the melodies in our book. Help children learn the names of the lines and spaces of the bass staff by moving down from Middle C, the line which appears between the two staffs.

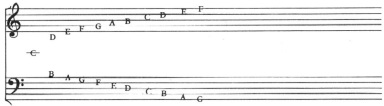

Give children an opportunity to practice reading the accompaniment from the bass clef. Some children who are studying piano will be able to play the accompaniment easily. For children with no piano experience, suggest that they practice alone.

Listen to the harmonica as it plays the introduction on the recording. Notate the last four measures of the introduction on the chalkboard and have children sing it on the "loo."

Brethren in Peace Together

Key: E minor   Starting Tone: G (3)
Meter: $\frac{6}{4}$ (♩)
Piano accompaniment on page 262

* RHYTHM: Notice that the meter signature is $\frac{6}{4}$. Discuss its meaning. The song will move in sixes and the quarter note is the beat note. However, this song will sound in twos, with accents falling on the first and fourth beats, as do many songs which are written in $\frac{6}{8}$.

$$(\; ♩ \; ♩ \; ♩ \; ♩ \; ♩ \; ♩ \;)$$

* MELODY: Guide children to discover that this song is in E minor. Discuss the fact that the key signature is the same as the key signature for G major. Help children realize why the same key signature is used for both scales. Arrange the bells for the G major scale. Review the fact that there is one sharp, F♯. Now arrange the bells for the E minor scale. Help children realize that exactly the same tones are used in both scales; only the sequence is different:

G Major: G A B C D E F♯ G
E Minor: E F♯ G A B C D E

In the first scale, G is heard as the home tone. Melodies written in G will center around G, B, and D, the first, third, and fifth tones of the scale. In E minor, E is heard as the home tone and melodies will center around E, G, and B. Scan the notation; notice that this song centers around E, G, and B. Establish tonality. Sing the melody on a neutral syllable; then sing it with words.

HARMONY: Follow the suggestion in the pupil's book and sing the song as a round. The following chant may also be sung, or played on the bells.

It is good to dwell in peace.

Brethren in Peace Together

Jewish Folk Song
Paraphrase of Psalm 133:1

The words of this Jewish folk song have meaning for people everywhere. After the double bar you can sing this song as a round. Group two should begin to sing when group one starts the third phrase.

How good-ly it is and how pleas-ant,

for breth-ren to dwell to-geth-er.

1. How good-ly it is and how pleas-ant,

for breth-ren to dwell to-geth-er.

2. Good-ly, pleas-ant, Breth-ren in peace to-geth-er.

How good-ly it is and how pleas-ant,

for breth-ren to dwell to-geth-er.

Record 6   Side A   Band 1. VOICES: children's choir.
ACCOMPANIMENT: clarinet, violin, harp.
FORM: Vocal (unison); Vocal (2-part round); Instrumental (2-part round).

This Train

American Folk Song

Listen to the recording. Notice the interesting rhythm. Look at the notation. In how many measures do you find this pattern?

Notice that the accent in this pattern comes on the second note instead of the first. Accents sometimes fall on notes which are usually unaccented. This is called **syncopation.**

1. This train is bound for glo - ry, This train, —
2. This train don't pull no ex - tras, This train, —

This train is bound for glo - ry, This train, —
This train don't pull no ex - tras, This train, —

This train is bound for glo - ry,
This train don't pull no ex - tras,

Don't ride noth - in' but the good and ho - ly,
Don't pull noth - in' but the mid - night spe - cial,

This train is bound for glo - ry, This train! —
This train don't pull no ex - tras, This train! —

Record 6 Side A Band 2. VOICES: children's choir.
ACCOMPANIMENT: harmonica, banjo, double bass, mandolin, violin, guitar.
FORM: Instrumental; Interlude, *2 meas.;* Vocal, *vv. 1-2;* Interlude;
Instrumental; Instrumental fade-out.

(135)

Key: E♭   Starting Tone: E♭ (1)
Meter: 4/4 (♩)
Piano accompaniment on page 264

This Train

* RHYTHM: In answer to the question in the pupil's book, determine that the pattern appears four times. Have the children practice clapping this pattern against a steady beat, emphasizing the syncopation. To help children understand the idea of syncopation, clap the following pattern, which begins with a long tone. Then clap the pattern from the song. Compare the sounds of the two patterns.

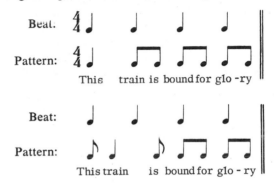

Beat.
Pattern:
This   train is bound for glo - ry

Beat:
Pattern:
This train   is bound for glo - ry

Chant the words softly. Observe all the syncopated patterns.

MELODY: Study the notation and notice that the melodic contours of measures five and one are similar, except that measure five is higher. Help the children discover that the first and last phrases are exactly alike. Listen to the recording and sing along softly until the melody is familiar.

HARMONY: Some children may sing the following chant. Emphasize the steady beat which contrasts with the syncopated melody.

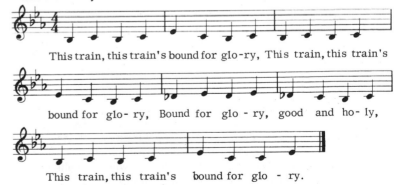

This train, this train's bound for glo-ry, This train, this train's

bound for glo - ry, Bound for glo - ry, good and ho - ly,

This train, this train's bound for glo - ry.

My Lord, What a Morning

Key: D   Starting Tone: F# (3)
Autoharp Key: C   Starting Tone: E (3)
Autoharp chords not in Pupil's Book
Meter: 4/4 (4/♩)
Piano accompaniment on page 266

* RHYTHM: To answer the question in the pupil's book, ask the children to study the notation. Guide them to recall, by reviewing page 135, that syncopation occurs when the accent falls on a normally unaccented beat. You can often determine that a pattern will be syncopated by looking at the notation. If the measure begins with a short tone followed by a long one, it probably will sound syncopated. Discover that this occurs at the beginning of each of the first six measures of the song. Listen to the recording to discover that these measures do, in fact, sound syncopated. The accent falls on the second, unaccented beat.

Draw attention to the dotted rhythms in the second section. Remind children that the relationship between quarter note and eighth note is now changed from two to one to three to one: ♩. = ♪♪♪

FORM: Study the design of the song. Notice that the first section is made up of four short **motives** or melodic patterns (each two measures long). Notice that the first three are similar, the last is completely different. The second section is made up of two phrases. Notice that the second phrase in this section ends with the same motive heard at the end of the first section. Review the meaning of the signs *D.C. al Fine* and *Fine*.

Children may enjoy reviewing these spirituals from third grade.

Michael, Row the Boat Ashore   Key: E

1. Michael, row the boat ashore, Hallelujah! (2 times)
2. Michael's boat's a musical boat, Hallelujah! (2 times)
3. Michael, row the boat ashore, Hallelujah! (2 times)
4. Sister, help to trim the sail, Hallelujah! (2 times)
5. Michael, row the boat ashore, Hallelujah! (2 times)

Get on Board   Key: G♭

Get on board, little children,
Get on board, little children,
Get on board, little children,
There's room for many a more.

The gospel train's a-coming,
I hear it just at hand;
I hear the car wheels rumbling and
rolling through the land.

My Lord, What a Morning

Spiritual

Sing this song in the joyous spirit of the words. Notice the rhythm often found in spirituals. Which measures include syncopated patterns?

My Lord, what a morn-ing, My Lord, what a morn-ing,

My Lord, what a morn-ing, When the stars be-gin to fall.

1. You'll hear the trum-pet sound
2. You'll hear the sin-ners mourn } To wake the na-tions un-der-ground,
3. You'll hear the Chris-tians shout }

Look-ing to my God's right hand, When the stars be-gin to fall.

Record 6   Side A   Band 3.   VOICES: baritone, children's choir.
ACCOMPANIMENT: guitar.
FORM: Introduction, *1 meas.;* Vocal, *vv. 1-3.*

Sing to Begin the Day! Sing in Assembly!

Begin your school day with singing. Join other classes and sing in assembly. As you sing at special times, sing with the style appropriate for the song. Begin your song in the correct tempo and on the correct pitch. Sing with different kinds of accompaniment. Sing these songs or others which you enjoy.

All Beautiful the March of Days	page 20
America	2
America for Me	184
A New Created World	158
Beautiful Savior	139
Brethren in Peace Together	134
Hiking, Laughing, Singing	6
Marching to Pretoria	148
My Lord, What a Morning	136
O Savior Sweet	78
Riding with the Cavalry	42
San Sereni	178
Sing for the Wide, Wide Fields	146
Stodola Pumpa	48
Swiss Roundelay	50
Waltzing Matilda	176
We Sing of Golden Mornings	14

This page is meant to be a reminder of songs that are most appropriate for singing at the beginning of the day or in assembly groups. The practice of beginning the day with singing is very worthwhile if the singing is done with spirit and with correct pitch and tempo. The quality of singing and the frequency of singing a song will largely determine its inspirational value. A song cannot fulfill inspirational purposes if it is sung so often that children lose their zest for singing it. A variety of songs is needed—seasonal songs, patriotic and sacred songs, and "favorite" songs. The songs should be studied and memorized before they become part of the "opening day" repertoire. You might keep a chart list of this repertoire, adding to it throughout the year and referring to it when making the choices each morning.

As an outgrowth of classroom singing, combining classes for large-group "sings" should be a frequent activity in the elementary school. This activity has inspirational and enjoyment values and it gives impetus to the singing program of the school. It has the possibility of impressing the children so that the songs are remembered and become a part of the lifetime repertoire.

An assembly sing should be prepared for in advance by having the children memorize the songs. For this purpose, a basic song list used by several teachers will assure that all children of a specific grade level or of several grade levels learn the same songs. Songs with a variety of mood and tempo should be chosen for each occasion. A variety of artistic accompaniments should be planned. A few teachers or children might play several autoharps simultaneously. The piano might be used to accompany some songs. An instrumental ensemble of adults or children might accompany some of the songs. A musical treat might be planned for the assembly—a performance by some professional or student musical group.

Windy Nights

Key: G minor   Starting Tone: D (5)
Meter: $\frac{6}{8}$ ($\frac{2}{\text{\musnote}}$)
Piano accompaniment on page 267

* EXPRESSION: Read this famous poem by Robert Louis Stevenson aloud to the children. Discuss the visual images suggested by the words. Listen to the recording and talk about ways the music helps to support the mood created by the words.

This poem is also effective as a choral reading activity. The class may be divided into high, medium and low voices. Read as follows:

Whenever the moon and stars are set,	medium voices
Whenever the wind is high,	low voices
All night long in the dark and wet,	medium voices
A man goes riding by.	low voices
Late in the night when the fires are out,	high voices
Why does he gallop and gallop about?	high voices
Whenever the trees are crying aloud,	medium voices
And ships are tossed at sea,	low voices
By on the highway, low and loud,	medium voices
By at the gallop goes he:	low voices
By at the gallop he goes, and then,	high voices
By he comes back at the gallop again.	high voices

Children may also enjoy adding an expressive accompaniment. Choose instruments for different phrases:

Phrase one: Play sand blocks to suggest the sound of the wind.

$\frac{6}{8}$ 𝅘𝅥𝅭 | 𝅘𝅥𝅭 | 𝅘𝅥𝅭 | 𝅘𝅥𝅭 |

Phrase two: Galloping rhythm may be played on wood blocks.

$\frac{6}{8}$ ♫♫♫ | ♫♫♫ |

Phrase three: Play a soft pattern on a drum with fingertips to suggest the sound of rain in the dark, wet night.

$\frac{6}{8}$ ♩ ♪♩ ♪ | ♩ ♪♩ ♪ |

Phrase four: Play the sand block pattern as in phrase one.
Phrases five and six: Repeat the rhythm pattern of phrase three.

MELODY: Observe the over-all contour of the melody. Each phrase begins high and moves gradually downward by steps. Study the key signature and the notation. Discover that the song is in G minor. Establish tonality by playing and singing up and down the G minor scale. Sing the song on "loo," then sing it with words.

Windy Nights

Music by William S. Haynie
Words by Robert Louis Stevenson

Robert Louis Stevenson wrote many poems for boys and girls. Choose another poem by Stevenson from a collection of poetry. Learn to read it aloud with expression.

Mysteriously

1. When - ev - er the moon and stars are set,
2. When - ev - er the trees are cry-ing a - loud,

When - ev - er the wind is high,_____
And ships ___ are tossed at sea,_____

All night long in the dark and wet,
By on the high - way, low and loud,

A man goes rid - ing by. _____
By at the gal - lop goes he: _____

Late in the night when the fires are out,
By at the gal - lop he goes, and then,

1. Why does he gal - lop and gal - lop a - bout?

Record 6 Side A   Band 4.   VOICE: child's voice.
ACCOMPANIMENT: bassoon, harp.
FORM: Introduction, *8 meas.*; Vocal, *vv. 1-2.*

By he comes back at the gal - lop a - gain.

For hundreds of years, people of many faiths have sung this hymn throughout the world.

Beautiful Savior

Silesian Melody
Translated by Joseph A. Seiss

Stately

1. Beau - ti - ful Sav - ior, Lord of the na - tions,
2. Fair are the mead - ows, Fair - er the wood - lands,
3. Fair is the sun - shine, Fair - er the moon - light,

Son___ of God and___ son of man;
Robed___ in flow'rs of ___ bloom - ing spring;
And ___ the twin - kling___ star - ry host;

Glo - ry and hon - or, Praise, ad - o - ra - tion,
Je - sus is fair - er, Je - sus is pur - er;
Je - sus shines bright - er, Je - sus shines pur - er

Now and for - ev - er - more be thine.
He makes our sor - row - ing spir - it sing.
Than all the an - gels heav'n can boast.

Key: Eb   **Starting Tone:** Eb (1)
Meter: 4/4 (4/♩)
Piano accompaniment on page 268

Beautiful Savior

EXPRESSION: This beautiful old hymn should be sung in a dignified style with proper phrasing and dynamics. Make sure that the meaning of the words is understood so that expressive singing can result. Remind children to sing the vowel sounds clearly. The song should be memorized in preparation for school assembly singing or singing with adults on many occasions.

* **MELODY:** Study the melody and discover first the four phrases. Call attention to the fact that the melody of phrase one contains a sequence. Measures three and four are the same as measures one and two, only three tones higher. Phrase one has a rising contour leading into phrase two, the climax phrase of the song. Phrases three and four have a declining contour. Phrase three also contains a melodic sequence. Measures eleven and twelve are the same as measures nine and ten, only one tone lower. Give class members a chance to practice and understand the melodic sequence patterns by playing the measures on bells or singing them with "loo." The dynamics of the song result from the melodic contour, with phrase two being sung the loudest.

Study the intervals of the melody. Help the class discover the many measures in which the melody is scale-wise (moving by steps of the scale). Practice singing particular intervals with numbers and letters: 2-7-1 of measure two, 4-2-3 of measure four, 5-1-6 of measure five, 5-3-4 of measure ten. Ask the class to sing the entire melody with numbers and later with letters.

Record 6   Side A   Band 5.   VOICES: children's choir.
ACCOMPANIMENT: organ.
FORM: Instrumental; Vocal, *vv. 1-3.*

Music and Other Arts

Poetry

Begin the discussion of this page by reviewing with the children some of the ideas regarding art given on page 22. Discuss the suggestion that any art is a means of expression and that ideas and feelings may be expressed in different art forms; only the materials are different. Review the kinds of materials used by the artist, the architect, and the composer.

As the class reads page 140, refer to the recordings of the two poems on page 141 and to the recordings of "Ionisation" on page 126 and "Syrinx" on page 142.

Listen to the poems. Read the second paragraph on page 140 again. Examine the first stanza of each poem, paying special attention to the differences in tone color. (Remember that sounds are not always identical with spellings.) In "Storm," notice the repetition of the *cr* sound in the words "crash," "crack," and "crushed." The words are related in meaning as well as sound and establish a kind of tone-meaning color to that stanza. In the first stanza of "Velvet Shoes," the *w* and *s* sounds recur (*w*alk, *w*hite, *w*ith, *q*uiet, tran*qu*il; u*s*, *s*now, *s*oundle*ss*, *s*pace, foot*s*tep*s*, *s*low, pa*c*e, la*c*e) lending a more subtle tone quality to the sound.

Listen to the tone colors of the two musical compositions. In "Syrinx," there is a single color, that of the flute. Its tone is clear and pure. In contrast, the tone colors in "Ionisation" are bold and clashing with great variety.

Discuss the differences in rhythm between the two poems. "Storm" moves in phrases. There is no fixed pattern that is standard for a line or a stanza. The only rhythmic similarity among the lines is that most of them have two accented syllables. "Velvet Shoes" has a more even rhythm. The four stanzas have similar, although not identical, rhythmic patterns. Rhyme is used in "Velvet Shoes" as one of the elements of pattern.

Music and Other Arts

Poetry

Poetry, like music, is expression in sound. The poet uses word sounds. The composer uses musical sounds. Listen to music and poetry. Discover what they have in common.

Tone color is important in music and in poetry. The composer uses musical sounds of different qualities to express musical ideas. He may use the tone color of a clarinet in contrast with that of a bassoon or a flute. The poet uses word sounds of contrasting color. He may use words that are short and crisp in contrast with words which have long vowels and soft consonants.

Rhythm is important in music and in poetry. Rhythm in poetry is similar to rhythm in music. It is created with long and short word sounds, with accents, and with silences.

Echoes are important in music and in poetry. In echoes, we again enjoy ideas and sounds already heard. Echoes help to create design in poetry and in music. The echoes may be exact or they may be changed in some way. The composer echoes melodies and rhythms in music. The poet echoes ideas and word sounds.

Listen to the recording of the poems on the next page. Listen for differences in tone color. Do you hear different rhythms in the two poems? Do you hear echoes of ideas and of word sounds?

Listen to "Ionisation," page 126, again and to "Syrinx," page 142. Discuss the tone color, rhythms, and echoes that you hear in each composition.

STORM

by Hilda D. Aldington

You crash over the trees,
You crack the live branch—
The branch is white,
The green crushed,
Each leaf is like split wood.

You burden the trees
With black drops,
You swirl and crash—
You have broken off a weighted leaf
In the wind,
It is hurled out,
Whirls up and sinks,
A green stone.

VELVET SHOES

by Elinor Wylie

Let us walk In the white snow
   In a soundless space;
With footsteps quiet and slow,
   At a tranquil pace,
   Under veils of white lace.

I shall go shod in silk,
   And you in wool,
White as a white cow's milk,
   More beautiful
   Than the breast of a gull.

We shall walk through the still town
   In a windless peace;
We shall step upon white down,
   Upon silver fleece,
   Upon softer than these.

We shall walk in velvet shoes:
   Wherever we go
Silence will fall like dews
   On white silence below.
   We shall walk in the snow.

Discuss the idea of **echoes**. In music, echoes may occur in the repetition of melodies, rhythms, or tone colors. Listen to "Syrinx" and "Ionisation"; talk about the ways the composer creates echoes in each.

In poetry, echoes may occur in the repetition of sounds, of ideas, of words, of repeated lines. LISTEN AGAIN TO THE POEMS. WE HAVE ALREADY NOTICED SOUND ECHOES. FIND OTHER ECHOES IN PHRASE STRUCTURE. ("You crash over the trees,/You crack the live branch"; "We shall walk . . .") Look for other kinds of echoes. Turn again to the poem on page 24. See how Blake has used both the word "laugh" and the idea of laughing throughout the poem.

Notice also the difference in the kind of form used in the two poems. "Storm" has a free form, not structured by rhyme or regular rhythm. The chief structural unit is the phrase, but there is no real repetition of rhythm from one phrase to the next. "Velvet Shoes" has a more formal structure. The lines have a definite pattern of rhyme and a fairly definite pattern of rhythm. Ask the class to recall musical compositions that have a free form ("Music for Instruments" by Isaac) and those that are more formally structured (*Piano Sonata in A Minor* by Mozart).

Suggest that the class choose a topic about which each child will write a poem. First discuss the kinds of tone color that a poem may have, the kinds of rhythm they may want to use, and the formal or free-form structures possible. Discuss the ways they can create echoes: sound patterns, rhyme patterns, rhythm patterns, repeated words, parallel phrasing. After the class has written the poems, examine the different ways the students used these elements. Some children like rhyme and regular rhythm. Others do not.

You may want to leaf through the book to notice the way artists have used tone color, rhythm, echoes, and structure in their paintings and sculpture.

Syrinx

BY CLAUDE DEBUSSY

BORN 1862   DIED 1918

The flute is one of the most ancient instruments. Every culture has its myth as to the origin of the flute. The story given in the pupil's book is based on a Greek myth. Read the story together. Children might also enjoy hearing the story "Pan's Pipes" by Ted Tiller, recorded by Columbia Records. It is a fantasy about the beginning not only of the flute, but of other instruments as well.

Listen to the first theme of "Syrinx," which is notated in the pupil's book. Play it on the piano or bells until children are familiar with it and can identify it when it appears again. The composition might be described as being divided in four sections, each beginning with a statement of the theme; each of the first three is longer than the last as Pan becomes more daring in his experimentation. The first section is very short, consisting only of a statement of the theme. The second statement is slightly longer and extends over a wider range. The third segment, which begins an octave lower, covers an ever-widening range, and is marked by use of trills and **grace notes** which ornament the main melodic line. The final statement of the theme begins on the same high note as the first statement and descends quickly to lowest range of the flute. This section closes with a descending pattern based on the **whole tone scale**, as shown in the pupil's book.

A whole tone scale is a six-tone scale in which each step is a whole step. Debussy often used this scale in his compositions. The effect which the scale produces at the end of this composition is one of incompleteness. It is as though Pan had only laid down his pipes momentarily, and the composition would soon continue.

Place the bells of the whole tone scale in order and invite children to experiment and improvise their own whole tone melody. Discuss the difference in sound between this scale and the major scale. With no half steps, no one tone sounds strongly as home tone.

Debussy lived during the late nineteenth and early twentieth centuries. His music has been described as **impressionistic** because in his music he tried to give his impressions of scenes, moods, or events. To create these moods he often used different scales, different kinds of harmonies, and freer rhythms than those employed by many of the composers of his time. Many of Debussy's compositions are based on scenes such as this one.

Syrinx

by Claude Debussy

The title of this composition for unaccompanied flute means "Pan's Pipes." Pan was the Greek god of the forest and meadows. He protected the shepherds and their sheep.

One day one of the nymphs, Syrinx, became frightened by Pan and fled from him. She called to her sisters for help. They changed her into some tall, hollow reeds.

Pan sat down by the reeds and sighed in disappointment. As he sighed, he noticed that the reeds gave forth a sweet sound. He cut the reeds into unequal lengths so that each reed would make a different sound and then tied them together. Pan's pipes, or syrinx, was the first musical instrument.

Debussy begins his composition with a plaintive, wandering little melody. It is as though Pan were experimenting with his reeds and was not sure of what notes to play.

Pan's melody is repeated several times. The melody is expanded and ornamented each time as if Pan were exploring all the possibilities of his new instrument.

Finally, Pan's solo comes to a close with a brief melody which moves down by whole steps.

Why do you think Debussy chose to end his piece with this pattern?

Record 10   Side B   Band 1.
William Kincaid, flutist.

Three Keyboard Pieces

The forerunner of the modern piano was the harpsichord. Since the strings of the harpsichord are plucked, rather than struck, the performer cannot regulate the loudness of the sound. In 1792 the piano was invented. Originally, the complete name for the piano was pianoforte, or "soft-loud" because it was capable of making both soft and loud sounds. All three composers represented here wrote music for the harpsichord. Two of them also composed for the new pianoforte. In concerts "here and now," the first piece is often played on the harpsichord. The other two are usually performed on the piano.

Sonata in A Minor, K. 175

by Domenico Scarlatti

Domenico Scarlatti was born in Italy, in the same year as Bach and Handel, and later lived in Portugal and Spain. In his piece for harpsichord, listen for the sudden changes of harmony, the contrasting melodies, and the exciting rhythms.

Rondo No. 2 in G Major

by Carl Phillip Emanuel Bach

Johann Sebastian Bach sons who were also famous composers. Both Mozart and Haydn said that they had learned much from the keyboard pieces of one of the sons, Carl Phillip Emanuel Bach. That son was a skilled performer, too, and it was probable that he played this piece on the piano.

Sonata in A Minor, K. 310

First Movement

by Wolfgang Amadeus Mozart

It is believed that most of Mozart's keyboard sonatas were written for the piano. Listen for majestic, flowing melodies in this sonata. What other Mozart music does this remind you of?

Three Keyboard Pieces

The composers in this lesson were contemporaries, but how different their music sounds! The musical period in which they lived was a transitional one, the bridge between the baroque and classical styles. Listen for the manner in which each composer used the keyboard instrument as a vehicle for his particular style.

Sonata in A Minor, K.175

BY DOMENICO SCARLATTI
BORN 1685   DIED 1757

The K.175 following the title refers to the catalogue of Scarlatti's harpsichord sonatas prepared by Ralph Kirkpatrick, a famous harpsichordist, who is the performer on your recording. In this sonata, children will hear many short melodies which use the entire range of the harpsichord. The melodies are often ornamented in order to create the illusion of sustaining the tone. Some of the melodies are heard more than once, in particular one which is in major.

Rondo No. 2 in G Major

BY CARL PHILLIP EMANUEL BACH
BORN 1714   DIED 1788

Carl Phillip Emanuel Bach was probably more renowned in his own lifetime than his now-famous father. In this piece, children will hear the eight-measure rondo melody many times in many different keys. **WHAT IS THE SURPRISE AT THE END?** (The rondo theme is begun once more very softly, and then suddenly interrupted by two loud chords.)

Sonata in A Minor, K.310

First Movement

BY WOLFGANG AMADEUS MOZART
BORN 1756   DIED 1791

K.310 refers to the catalogue of Mozart's complete works by L. von Koechel in 1862. The movement is in a large three-part form. Children should hear that this composition is more unified than the other two, that the melodies are fewer and longer, and that the harmonies do not change as abruptly.

How Does My Lady's Garden Grow?

Key: C   Starting Tone: E (3)
Meter: $\frac{6}{8}$ (♩.)
Piano accompaniment on page 269

* **COMPOSER'S STYLE:** This song, as well as a number of others in this section, was written by a composer of today. Composers often turn to the past for musical ideas. The composer who wrote "Psalm 100" turned to the past for the words of his song. Frackenpohl turned to the past for the design of this composition. This song is in the form of a canon, a musical form which was first developed by composers five hundred years ago. Review the canon "Follow Me" on page 96.

* **FORM:** Ask children to study the song page and discuss the design of the song. Help them to become aware that the bottom part is an exact repetition of the top part. This design is known as a canon. A round is a type of canon with which the children are familiar. In a round the music is written so that the last phrase will harmonize with the first phrase; thus, the song can be repeated over and over and will continue to sound right harmonically. This is not true of this canon. It is to be sung from beginning to end, in the same way any other two-part song is sung.

* **MELODY:** Study the melodic notation; discover that the melody in measures three and four is an inversion (upside down) of the melody for measures one and two. Notice that the melody in measures five and six moves gradually upward. Most of the song moves by steps. Sing the song with numbers, then sing it with words. Sing it first in unison.

HARMONY: When children know the melody well, divide the class into two groups and sing the song as a canon.

How Does My Lady's Garden Grow?

Music by Arthur Frackenpohl
Words from Mother Goose

Smoothly

How does my la - dy's gar - den grow? How does my la - dy's
How does my la - dy's gar - den grow?

gar - den grow? With sil - ver bells and cock - le - shells, And
How does my la - dy's gar - den grow? With sil - ver bells and

pret - ty maids all in a row.
cock - le - shells, And pret - ty maids all in a row.

Today, people still enjoy the wonder and beauty of nature. People have more time for recreation and are drawn to the outdoors when working days are done. Songs of nature's loveliness from other countries still have meaning for us today.

Record 6   Side A   Band 6. VOICES: children's choir.
ACCOMPANIMENT: piano, bells.
FORM: Introduction, *1 meas.;* Vocal; Instrumental (2-part round);
Vocal (2-part round).

Study the notes and discover which bells you need to play the second section of this melody. Do you recall the name of the scale with five tones?

Jasmine Blossoms

Chinese Folk Melody
Words by Beth Landis

Voices:

1. White stars on the hill - side there,
2. White stars with the light of morn,

Sweet a - ro - ma, jas - mine fair,
Like bright gems of dew - drops born,

I will wear you in my hair,
I will wear you in my hair,

Fine

All may then your fra - grance share.
All will see my jew - els rare.

Bells:

D.C. al Fine

Record 6 Side A Band 7. VOICE: soprano.
ACCOMPANIMENT: recorder, koto, temple blocks, drums, bells, bell tree, cymbal, triangle, finger cymbal.
FORM: Introduction, *4 meas.;* Vocal; bell part; Vocal; Coda, *4 meas.*

Tonality: Pentatonic (F G A C D)
Starting Tone: A
Meter: $\frac{2}{4}$ ($\frac{2}{\,\downarrow}$)
Piano accompaniment on page 270

Jasmine Blossoms

EXPRESSION: Read the paragraph in the pupil's book. Ask children to recall other songs that describe the beauty of nature which they have learned this year. Children might suggest "We Sing of Golden Mornings," "Snug 'neath the Fir Trees," or "The Butterfly."

It is also interesting to note that this old Chinese melody was used by Puccini in his opera, *Turandot.*

* MELODY: Follow the directions in the pupil's book and locate the necessary bells:

These tones, F G A C D, make up the pentatonic scale for this song. Help children discover that the pattern of steps for this scale is:

1	2	3	4	5
whole	whole	whole and half	whole	

The pentatonic scale is used in many Oriental folk songs. Review the songs from Japan on pages 58, 59, and 60. WHICH OF THESE SONGS ARE BASED ON THE PENTATONIC SCALE? ("Song of Itsuki" and "A Good Day in Japan.")

Sing up and down the pentatonic scale several times until children are comfortable with its sound. Suggest that they try to read the melody at sight, singing with "loo." Choose one child to learn the bell part. Give him an opportunity to practice it alone.

When children know the melody they may wish to write a verse of words to sing with the bell melody.

Sing for the Wide, Wide Fields

Key: Bb   Starting Tone: Bb (1)
Autoharp Key: C   Starting Tone: C (1)
Autoharp chords not in Pupil's Book
Meter: $\frac{2}{4}$ ($\frac{2}{}$)
Piano accompaniment on page 272

EXPRESSION: Some children in your classes may be familiar with this song. The 4-H is one of the largest youth organizations in this country. It was originally an organization for boys and girls who lived on farms. Today there are also clubs in many cities and even in some foreign countries. Children may join when they are ten so many fourth-graders are eligible to be members. The four H's stand for Head, Hands, Heart, and Health.

Read the words of the song aloud. Review the discussion about music as an expression of the people found on page 1 of the pupil's book. WHAT KIND OF SONG IS THIS? It is a song about nature, a hiking song. Nature is a common topic for folk songs. Singing as we hike is one of the many ways we use music for recreation.

* RHYTHM: Tap the rhythm of the melody while one child plays the beat softly on sticks. Notice the ties at the end of each phrase. Discuss the importance of sustaining these words for the full value of both notes. Draw attention to the uneven patterns in measures thirteen and twenty-nine.

Sing with strong accents in a steady tempo which would be suitable for hiking.

* DESIGN: Study the design of the song. It is made up of eight four-measure phrases. Look for same and different phrases. Discover that phrases one and two are the same as phrases five and six, except for the "pick-up notes" at the beginning of phrase five.

Invite children to follow the suggestion in their book and write a song for their club or their class. They may make up new words for this melody, or they may compose both melody and words.

Sing for the Wide, Wide Fields

Music by Rena M. Parish
Words by Fannie R. Buchanan

This is truly a song for here and now. It is the official song for the 4-H Clubs of America. Boys and girls all over the United States belong to the 4-H Clubs. They sing this song at their meetings. You might like to compose a song for your club or write a school song.

Record 6   Side A   Band 8.   VOICES: children's choir.
ACCOMPANIMENT: brass ensemble, percussion.
FORM: Introduction, 8 meas.; Vocal; Coda, 8 meas.

Sing   for   the   friend-ship   sweet; ___

Sing   as   to-geth-er   we   swing   a-long

With   the   turf   be-neath   our   feet. ___

Nature is a subject used by all artists—painters, composers, writers, etc. Here is a poem that expresses the author's feeling about nature.

Out in the Fields with God

by Louise Imogen Guiney

The little cares that fretted me,
   I lost them yesterday
Among the fields above the sea,
   Among the winds that play,
Among the lowing of the herds,
   The rustling of the trees,
Among the singing of the birds,
   The humming of the bees.

The fears of what may come to pass,
   I cast them all away
Among the clover-scented grass,
   Among the new-mown hay,
Among the rustling of the corn,
   Where drowsy poppies nod,
Where ill thoughts die and good are born,
   Out in the fields with God.

Marching to Pretoria

Key: D   Starting Tone: F# (3)
Autoharp Key: C   Starting Tone:
E (3)
Autoharp chords not in Pupil's Book
Meter: $\frac{2}{2}$ $\left(\frac{2}{}\right)$
Piano accompaniment on page 274

FOLK STYLE: This song was originally sung by the Dutch who had come to South Africa to work in the diamond mines. Many of them had left their families in Holland and were very lonely. Thus, they did sing, eat, and live together, as the words of the song suggest. Some children may do research to discover where Pretoria is, how the Dutch came to be in South Africa, and so on.

*__RHYTHM:__ Observe the meter signature; determine that the rhythm will move in twos, with the half note as the beat note. Examine the notation. WHERE DO YOU FIND MEASURES THAT SOUND WITH THE BEAT? (Measures 13, 14, 17, 18, 25, 26, 29, 30.) HOW DOES THE RHYTHM SOUND MOST OF THE TIME IN RELATION TO THE BEAT? (Two tones to a beat on the verse and with the beat on the refrain.) FIND A PATTERN WHICH INCLUDES TONES THAT ARE LONGER THAN THE BEAT. (Next to last measure in the verse and the last two measures of the refrain.) Identify the dotted rhythm in measures 3, 5, 7, and 11. Remind children to observe the quarter note rest.

MELODY: Draw children's attention to the melodic contour. Notice the **sequence**. The melody for the words "so we are all together" is sung three times, each time one step lower. Notice the repeated pattern on the word "Pretoria" in the refrain.

Guide children to establish tonality by singing 1-3-5-3-1. Encourage them to sing the melody with numbers.

HARMONY: When children know the melody, draw attention to the two-part harmony on the refrain. Discover that the harmonizing part is a third lower than the melody. Listen to the recording, paying special attention to the harmony on the refrain. Divide the class into groups and sing the two parts. Some children may also learn to play the harmonizing part on the bells or piano.

Marching to Pretoria

South African Folk Melody
Words by Josef Marais

Pretoria is a city in South Africa. The men sang this song as they returned home from work in the diamond mines. Today it is sung as a marching song.

I'm with you and you're with me, And so we are all to-geth-er, So we are all to-geth-er, So we are all to-geth-er. Sing with me, I'll sing with you, And so we will sing to-geth-er As we march a-long._____

Record 6   Side B   Band 1.   VOICES: tenor, baritone, bass.
ACCOMPANIMENT: accordion, guitar, double bass.
FORM: Introduction, 4½ meas.; Vocal; Instrumental; Vocal.

Refrain

F   F   C   C

We are march-ing   to   Pre - to - ri - a, ____

G7   G7   C

Pre - to - ri - a, ____   Pre - to - ri - a, ____

C   F   F   C   C

____   We are march- ing   to   Pre - to - ri - a, ____

F   C   G7   C   C

Pre - to - ri - a,   hur - rah! ____

Notice that the **refrain** is in two-part harmony. Learn the melody in unison. Some class members may then sing the same melody a third lower as a harmonizing part.

When you know the song, make up a new verse.

Ask children to help you plan an autoharp accompaniment for the song. When sung with the autoharp, the song must be transposed to the key of C. WE CAN PLAY AN ACCOMPANIMENT FOR THIS SONG USING THE CHORDS FROM THE KEY OF C: C, G7, AND F. SING THE MELODY SOFTLY AND LISTEN TO THE AUTOHARP. TELL ME WHEN TO CHANGE CHORDS. As children determine the necessary chords, put the names on the chalkboard, showing one chord per measure. (Notice that you will need two chords in the third from the last measure of the refrain.) When children have determined the necessary chords, put the sequence on a chart so that they can practice it and accompany the class:

```
C | C | C | C | G7 | G7 | C | C |
C | C | C | C | G7 | G7 | C | C |
F | F | C | C | G7 | G7 | C | C |
F | F | C | C | F  | C G7| C | C ‖
```

When children know the song well, suggest that they follow the suggestions in their book and make up a second verse.

Petrouchka Ballet Suite

Scene One, "The Shrovetide Fair"

BY IGOR STRAVINSKY
BORN 1882

The contemporary composer, Igor Stravinsky, is one of the most remarkable composers of our time. His name is well known to people of different musical interests the world over. His works are more frequently performed than those of any other contemporary composer. He has written music for voices and instruments in almost every possible combination. Born in Russia, the composer has lived in the United States since 1940. He has conducted numerous concerts of his compositions in many cities of the world.

The children may recall other Stravinsky compositions, such as "A Soldier's Tale" (*Exploring Music 3*) and "March, Waltz, Polka and Galop" from *Suite No. 2 for Small Orchestra (Exploring Music 2)*. It would be good to borrow the records and review these some time after children have studied *Petrouchka* so that impressions of the composer's style will be deepened.

The music for the ballet, *Petrouchka,* is delightful in itself, apart from the staged dance. It is program music of great charm. Although it was written when the composer was only twenty-nine years of age, the instrumentation and new melodic and harmonic sounds found in the music were already typical of his style.

Petrouchka is a legendary marionette in Russian folklore. The fair of the ballet is the Shrovetide Fair and the stage setting is a snowy scene. The composition opens with "crowd music" with woodwinds and strings in prominence. The brasses join to build excitement. Then the bell-like main theme printed in the children's book is heard. It is played first by the full orchestra and then by woodwinds, harp, and strings with tambourine. The rhythm and harmony of this theme are used again and again in the music associated with the happy mingling crowd at the fair.

◉

As the crowd is entertained by an itinerant musician and a dancer, the barrel organ is ingeniously imitated by the woodwinds. The "organ" melody is played by clarinets with the flutter played by

Petrouchka Ballet Suite

Scene One, "The Shrovetide Fair"

by Igor Stravinsky

This music was written for a **ballet.** The main character of the ballet is a clown puppet named Petrouchka. The first scene is that of a fair in Leningrad. We see the dancers in the stage setting representing the crowd at the fair. On the stage are stalls, sideshows, and the showman's small wooden stage with closed curtains. The music of merriment begins with the carnival sounds played on the flutes and other instruments. The composer uses a folk song as the basis for the melody and rhythm he develops in the carnival music. The folk song begins:

(sounds an octave higher)

150

Record 11   Side A   Band 1.
Columbia Symphony Orchestra,
Igor Stravinsky, conductor.

The crowd mingles happily, hearing the music from the different booths. A man plays a hand organ as a girl dances for pennies. The composer based his music on a tune which he once heard an organ grinder play:

(sounds an octave higher)

The orchestra plays the first section of the music again while the dancers continue to dramatize the merriment of the crowd.

Suddenly the showman draws the curtain and we see his puppets: the Ballerina, a doll with red cheeks; the Moor, a big dark fellow; and floppy Petrouchka. The showman plays his flute as he introduces the puppets. As he touches them, the puppets spring to life. When all three are in motion, they dance together in a wild Russian dance.

(sounds an octave higher)

flutes. There are interruptions when the "crowd music" and music of other acts are heard. The girl dances to a flute and clarinet duet and she plays the triangle as she dances. The music of the crowd as heard at the beginning of the ballet builds to a loud climax.

◉

The snare drum and timpani are heard, and then a quiet mysterious passage leads into the flute cadenzas of the showman. He opens the curtain to reveal the lifeless, sprawling figures of the three puppets. A two-note motive of the flute echoed by the piccolo accompany the touch that animates the puppets. The three puppets begin to dance, and as the music becomes more brilliant, they leap from the booth into the snow. The woodwinds, French horns, trumpets, and piano introduce the Russian Dance. The xylophone and piano punctuate with rising glissandos. (This theme is in the pupil's book.) The music based on the theme builds to a climax. A new melody is played by oboe, then violins, then piano. The first melody quickly passes from xylophone to clarinet to English horn and then to piano. The full orchestra brings the music to a colorful close.

Music and Other Arts
Dance

Dance is one of the oldest of art forms. In primitive societies, dance and music undoubtedly developed side by side, with each art growing with the other. Discuss with the children their own experiences with dancing. Recall times in the classroom when they have participated in various kinds of dancing: folk dance, developing interpretive dance to music, and so on. Ask children to suggest other kinds of dancing, such as ballroom dancing, which their older brothers and sisters enjoy. Some of their parents may belong to square dance clubs.

Ballet is a highly specialized type of dance art. Some children may have taken ballet lessons and will be able to demonstrate some steps for the class. If possible, invite a local ballet teacher to class to talk about ballet and to demonstrate for the children. Many children may have seen ballets performed on television or at the theatre.

Discuss the ideas presented in the final paragraph. Stress the fact that a ballet often is the result of many different artists working together. Invite children to work together to produce their own ballet based on *Petrouchka* or another composition which they have studied this year.

Divide the class into various artistic groups. One group may plan the story line; another may outline the dance movements to be used; another may plan and execute stage settings and costumes. Everyone may participate in the final dance production. Present the completed ballet for another class.

Music and Other Arts

Dance

The arts of music and dance often express feelings that cannot be put into words. The dancer uses gesture and movement to be seen. The musician plays or sings musical sounds to be heard. Both artists create compositions which communicate an idea or a feeling to the audience.

Ballet is an important form of artistic dancing. It is a theater dance which is performed in costume and accompanied by music. The ballet dancer must begin to study when he is a young child. He must learn the many different patterns of movement which are basic to all ballet dances. The artist who plans the ballet is called the **choreographer.** He creates different ballets by combining the basic dance movements in many ways.

Music and ballet are sister arts because ballet seldom exists without music. Sometimes the composer writes music for a dance idea which the choreographer has already developed. Sometimes the choreographer hears a musical composition which he likes and creates a dance for the music.

The arts of dance, music, painting, and story are combined in ballet. The original story may be developed by a writer; a musician composes the music; a choreographer plans the dance movement. Other artists design and create the stage settings. The final production is the result of many artists working together.

Dancers

BY EDGAR DEGAS (DUH-GAH)
BORN 1834   DIED 1917

DEGAS, Hilaire-Germain-Edgar, *Dancers* (C. 1899), Pastel, 37¹/₄″ x 31³/₄″,
Collection, The Museum of Modern Art, New York, Gift of William S. Paley

Edgar Degas was fascinated by the behind-the-scenes world of the ballet dancer. Backstage he could observe the dancers without any theatrical illusion. He recognized and admired the combination of athletic strength and almost weightless grace that any good dancer must have. Here in this pastel, he suggests the strength of the dancers in their firmly planted legs. In the iridescent colors of the **tutus** (ballet skirts), he is able to suggest lightness and grace.

Backstage, we can see how the patterns of ballet movements have become part of the habitual poses of the dancers. When a person practices his art over and over, the technical details become almost automatic. The hard work that has gone into the training of a dancer helps the dancer seem to move without effort.

The musician and the artist also train themselves to master the technical parts of their art so that they are free to express themselves without always struggling with the most basic elements of learning. A composer studies harmony and orchestration. A painter studies color and balance. A dancer studies the classical dance movements. When they have mastered these elements, they are able to produce a finished piece that seems to have been created without effort. We do not often see the behind-the-scenes work, but without it the result would seem unfinished.

As children work out their own dances, encourage them to discuss the kinds of thinking and experimenting that go into their creative work. They will probably notice that the more work they put into a dance, the more finished it will seem when presented.

Weggis Dance

Key: E♭   Starting Tone: B♭ (5)
Autoharp Key: F   Starting Tone: C (5)
Autoharp chords not in Pupil's Book
Meter: $\frac{2}{4}$ $\left(\frac{2}{}\right)$
Piano accompaniment on page 276

FOLK STYLE: The "Hol-di-ri-di-a" figure is typical of many Swiss yodeling songs. The Swiss "talk" with each other across the valleys by yodeling because the yodel will carry farther and is more easily understood than words. The Swiss men usually sing the yodeling refrain. The children may imitate this custom by having the girls sing the words while the boys yodel. Review other Swiss songs learned this year on **pages 50 and 52.**

FORM: Study the design, as requested in the pupil's book. There are two sections, a verse and a refrain. Discover that in each section there are two phrases. Each phrase is made up of three motives. The first motive in the first phrase is two measures long: $\frac{2}{4}$ ♩♩ ♪♩ | ♪♩ | and is the same in both phrases of the verse. The second and third motives of phrase one are each one measure long: $\frac{2}{4}$ ♫♫♩ ‖ ♫♫♩ ‖ The second motive stays the same in both phrases but the third motive is different in each phrase. Here is the rhythm of the first motive in the second section (refrain): $\frac{2}{4}$ ♩ ♩ | ♩ ♪♩ | The second and third motives are exactly the same as the second and third motives of the first section. The design of the complete composition would be as follows when written in letters: A: a a' B: a a'

As children learn the dance described in their books, notice that the design of the dance matches the design of the music. In answer to the question in the pupil's book, help the children realize that the dance steps for the verse and refrain are different because the music for each section is different.

Use the following formation for the dance: Double circle of partners, holding crossed hands. Girls toward center of circle.

Weggis Dance

Swiss Folk Dance

Ballet dancing is an art that must be studied for years before the dance steps can be mastered. Folk dances, such as this one from Switzerland, can be quickly learned and enjoyed by everyone.

1. From Lu - cerne to ___ Weg - gis fair,
2. When we row a - cross the bay,
3. Weg - gis leads to a moun - tain high,

Hol - di - ri - di - a,   hol - di - ri - a,

Shoes and stock - ings we need not wear,
There we see pret - ty maid - ens gay,
Gai - ly sing as ___ we go by,

Hol - di - ri - di - a,   hol - di - a.

Refrain

Hol - di - ri - di - a, Hol - di - ri - di - a,   hol - di - ri - a;

Hol - di - ri - di - a, Hol - di - ri - di - a,   hol - di - a.

Record 6   Side B   Band 2.   VOICES: 2 sopranos, 2 tenors.
ACCOMPANIMENT: clarinet, accordion, guitar, double bass, percussion.
FORM: Introduction, *4 meas.*; Vocal, *vv. 1-3.*

When you know the song, learn the dance steps. With the verse, dance a heel-toe polka: heel-toe-step-step-step. With the refrain, take sliding steps away from your partner. Then step-hop in a circle around your partner. Why are the dance patterns different for the verse and the refrain?

Study the design of this song. Find motives, phrases, and sections. Write the design of the phrases and sections with letters.

Lines Written for Gene Kelly to Dance to

by Carl Sandburg

Spring is when the grass turns green and glad.
Spring is when the new grass comes up and says, "Hey, hey! Hey, hey!"
Be dizzy now and turn your head upside down and see how
     the world looks upside down.
Be dizzy now and turn a cartwheel, and see the good earth
     through a cartwheel.

Tell your feet the alphabet.
Tell your feet the multiplication table.
Tell your feet where to go, and watch 'em go and come back.

Can you dance a question mark?
Can you dance an exclamation point?
Can you dance a couple of commas?
And bring it to a finish with a period?

Can you dance like the wind is pushing you?
Can you dance like you are pushing the wind?
Can you dance with slow wooden heels
     and then change to bright and singing silver heels?
Such nice feet, such good feet.

Record 7   Side B   Band 6.

Lines Written for Gene Kelly to Dance to

Excerpts

This poem has been recorded for the children to hear. Listen to the poem; discuss the many images suggested by the words. Refer to the discussion on poetry, page 140. CAN YOU DESCRIBE THE TONE COLOR OF THIS POEM? THE RHYTHM? DO YOU HEAR ANY ECHOES?

Talk about the combination of art forms. Review the discussion on page 152 about the combination of music and dance. In this poem the arts of poetry and dance have been joined. What kind of dance do you think Gene Kelly danced with this poetry? As children listen to the poem again, ask them to think of dance movements they can show the rest of the class. Give individuals an opportunity to "dance a question mark," "an exclamation point," and so on.

Some children might prefer to create a "question mark" in music by improvising a melody or a rhythm that they feel is appropriate.

Ask children to think of other arts that could be combined. CAN YOU FIND A PAINTING IN YOUR BOOK WHICH YOU COULD "DANCE"? Some children might paint a picture illustrating a favorite poem, or they may decide to write a poem to go with a favorite painting. They could paint a picture to illustrate an instrumental composition, or write a poem that has the same mood.

Subduing an Elephant

ARTIST UNKNOWN

The importance of relying upon what we already know as we further explore a subject can be discussed in terms of this painting from India. Some of the children may know something about India. Have one student locate the country on a map.

The elephant was to most of India what the horse was to Europe and America: a means of transportation and a beast of burden. Children in the class may be familiar with stories about the need to tame horses before the animals could help men. Elephants, too, had to be tamed and trained.

Notice the size of the elephant. We know that an elephant is not really that much larger than men or flowers or trees. But to men who are trying to control the animal, it seems enormous. The artist used size to indicate the strength and importance of an elephant.

The artist used different kinds of design elements. The shape of the trees seem to echo the curves of the elephant. The gold ornaments strung along the elephant form an ornamental design.

The artist also used color in a strong and distinct way. Spots of red carry the eye from one human being to another. Each shape is distinctly separated from the background as well as from other shapes by color.

Although the artist comes from a different age and a different culture, we can understand and appreciate his devices for expressing his ideas. As we learn more about art and more about an artist's country, we are able to increase our understanding of his work. But even using what we already know, we can begin to explore his world despite our different cultural background.

Subduing an Elephant (C. 1690), Artist unknown, Francis G. Mayer
Art Color Slides, Inc., Private Collection

More Music to Explore

As you explore more music, try to make use of what you have learned. What do you know about the songs of long ago, far away, and here and now? What do the songs of each have in common? What is different?

What do you know about the music of the composer? Review compositions from far away, long ago, and here and now.

What do you remember about the arts of architecture, painting, dance, poetry, and sculpture? Discuss what the different kinds of art have in common with music.

What do you know about rhythm, melody, and harmony in music? Discuss what you know and what you can do by yourself as you sing, play, or listen to music.

What do you know about design in music? How many designs do you know? Find examples you have studied.

What important words have you learned to use when you speak of music? Make a list of important words that are found in your book. Use these words whenever you want to tell others what you hear and see in music.

People will continue to express their feelings and interests in music. They will continue to make music at work, at play, and in worship. There will always be "more music to explore"!

As children discuss the things they have learned about songs of long ago, far away, and here and now, stress the similarities and the differences. The topics of songs are often the same, no matter when or where they were first sung. The ways people use music has also remained consistent: for worship, work, recreation, and so on. The musical sounds themselves are sometimes very different. We can often tell when or where a song was composed by the kind of melody, rhythm, and harmony that we hear.

Help children locate the music of composers which they have studied this year. They might make a bulletin board which includes a time-line. Attach the names of the composers to the time-line in correct sequence from long ago until today. Another time the children may make a display using a map of the world. Attach the composers' names to the appropriate countries.

Reread the pages about the various arts (22, 70, 116, 140, 152). Stress the similarities: all arts may express similar kinds of ideas; all have form; rhythm of some type may be found in many arts; "color" is also used in different ways in the various arts. The differences lie primarily in the kind of material each artist uses.

As children discuss the last four paragraphs, review the pages about melody, rhythm, harmony, and design in their book. Ask children to choose favorite songs and discuss the rhythm, melody, harmony, or design of each song. Help them to build a vocabulary list of musical terms and to define each. Encourage the children to use these terms as they talk about the music they study.

A New Created World

Key: G   Starting Tone: D (5)
Meter: 4/4 (♩)
Piano accompaniment on page 277

COMPOSER'S STYLE: This song is part of a longer chorus from the oratorio, "The Creation." An **oratorio** is a composition for soloists, chorus, and orchestra. It usually consists of choral numbers, solos, quartets, duets, and so on. Most oratorios are based on a sacred subject. This one deals with the creation of the world.

* EXPRESSION: Listen to the music; discuss the words. Suggest to the children that this is a good song to sing in the spring because the words remind us that the world seems to be newly created each spring. Discuss ways that the music supports the ideas of the words. Notice how the melody moves gradually upward, with the highest point in the sixth measure on the word "up."

Lo, the Winter Is Past

Key: F   Starting Tone: F (1)
Meter: 4/4 (♩)
Piano accompaniment on page 278

COMPOSER'S STYLE: This composition and "A New Created World" both use ideas from the Bible. Both deal with the same topic, the return of spring. The music for "Lo, the Winter is Past" was created by a composer of today. The composer of "A New Created World" lived two hundred years ago. Compare the two compositions.

* MELODY: Study the key signature, scan the notation and determine the home tone of this song. Locate patterns that move by steps of the scale. Notice that the melody begins with 1-5 and ends with the same interval in the opposite direction: 5-1. Ask children to sing the melody on "loo," then with words.

* EXPRESSION: Listen to the recording; the melody is played first by the cello. Notice the sustained legato tone with which the melody is played. The singers perform with the same legato tone. Beneath the flowing melody the piano accompaniment provides contrast by stressing the steady on-going beat.

Some children will be able to hear that the cello plays the melody of the opening phrase at the end of the song, while the singers sustain the word "come."

A New Created World

This song is an excerpt from *The Creation,* an oratorio by Joseph Haydn.

by Joseph Haydn

A new cre-a-ted world, a __ new cre-a-ted world,

Springs up,   springs up   at __ God's com-mand.

Lo, the Winter Is Past

Music by Walter Ihrke
Words from the "Song of Solomon"

Study the meter signature. What does it tell you about the rhythm of the song? Observe the rests as you tap the rhythm of the melody.

Very smoothly   *p*

For, lo,   the win-ter is past;   the rain is __

o-ver and gone.   The flow-ers ap-pear on the earth; the

time of the sing-ing of birds is come. _____

Look at the key signature and discover the home tone. On what scale is the song based? Look for melody patterns that move by steps of the scale. Look for patterns made up of tones of the I chord. Sing the song with "loo." Sing it with words.

You may sing this song as a round, or one person may play the second part on the bells. Notice how the two melodies move in opposite directions with different rhythms.

White Coral Bells

Traditional Round

1. White cor-al bells up-on a slen-der stalk,
2. Oh, don't you wish that you could hear them ring?

Lil-ies of the val-ley deck my gar-den walk.
That will hap-pen on-ly when the fair-ies sing.

Listen to the recording to learn the German words.

Lachend Sommer

German Canon

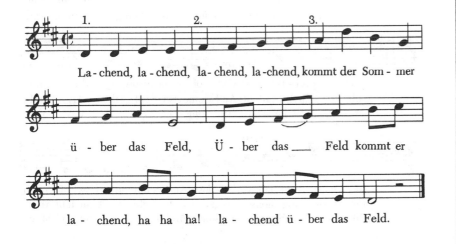

La-chend, la-chend, la-chend, la-chend, kommt der Som-mer

ü-ber das Feld, Ü-ber das___ Feld kommt er

la-chend, ha ha ha! la-chend ü-ber das Feld.

Record 6   Side B   Band 5.   VOICES: boy choir.
ACCOMPANIMENT: autoharp, bells.
FORM: Instrumental; Vocal (2-part round); Vocal (bells on 2-part round).

Record 6   Side B   Band 6.   VOICES: children's choir.
ACCOMPANIMENT: flute, clarinet, bassoon.
FORM: Vocal (unison); Vocal (3-part round); Instrumental (3-part round).

Key: C   Starting Tone: C (1)
Meter: 4/4 (4/♩)
No piano accompaniment

White Coral Bells

* MELODY: Determine that the melody is in C. Notice the general melodic contour. It moves downward during phrase one, upward during phrase two. Sing the song with numbers. Learn to play the melody on the bells. Sing the song as a two-part round when the children feel secure with the melody.

RHYTHM: Divide the class into two groups. Choose contrasting percussion instruments for each group and play the rhythm of the melody as a rhythmic canon.

Key: D   Starting Tone: D (1)
Meter: ¢ (2/♩)
No piano accompaniment

Lachend Sommer

* RHYTHM: Draw attention to the meter signature (¢). Review the meaning of (C). The line through the C indicates that the two numbers of the 4/4 meter signature are to be cut in half; therefore this meter signature stands for 2/2. The half note is the beat note. Scan the notation and find measures that move with two tones to a beat. (Measures 1, 2, 3.) WHERE WILL YOU FIND A PATTERN THAT MOVES WITH FOUR TONES TO THE BEAT? (Beginning of measure five.) Tap the rhythm of the melody lightly.

* MELODY: Determine the key signature and ask a child to establish tonality by playing the D scale. Discover that the melody moves primarily step-wise. Sing the song with numbers. Listen to the recording and learn the German words.

HARMONY: Sing this as a three-part canon. One part may be played on the bells. The German words mean: "Laughing, laughing comes the summer over the field. It comes over the field laughing, 'ha! ha! ha!,' laughing over the field."

May Day Carol

Key: D♭   Starting Tone: A♭ (5)
Meter: 4/4 (4/♩)
Piano accompaniment on page 279

* EXPRESSION: May Day is one of the most ancient of the spring festivals. It originated in England, where the custom of leaving flowers on the doorstep on May Day morning has been observed for centuries. Boys and girls in some sections of the United States still enjoy this tradition.

Read the words of the carol aloud to the children. Listen to the recording. When children are familiar with the melody, ask them to decide what marks of expression could be included in the song. Discuss tempo; it should be moderately fast. WHERE WILL THE LOUDEST SECTIONS OF THE SONG BE? (Perhaps on "heavenly Father," measure 5, and "And step into," measure 13.) WHAT EXPRESSION MARK WOULD INDICATE THIS? (f) WHAT MARK MIGHT PRECEDE THIS SECTION? (A crescendo mark, to indicate that the phrase should grow gradually louder.) WHERE WOULD THE QUIETEST PART OF THE SONG BE? ("and bade us awake and pray," measure 7, and "fetch me a bowl of cream," measure 15.)

* MELODY: Examine the melodic notation carefully. Help children realize that phrases one and three are almost the same. Discuss the differences between phrases two and four. Phrase two moves to the highest point by step, phrase four moves to the same point by skip. The two phrases end differently. Listen to the recording; then sing the song lightly on a neutral syllable. Listen again to the recording to be sure the children sang the melody correctly. Then sing it with words.

May Day Carol

English Folk Song

May Day has been celebrated as a special holiday since primitive times. This carol is an English folk song. What May Day customs do you know?

1. The moon shines bright, the stars give a light, A lit-tle be-fore 'tis day; Our heav-en-ly Fa-ther, he called to us, And bade us a-wake and pray. A-wake, a-wake, oh, pret-ty, pret-ty maid, Out of your drow-sy dream! And step in-to your dair-y be-low, And fetch me a bowl of cream.
2. If not a bowl of thy sweet cream, A cup to bring me cheer; For the Lord knows when we shall meet a-gain, To go May-ing an-oth-er year. I have been wan-d'ring all this night, And some time of this day; And now, re-turn-ing home a-gain, I've brought you a branch of May.
3. A branch of May I've brought you here, And at your door I stand; 'Tis noth-ing but a sprout, but well bud-ded out By the work of our Lord's hand. My song is done and I must be gone, No long-er can I stay; So it's God bless you all, both great and small, And send you a joy-ful May.

Record 6 Side B Band 7. VOICE: tenor.
ACCOMPANIMENT: 2 violins, cello, harpsichord.
FORM: Introduction, *4 meas.;* Vocal, *v. 1;* Interlude, *4 meas.;*
Vocal, *v. 2;* Interlude, *4 meas.;* Vocal, *v. 3;* Coda, *4 meas.*

The melody of this song includes patterns that you know. Locate the familiar note groups. Sing the patterns with numbers and with letters.

Nightingale's Song

Somerset Folk Melody
Words by Beth Landis

1. How brief is the night, O how ear-ly the light
2. O tell me how soon, Will the light of the moon

When the tones of the night - in - gale flow! ____
The ____ sun - light re - place with her glow? ____

O ____ could we pro - long The ____ night - in - gale's song,

As she sings in the mead-ow be - low, ____

As she sings in the mead - ow be - low. ____

On the word "below," the melody patterns sound the same. However, they begin on different notes. This is called a **sequence.** Locate the measures containing the sequence. Sing the notes with numbers and letters.

Key: G   Starting Tone: D (5)
Autoharp chords in Pupil's Book
Meter: $\frac{3}{4}$ ($\frac{3}{4}$)
Piano accompaniment on page 280

Nightingale's Song

* MELODY: The class should learn this song by reading the notes. As the children study the text, they should discover the rhythm and phrasing of the words and the word syllables that are sung on more than one tone. As they study the notation, they should notice the scale-wise melody pattern in measures 12, 13, and 14. Help the children locate melody patterns from the I chord in measures 1, 4, 5, 9, and 19. They should locate the melodic sequence in the fourth line, noticing that in the first measure of the sequence the three-note motive begins on D, then on C, and then on B.

After practicing the melody patterns, tapping the rhythm of the song, and chanting the words in rhythm, the class should be asked to read the melody of the entire song, singing it with numbers, letters, and words.

HARMONY: Assist the class in composing a harmony part in thirds with the melody on the fourth line of the song ("sings in the meadow below"). Write the notes of these measures of the melody on the board. Suggest that the parts begin on the word "in" when one group of singers sings down to F sharp while the other group continues on the melody. The lower part would continue a third below the melody. Write the notes as the class names them. Practice singing the measures in two parts. Incorporate the measures into the singing of the entire song.

Record 6   Side B   Band 8.   VOICE: soprano.
ACCOMPANIMENT: woodwind quintet.
FORM: Instrumental; Vocal, *vv. 1-2.*

The Crow

Key: F   Starting Tone: C (5)
Meter: $\frac{2}{4}$ ($\frac{2}{\downarrow}$)
No piano accompaniment

MELODY: Before children hear the recording of the song, play the melody on the piano while they follow along in their books. DO YOU HEAR PARTS OF THE MELODY MORE THAN ONCE? Help them to discover that the design of the melody is A B C A B C.

Play the first four measures of the melody harmonizing it with an F major chord on the downbeat of each measure. DOES THIS HARMONY SOUND CORRECT WITH THE MELODY? (The tone of the melody in the first four measures clearly outlines an F major chord.) Similarly, the other phrases could be harmonized with a simple chord pattern.

EXPRESSION: Listen to the recording of the song with books still open. Guide children to hear that Stravinsky's accompaniment is more complex than they might have expected. It does not sound like a song of long ago or a folk song because the accompaniment is composed of unusual chords and rhythmic patterns. As if to reinforce the meaning of the words, when the melody repeats for the last three lines, the accompaniment is slightly different.

The Crow

Music by Igor Stravinsky
Words by Linda Rosenbloom

This song was written by Igor Stravinsky who also composed the "Petrouchka Ballet Suite" on page 150. Listen to the recording of the song. Discuss what you hear in the music that tells you that this is neither a song of long ago nor a folk song.

On a bridge a-bove the bay Sat a crow one sun-ny day.

I took him by the tail and heel, Then up-on the bridge I _ kneel'd.

In the bay I set him To watch the wa-ter wet him.

Next day I came back to see, Un-der-neath the bridge was he.

I took him out and with a sigh, Put him in the sun to _ dry.

Yes-ter-day I saw him; The sun's still shin-ing on him.

Record 7   Side A   Band 1.   VOICE: soprano.
ACCOMPANIMENT: piano.
FORM: Introduction, *4 meas.;* Vocal; Interlude, *4 meas.;* Vocal.

Bird Songs in Music

As nature's musicians, birds have fascinated many composers. Some birds sing in tones that can be written in notes. The composer Mozart kept a notebook of bird songs he heard. Many composers have included an imitation of bird songs in their music. One composer even used a recording of the true singing of a bird in his composition!

The Cuckoo and the Nightingale
from *Organ Concerto No. 13 in F Major*
by George Frideric Handel

The songs of two birds are imitated in this composition by a composer of long ago. Listen to the music and notice how the sounds are made. Discuss all the other interesting sounds you hear in this music. See if you can use these words in describing what you hear: repeat, imitate, scale, melody, harmony.

What large design has the composer given his music?

The Pines of the Janiculum
from *The Pines of Rome*
by Ottorino Respighi

A more recent composer had another way of using a bird's song. He made a recording of a nightingale's singing. While the orchestra plays an accompaniment, the recording gives us the natural song of a bird. Listen to the music several times. It is a description of a scene in a pine woods near Rome. Discuss special purposes these instruments have in the music: the clarinet, the harp, the strings.

Record 11   Side A   Band 3.
E. Power Biggs, organist
London Philharmonic,
Sir Adrian Boult, conductor.

Record 11   Side A   Band 2.
Philadelphia Orchestra.
Eugene Ormandy, conductor.

Bird songs in nature are varied and sometimes quite elaborate. The blackbird has been called the most musical of the birds. Birds have been observed in what seems to be "practice." An individual bird will "compose" a tune that he likes and sing it from year to year.

Numerous composers have written "bird music." Bach wrote a fugue with a cockcrow as subject. Haydn's *Creation* and *The Seasons* include bird sounds as does *The Four Seasons* of Vivaldi. Respighi wrote an entire suite called *The Birds* as well as including the bird song recording in his *The Pines of Rome*.

The Cuckoo and the Nightingale
from *Organ Concerto No. 13 in F Major*

BY GEORGE FRIDERIC HANDEL
BORN 1685   DIED 1759

The music is one movement of a composition for organ and orchestra. The movement is a rondo, the short first section alternating with several "bird song" sections played by the organ alone. The theme of the first section is itself suggestive of bird songs and is especially interesting for the quick changes between major and minor. The cuckoo sounds are imitated on the organ in different registers and the trills of the nightingale are imitated on the organ.

There is imitation and repetition in the music when passages are played by the orchestra, then by strings, then by organ, and when short melodic patterns pass from one to another. A melodic figure is repeated in sequence beginning in higher pitches. The organ plays a long scale melody near the end of the music and interesting harmony results from imitation when the scale melody is played as a second voice with itself, as in a round.

The Pines of the Janiculum
from *The Pines of Rome*

BY OTTORINO RESPIGHI (RESS-PEEG'EE)
BORN 1879   DIED 1936

This brief composition is one of four parts of a composition which describes scenes near Rome and memories related to the scenes. The clarinet solo seems to establish the quiet mood of the pine woods. The strings and harp are played as accompaniment, enhancing the bird song. In concert performances, a recording of natural bird songs is played.

The Wielewaal

Key: E♭ Starting Tone: B♭ (5)
Meter: $\frac{4}{4}$ ($\frac{4}{\text{♩}}$)
Piano accompaniment on page 281

* EXPRESSION: Read the words of this Dutch song. WHAT KIND OF A SONG IS IT? (A song about a bird.) WHAT SONGS HAVE YOU LEARNED FROM OTHER COUNTRIES THAT ARE ABOUT THIS SAME TOPIC? ("The Nightingale's Song," "The Crow.")

* MELODY: Follow the directions in the pupil's book and study the melodic notation. Discover that the last four measures are based entirely on the tones of the I chord: E♭ G B♭. Notice that the first melodic pattern, "Come to the country, join us all" is also primarily based on tones of this chord. Ask children to sing the melody with numbers, with letters, then with words.

* HARMONY: Sing the song as a two-part round when the melody is familiar. Since the melody of the last four measures is based entirely on the I chord, children can easily add a harmonizing part and play it on the bells as an accompaniment. Locate the bells of the I chord; invite children to improvise their own patterns. Remind them that the pattern must include the same number of beats as the melody and must move in fours. The pattern might be as follows:

The Wielewaal

Dutch Folk Song

"Wielewaal" means "oriole." Study the notation. In which measures is the melody based on tones of the I chord? Sing the song as a round. Notice that the second group enters just one measure after the first group begins to sing.

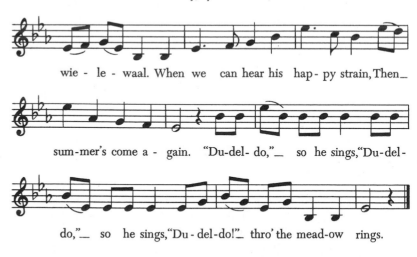

Come to the coun-try, join us all, And let us find the wie - le - waal. When we can hear his hap-py strain, Then sum-mer's come a - gain. "Du-del- do,"_ so he sings, "Du-del-do,"_ so he sings, "Du- del-do!"_ thro' the mead-ow rings.

From *Folk Songs and Games from Holland*, collected and arranged by Ann E. Roeder, copyright, 1956 by G. Schirmer, Inc. Used by permission.

Record 7 Side A Band 2. VOICES: children's choir.
ACCOMPANIMENT: flute, clarinet.
FORM: Vocal (unison); Vocal (2-part round).

Study the notation. Find melody patterns that move by steps. In which measures does the melody move by skips and use the tones of the V7 chord?

The Upward Trail

Words and Music Traditional

We're on the up-ward trail, we're on the up-ward trail,

Sing - ing, sing - ing, ev - ery - bod - y sing - ing, as we go.

We're on the up-ward trail, we're on the up - ward trail,

Sing - ing, sing - ing, ev - ery - bod - y sing - ing, home-ward bound.

Record 7   Side A   Band 3.   VOICES: children's choir.
ACCOMPANIMENT: piccolo, trombone, percussion.
FORM: Vocal; Vocal (2-part round).

Key: G   Starting Tone: G (1)
Meter: 4/4 (♩)
Piano accompaniment on page 282

* **RHYTHM:** Study the rhythmic notation. HOW MANY DIFFERENT MEASURES OF RHYTHM CAN YOU LOCATE? (Five.) Divide the class into five groups; tap the five patterns simultaneously. Discuss the relationship of each pattern to the beat:

Practice tapping the rhythm of the melody. When children can tap it correctly, divide them into two groups and tap it as a rhythmic canon. Group 2 starts one measure after Group 1.

Invite the children to create their own rhythmic canon. Divide the class into several groups. Each group may create a rhythm pattern for one measure in 4/4 meter. Combine the measures into a complete rhythmic composition. Learn to clap the composition; then clap it as a canon.

* **MELODY:** Answer the questions in the pupil's book. The melody moves by steps on the words "we're on the upward." Draw attention to the difference in the upward skip on the word "trail" in measures two and four. The first time it is a skip of a sixth (D-B); on the repeat it skips up a seventh (D-C). Practice singing these two intervals. The melody moves by skips in measures 5-6 and 13-14, using tones of the V7 chord. Practice these patterns. Sing the entire melody with "loo," then sing it with words.

HARMONY: Sing this song as a canon. Review the difference between a canon and a round. In a round the first voice may return to the beginning while the second voice is still singing the last phrase. In a canon the harmonies will not sound right if this is done.

Music and Other Arts
Design

Throughout this book, the similarities and differences between music and other arts—painting, architecture, poetry, and dance—have been presented. On this page one of the similarities among all the arts is discussed.

As children read this page, help them begin to understand that design in art can be provided in many different ways. Through the years artists have searched for various means of giving form to their works of art. Traditional designs are often carefully balanced, and the design is easy to hear and see, as in "Carillon" on page 68, "Laughing Song" on page 24, the cathedral on page 71 and the painting opposite page 1.

Many contemporary artists, however, create designs that are more free and less carefully balanced. They make use of repetition and variety in such subtle ways that the design is sometimes difficult to detect and almost impossible to describe precisely.

To help children become aware of the differences between formal and informal designs, compare examples of formally balanced designs (as suggested above) with examples that are more subtle. In each of the first named examples the artist has combined his materials to create a perfectly balanced design which we can easily observe and sometimes describe with a particular name.

Review "The Laughing Song." One can tell something about its design simply by looking at it: it is divided into three sections, each four lines long. All of the lines have about the same number of syllables. All have four accented syllables. As you read the poem, notice that the same general idea is stressed throughout the poem, giving it a sense of strong unity. Discuss ways Blake has provided contrast by developing "variations" on his basic theme: "When the *green woods* laugh," "When the *meadows* laugh," "When the *painted birds* laugh." Each new section begins with a variation on the same idea. One might almost describe this poem by the musical term, "theme and variations."

Music and Other Arts

Design

Design or form is important in every work of art. An artist organizes his materials by means of a design. As we look at a painting, read a poem, or listen to music, we can study the artist's design. Discovering the design will help us to understand and enjoy the artist's ideas.

An artist creates a design by repeating some of his ideas. **Repetition** helps to give **unity** to works of art. In music, unity is created by repeating melody, rhythm, or tone color. In painting or weaving or making pottery, the artist achieves unity by repeating color, line, or shape. Unity in poetry can be created by repeating word sounds or by echoing ideas.

Variety is important in design. The artist may create variety by introducing a new idea. He may use contrasting color, shape, rhythm, or sound. He may alter his original idea in some way.

Listen to the poem "Chanson Innocent" by E. E. CUMMINGS. Look at the Inca pottery and the Navajo blanket on page 168. Listen to the composition by Webern on page 169. Discuss how each artist developed unity and variety in his composition.

CHANSON INNOCENT

by E. E. CUMMINGS

in Just-
spring   when the world is mud-
luscious the little
lame balloonman

whistles   far   and wee

and eddieandbill come
running from marbles and
piracies and it's
spring

when the world is puddle-wonderful

the queer
old balloonman whistles
far   and   wee
and bettyandisbel come dancing

from hop-scotch and jump-rope and

it's
spring
and
          the

               goat-footed

balloonMan   whistles
far
and
wee

Review the ways that Bizet created a carefully balanced design for "Carillon" with the first and last sections repeated exactly; the middle section provides contrast.

In other compositions the design is more difficult to determine because the artist does not use exact repetitions, or because he makes use of repetition in unexpected ways.

Compare the way "Chanson Innocent" (page 167) is arranged on the page with the way "Laughing Song" is arranged. One knows immediately that the design of this poem will be free rather than carefully balanced. The several sections are of different lengths. Lines vary in length from a single word to a complete thought.

However, as one listens and studies the poem more carefully, he discovers that the artist has provided us with a very clear design, even though it is not exactly balanced. Ask children to look for repeated phrases, such as "far and wee." Notice the different placement on the page and the different placement in the sequence of ideas each time it is repeated.

Discuss the ways that E. E. CUMMINGS has given this poem variety. Again discuss the shape of the poem on the page. Notice that, even when he uses repetition, contrast can also be observed. For example, each time the statement that the balloonman whistles is repeated, the idea is varied: he is a little lame balloonman; he is queer and old; he is goat-footed.

Compare "eddieandbill come/running from marbles and/piracies" with "bettyandisbel come dancing/from hop-scotch and jump-rope." ARE THESE TWO THOUGHTS CONTRASTING? IS THERE ANYTHING IN THE TWO IDEAS THAT ADDS UNITY TO THE POEM?

Listen to the Webern composition. Its design is discussed in detail on page 169. Discuss the fact that this composition also has a design which is not easily observed. However, just as with "Chanson Innocent," as one listens again and again one realizes that the composer has given us a very carefully planned design.

Examine Moore's *Two Forms* on page 117. Discover that it also has a free design which can be observed with careful study. It has the design element of two complementary forms.

Review the quartet by Mozart (page 111), the poem "Velvet Shoes" (page 141), and Michelangelo's *Moses* (page 117) for additional examples of formal designs.

Ask children to locate other compositions, poems and paintings in their book where the design is freer. "Ionisation," "Lines Written for Gene Kelly to Dance to," and "Girl with Lantern" (page 30) are all examples of art work where the design is more subtle.

In the Navajo blanket, unity of design was achieved by repeating a pattern and colors. The diamond elements against the stripes could be extended, and we would know just how to continue the pattern if we wanted to. Variety is achieved by the use of contrasting colors and of more than one pattern element. There is the diamond element and the stripe element. Even the diamonds and stripes vary in size.

The Inca water jar uses the circular form of the piece itself in the design. The pattern elements are all similar and they themselves form circles or parts of circles. Here the shape of the piece and the pattern painted on the piece complement each other in design.

Both of these pieces of craft work have a fairly balanced design.

Six Pieces for Orchestra, Opus 6
Third Piece

BY ANTON WEBERN (VAY'BURN)
BORN 1883   DIED 1945

Read the first paragraph aloud and discuss the ideas. Ask children if they have recognized a person by the sound of his voice, without seeing him. Emphasize the fact that it is the characteristic tone color or timbre of the sound which makes such identification possible.

As children listen to the brief composition and follow the color chart, stress the fact that these colors are not intended to represent specifically the instrumental sounds. Although some people associate particular colors with certain sounds, each person will have different choices of colors.

DESIGN is important, too, in crafts and in music.

How were unity and variety achieved in the design of the Navajo blanket (right) and of the Inca pottery (below)?

The chart on the opposite page shows by colors the unity and variety one composer had in part of his design for a piece of music.

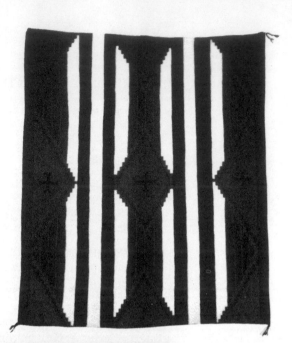

Indian chief's blanket, Photograph courtesy Museum of the American Indian, Heye Foundation

Double-spouted water jar—Inca pottery, Photo Courtesy of The American Museum of Natural History

Six Pieces for Orchestra, Opus 6

Third Piece

by Anton Webern

The "Six Pieces for Orchestra" by Webern are sometimes described as **tone-color music.** An artist uses color, shades of paint, and a variety of brush strokes to express his ideas in paintings. A composer uses the sound of each instrument. He puts them together in various combinations to produce the special effect which he wants us to hear. The particular sound of an instrument or a voice is its **"tone color."** Just as you can recognize a friend by the sound of his voice, you can recognize an instrument by its tone color.

Listen to the third piece from "Six Pieces for Orchestra." Why do you think it is called tone-color music? Suggest words which describe the tone color of this short piece.

Glock., Celesta										
Viola, Violin										
Strings										
Clarinet										
Bassoon										
Woodwinds										
Trumpets, Horn										
Bass drum										

Here is a chart representing Webern's selection of instruments in the composition. Listen again as you watch the chart. Which instrument do you hear first? Although the whole orchestra is used for the piece, you seldom hear all of the instruments together. You hear only one or a few sounds at a time as the instruments pass the melody patterns back and forth. This melody moves over a wide **range** from high to low as it passes from instrument to instrument. As you listen, notice how the composer makes his musical design by contrasting and repeating tone colors, ranges, and patterns.

Discuss the fact that the melody consists of many short fragments, each played by a different instrument or combination of instruments. In addition, the natural tone quality of the instruments is often altered through the use of mutes and playing techniques, such as harmonics. The result is a kaleidoscopic view of a terse, highly-organized melodic line. The melody and rather sparse harmony are dependent primarily on two intervals, the second and third, and their **inversions**, the seventh and the sixth. (An inversion of an interval is created by transferring the lower note an octave higher, or the higher note an octave lower. For example, the interval C-E, a third, would become a sixth if the same pitches were written E-C.)

Notice the seconds and thirds in the opening melodic fragment played by the viola:

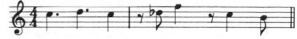

Later the glockenspiel and French horn play this succession of intervals:

Webern, because of his skillful handling of tone color, his love of sound for its own sake, and his use of free rhythmic patterns, has been compared to the French composer, Claude Debussy. Listen again to "Syrinx" (page 142). Notice how Debussy exploits the high and low ranges of the flute and the distinctive qualities of the instrument in these ranges. Debussy's orchestral works demonstrate even more clearly his instinctive use of tone color.

When the children are familiar with the composition they may wish to make their own color chart, using colors of their choice to represent each segment of the composition. Another time, suggest that they create a design with water colors or colored chalk which reflects the melodic contours or rhythmic patterns which they hear.

Record 11   Side B   Band 1.
Columbia Symphony Orchestra,
Robert Craft, conductor.

Let's Explore Tone Color

Review the discussion regarding tone color which is included in the lesson on page 169. Ask children to list the instruments which they feel they could recognize by the sound, that is, by the tone color. As children study this page and listen again to compositions featuring various instruments, help them develop a vocabulary of terms with which to describe the distinctive color of the instruments within the four families. The children may develop a bulletin board display which illustrates the families, with a brief descriptive paragraph about each family.

As children review *Hary Janos Suite* they will be able to hear instruments from each family. Draw particular attention to the strings at the beginning of the Overture; notice the percussion instruments, as well as woodwinds and brass, in "Viennese Musical Clock." Brass instruments are also featured in "The Battle and Defeat of Napoleon."

Listen again to the Webern composition. Discuss the interesting contrasts of color which Webern creates through his choice of instrumentation and the sequence in which he places the instruments. Again, members of every family in the orchestra are used. However, the character of this composition is very different from the Kodaly piece. Here the instruments are heard one after another, instead of simultaneously. The total effect is very different.

Learn the names of the four families. Help children decide reasons why each family is named as it is. Read the next four pages for information regarding each family.

Review the names of the various traditional instrumental ensembles; discuss the instruments which make up each group. The orchestra includes members of all four families. The band is made up of three families and excludes the strings. (A string band and/or harp are sometimes added for specific compositions.)

Each family has its own small ensemble. The string quartet includes two violins, a viola, and a cello. The woodwind quintet includes flute, oboe, bassoon, clarinet, and French horn. The brass quintet is usually made up of two trumpets, French horn, trombone, and tuba. Percussion ensembles include various instruments, depending on the demands of the specific composition.

As children listen to different ensembles, discuss the differences in tone color and in the type of music played by each group.

Let's Explore Tone Color

The particular sound of an instrument or a voice is its **tone color.** You read about that on page 169. After you hear an instrument a few times, you can begin to recognize it by its tone color.

When a composer writes an instrumental composition, he chooses certain instruments because of their distinctive tone color. He puts them together in different combinations to produce the special effect he wants us to hear.

Sometimes the composer uses all of the instruments and writes a composition for the full orchestra. Listen again to the parts of the "Hary Janos Suite" that you studied on page 40. Look at the instruments pictured on the following pages. How many of them did you hear in "Hary Janos"?

Sometimes a composer writes for a small group of instruments. Mozart used only four instruments for his composition discussed on page 111.

A composer may wish to use only a single instrument, as Debussy did in "Syrinx" on page 142. Can you imagine how that composition would sound played on a trumpet, or a cello? Would it have been as effective?

The instruments of the orchestra are grouped in the families shown on the following pages: Brass, String, Percussion, and Woodwind. The piano, harp, and celesta, though not in a family, are also parts of the orchestra. Discuss reasons why the instruments of each group belong in the same family.

Listen to "Sweet and Low" on page 103. The accompaniment is played by a string quartet. Listen to the woodwinds play the accompaniment of "Nightingale's Song" on page 161. Brass instruments can be heard in the accompaniment of "America" on page 2. Why were these instruments good choices to play the accompaniment for each of these songs?

THE BRASS FAMILY

Trombone

Trumpet

Tuba

French Horn

For additional information on the brass instruments see page 174c.

Listening compositions in the pupil's book in which brass instruments may be easily identified include:

    Carillon (French horn), page 68

    Hary Janos Suite, Third Movement, Battle and Defeat of Napoleon (trombones, tuba, trumpet), page 41

    Gavotte (trumpet), page 8

Recordings of songs in the pupil's book in which brass instruments may be easily identified include:

    De Bezem (trumpet), page 37

    Come, Ye Thankful People, Come (trumpet), page 77

    De Bezem (trombone), page 37

    The Upward Trail (trombone), page 165

    Cherries So Ripe (French horn), page 35

    French Cathedrals (French horn), page 69

    Swiss Roundelay (French horn), page 50

    Cherries So Ripe (tuba), page 35

    Once (tuba), page 46

The String Family

For additional information on the strings, see page 174a.

Following are some compositions included in the pupil's books in which string instruments are featured:

Quartet No. 10 in C Major (string quartet), page 111
Concerto in D Major (violin), page 72
Trio in A Minor, Opus 114 (cello), page 29

Song recordings featuring string instruments are:

May Day Carol (violin), page 160
Wraggle-Taggle Gypsies (violin), page 92
Joseph Dearest, Joseph Mild. (viola), page 83
Sweet and Low (cello), page 103
Lo, the Winter Is Past (cello), page 158
De Bezem (double bass), page 37

THE STRING FAMILY

Violin   Viola   Cello   Double Bass

THE
PERCUSSION
FAMILY

Timpani being played

PIANO

HARP

CELESTA

The Percussion Family

For additional information on percussion instruments, see page 174d.

Listen to the following compositions in which percussion instruments may be identified:

Hary Janos Suite, Viennese Clock, pages 40-41
Ionisation, page 126
Petrouchka, pages 150-51

The following song recordings feature the four percussion instruments:

Lullaby (piano), page 26
The Crow (piano), page 162
It's Quiet on the Moon (timpani), page 122
It's Quiet on the Moon (celesta), page 122
O Give Me a Cot (harp), page 62
Brethren in Peace Together (harp), page 134

The Woodwind Family

For additional information on the woodwinds, see page 174b.

Compositions in the pupil's book which feature woodwind instruments are:

Song recordings featuring woodwind instruments are:

THE WOODWIND FAMILY

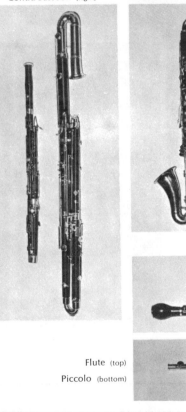

Bassoon (left)
Contra Bassoon (right)

Bass Clarinet (left) Clarinet (right)

Alto Saxophone

Oboe (top) and English Horn (bottom)

Flute (top)
Piccolo (bottom)

The String Family

The string section is the backbone of the orchestra or, as it is sometimes called, the heart of the orchestra. Without the full-throated strings, the musical sound lacks richness.

When string instruments are played, the sound is created by bowing or plucking a taut string. The player "stops" the string by pressing his finger at a particular point, thus changing the length of the string which is free to vibrate. As the length of the vibrating string is altered, the pitch is changed: the shorter the string, the higher the pitch.

Much of the versatility of the string family arises from the fact that the instruments can be played in a variety of ways. They may be bowed either **legato** (smooth and connected) or **staccato** (short and detached). For special effects they may be played **pizzicato** (plucked). The player may also create a **vibrato** (a slight variance in pitch caused by moving the finger back and forth quickly on the string). A **glissando** can be created by sliding the finger quickly up or down the length of the string. The player may produce a **tremolo** by moving the bow rapidly back and forth across the string. **Double-stopping** refers to playing two strings simultaneously, thus changing a melody instrument to one capable of producing harmony. **Harmonics,** which are flutelike tones in the very high register, are produced by lightly touching the string at certain points instead of pressing it firmly in the usual way. The tone quality of a string instrument may be softened by placing a **mute** on its bridge.

Violin: Often called the soprano of the string family, the violin owes its important position in the orchestra to its remarkably versatile qualities. It can produce expressive sounds ranging from the softest lyricism to the highest dramatic excitement.

This instrument is capable of great agility, and rapid and complex passages can be played with amazing rhythmic precision.

The violin's four strings are tuned in fifths: G D A E. The brilliant or ethereal melodies (depending on the composer's demands), produced on the high E string, are in striking contrast to the warm, full, sonorous tones created on the low G string.

Viola: Known as the alto of the string section, the viola is larger than the violin; and its four strings are tuned in fifths: C G D A. The upper three strings of the viola correspond in pitch to the three lower strings of the violin. The tone quality is the least assertive of the string family. The low register can be somber or mysteriously veiled. The higher register is eloquent and can be romantic but with less brilliance than the violin. The viola is not often used as a solo instrument but usually plays harmony or accompaniment parts in the orchestra.

Violoncello: Popularly known as the cello, this deep-throated string is a favorite of composers. While its vibrant tone quality is darkly resonant in the lower register, it is songful and lyric on its higher strings. The cello often plays intense, soaring melodies; at other times it supplies the harmonic foundation for the string choir. The cello is about double the length of the violin; the player rests it between his knees. The cello's strings are each tuned an octave lower than those of the viola.

Double Bass: The double bass is the largest and deepest-voiced of the string family. The instrument stands over six feet high, and the performer sometimes sits on a high stool while playing. The strings on a double bass are tuned in fourths: E A D G. Rarely, for weird or comic sounds, the double bass is singled out as a solo instrument. However, its function in the orchestra is primarily to provide a harmonic foundation. It is very often played pizzicato to good effect.

Harp: The harp is one of the most ancient of musical instruments. It remained in much the same form from primitive times until the eighteenth century when various improvements were made which allowed the harpist to play all the tones in the chromatic scale. It has over forty strings, each of which can be altered by foot pedals to play three tones: the pitch of the open string, the pitch one-half step higher, and the pitch a whole step higher. The tone of the harp cannot be confused with any other instrument. The lower and middle strings produce a warm, lush tone while the upper strings are more brilliant. The characteristic utterance of the harp is the **arpeggio** (a chord in which the notes are played in rapid succession rather than simultaneously).

The Woodwind Family

Members of the woodwind family include instruments whose tone is produced by blowing into a tube or pipe. They are, or were originally, made of wood. There are four main members of the woodwind family: **flute, oboe, clarinet,** and **bassoon.** To each of these, another instrument is closely related: the **piccolo** is related to the flute; the **English horn,** to the oboe; the **bass clarinet,** to the clarinet; and the **contrabassoon,** to the bassoon. As the children listen to woodwind instruments on various occasions, help them to develop their own vocabulary of descriptive words by which they can identify the characteristics of each instrument.

Flute: The flute is held horizontally and the player blows across a hole near the upper end. In the high register the flute is brilliant and penetrating, while the low register is soft and velvety. The middle register is smooth and clear. The flute is used for important melodic passages in the middle and upper registers and brilliant decorative figures.

Piccolo: The piccolo is a small flute, played in the same manner, but pitched an octave higher. Its tone is piercing and easily heard in the upper register, but it is rarely used in its lowest octave. The piccolo's gay, sparkling quality adds color to orchestral climaxes.

Oboe: The oboe is a double-reed instrument. It is almost as agile as the flute. Its intense tone and versatility of expression make it one of the important members of the orchestra. In the upper range the tone is bright and reedy; the low tones are round and haunting. The oboe gives the A to which the whole orchestra tunes.

English Horn: The English horn is actually an alto oboe. Its pear-shaped bell accounts for the unusual timbre. The dark, nasal quality is somewhat melancholy and meditative in character with a plaintive quality which is peculiarly its own. It is a most effective solo instrument if not required to play too loud.

Clarinet: The clarinet is a single-reed instrument. Its sound is caused by vibrations of the reed against the mouthpiece. It creates a tone which is fuller than that of the double-reed instruments and yet markedly different in different ranges. In the low range the clarinet is dark, and its sonorous tone is sad and haunting. The bright quality of the clarinet in the middle or "clarion" register is polished and capable of singing pure, clear melodies. The high register is brilliant and penetrating.

In the orchestra the clarinet adds a variety of tonal colors that no other woodwind can contribute. It is also noted for its agility. The clarinet holds the place of importance in the modern band that the violin holds in the orchestra.

Bass Clarinet: As its name implies, this clarinet adds to the bass of the woodwind choir. Its tone is more powerful, rounder, and less reedy than its higher-pitched brother. The low tones, used most often, are remarkably rich and resonant.

Saxophone: The saxophone has only comparatively recently become a part-time member of the symphony orchestra. Today it is a regular member of popular or jazz bands. The saxophone, a single-reed instrument, is built in different sizes, including soprano, alto, tenor, baritone, and bass.

Bassoon: A double-reed instrument, the bassoon is a long wooden pipe doubled back on itself. It is often called the clown of the orchestra, yet it is also capable of many other moods. It provides the bass for the woodwind choir but is also assigned melodic parts. Its tone color varies considerably in different registers.

Contrabassoon: This instrument has a tube over sixteen feet long, doubled back on itself four times. It has a dark, growling quality peculiar to itself. It can play lower notes than any other orchestral instrument.

The Brass Family

Members of the brass family include those instruments whose tones are produced by blowing through cup-shaped mouthpieces into long metal tubes which are coiled in one of several different shapes. The player can, by pressing the valves in various combinations, change the length of the air column and thus alter the pitch.

Brass instruments existed in ancient cultures but were not useful as musical instruments because of their limited range. Because they lacked valves, the primitive instruments could play only a few tones, mostly those making up the tonic chord (1-3-5-8). For this reason, most military and hunting calls are made up of just these four tones. The modern valved instruments were developed during the nineteenth century, making it possible to sound all of the pitches within the range of the instrument.

Ancient instruments were used primarily for signals during military maneuvers, in religious ceremonies, and during the hunt. The Jewish shofar is described in the Old Testament. Its terrifying sound was commanding and hoarse in great contrast to the tones of modern-day instruments. The earliest horns were made from animal horns.

The brass choir adds color, accent, richness, and body to the orchestral texture. A cone-shaped **mute** inserted into the bell makes the sound of a brass instrument become more nasal or more subdued, depending on how loud it is played.

Trumpet: The trumpet is the soprano of the brass choir. Its tubing is four and one-half feet long, coiled into a narrow rectangle, with three valves. Its tone can be noble, defiant, sharp, and heroic.

The **cornet** is very much like the trumpet with shorter, thicker tubing. Its tone is less brilliant but it is more agile and easier to blow. It is found more often in bands than in orchestras.

French Horn: Often described as the most beautiful of all the brass instruments, the French horn is also the most difficult to play. Its seventeen feet of tubing are wound into a circle, and it may have three or four valves. The French horn is a descendant of the ancient hunting horn; and its tone still suggests the out-of-doors, the remote, the romantic. Its mellow, full tone can be exceedingly powerful and majestic; it can also be dreamy and mysterious. The tone of the French horn blends equally with either woodwind or brass, and it is often used as if it were a member of the woodwind family.

Trombone: The trombone is unique among the brass instruments in that the player changes pitch by moving a slide, thus lengthening or shortening the air column. The trombone can be pompous and heavy or majestic and noble. Its tone is very powerful and most effective when played in groups. The bass trombone contributes strength to the lower register of the brass choir.

Tuba: This "brass bass" is the largest and lowest member of the brass family. It can add robust power and weight to the entire orchestra. When played softly, it adds a plush smoothness to the bass line.

The Percussion Family

The most ancient instruments are in the percussion family (whose sounds are made by striking or shaking). The earliest percussive sound-makers were our hands and feet. There is evidence that primitive man made much use of these in his first experiments with rhythmic sound. Next came sound-making instruments of wood, gourds, skin, clay, and metal, depending on which materials were easily available.

Percussion instruments in the modern orchestra are of two types: those of definite (tuned) pitch and those of indefinite (non-tuned) pitch.

Instruments of Definite Pitch

Timpani: The timpani, the only drums of definite pitch, are some of the most important percussion instruments in the orchestra. They are like huge copper kettles with skins stretched over the tops; hence, they are also called "kettledrums." Screws placed around the top change the tension of the skin head and alter the pitch. Foot pedals are also used to alter the pitch and may be employed for rapid pitch change.

A minimum of two timpani are found in the orchestra. They are used to build up the orchestral volume of sound, to create dramatic suspense, and to add to thunderous climaxes. Mallets of different types—made of sponge, felt, rubber, or wood—are used to produce special effects.

Glockenspiel (Orchestra Bells): Horizontal steel bars are arranged ladder-like in two parallel rows and are struck with various kinds of mallets. Orchestra bells have a bright, crystalline quality. The penetrating tone color is used sparingly for special effects.

Xylophone: The xylophone consists of a series of tuned wooden bars struck with wooden mallets. Its dry, hollow sound is somewhat grotesque and wooden in quality. The **marimba,** a type of xylophone, has a softer tone quality.

Chimes: Metal tubes are suspended from a metal frame and struck with a hammer. They produce a solemn sound reminiscent of church bells.

Celesta: The celesta looks like a miniature upright piano. Its sound is created by striking a series of steel plates with tiny hammers which are controlled by a keyboard. Its silvery, liquid tone is delicate and is especially suitable for light, ethereal effects. One of its first appearances was in the "Dance of the Sugar Plum Fairy" from *The Nutcracker Suite* by Tchaikovsky.

Instruments of Indefinite Pitch

Snare or **Side Drum:** The snare drum is a shallow cylinder closed at both ends by skin. Gut or wire snares are stretched across one head of the drum. They vibrate against the skin when the other head is struck. The crisp, rattling tone of the snare drum is often used for martial effects. It accentuates the rhythm and can also create suspense.

Bass Drum: The bass drum is essentially a huge snare drum without snares. The pitch is very low and, because of the great body of vibrating air enclosed, the sound is exceedingly resonant and powerful.

Cymbals: Cymbals have come to us virtually unchanged in form since Biblical times. The two large, slightly cupped discs of brass add to the brilliance of an orchestral climax when struck together.

Triangle: The triangle is a rod of steel bent into a triangular-shaped form and open at one of the corners. It is struck with a thin steel bar, producing a light, tinkling sound which can cut through the sound of the full orchestra.

Gong: This large disc of hammered metal is of Chinese origin and is struck with a soft mallet. Its sound can be ominous and solemn or soft and mysterious.

Tambourine: This instrument is actually a miniature drum with a single parchment (skin) head. Small metal discs are inserted into the wooden hoop, creating a metallic jangling sound when shaken or struck.

Other percussion instruments are discussed on pages viii and ix.

Au clair de la lune

French Folk Song

1. Au clair de la lu - ne, Mon a - mi Pier - rot,
2. Au clair de la lu - ne, Pier - rot ré - pon - dit:

Prê - te - moi ta plu - me, Pour é - crire un mot;
Je n'ai pas de plu - me, Je suis dans mon lit.

Ma chan - delle est mor - te, Je n'ai plus de feu;
Va chez la voi - si - ne, Je crois qu'elle y est,

Ou - vre - moi ta por - te, Pour l'a - mour de Dieu.
Car dans la cui - si - ne On bat le bri - quet.

Study this song as you review what you know about reading music. Study the design. How many phrases do you find? Which phrases are repeated? Write the design with letters.

Study the rhythm. What does the meter signature tell you? Find measures where the tones of the rhythm sound with the beat. Find measures where the tones are two beats long.

Learn the melody. Study the key signature. Locate the home tone. Look for patterns of melody that move by steps of the scale. Sing the melody with numbers, letters, and "loo."

Record 7 Side A Band 4. VOICE: tenor.
ACCOMPANIMENT: oboe, clarinet, guitar, celesta, xylophone.
FORM: Instrumental; Vocal, v. 1; Vocal, vv. 1-2 (singer pauses after each phrase; instruments repeat each phrase); Vocal, vv. 1-2.

Key: G   Starting Tone: G (1)
Autoharp chords in Pupil's Book
Meter: $\frac{2}{4}$ ($\frac{2}{\text{♩}}$)
Piano accompaniment on page 283

Au clair de la lune

FORM: Follow the instructions on the pupil's page. Challenge children to make use of all they have learned about music this year as they learn the song. Help them determine that there are four phrases. Phrases one, two, and four are the same. Phrase three is different. The design in letters is A A B A.

RHYTHM: The rhythm sounds in twos; the quarter note is the beat note. In many measures the rhythm of the melody sounds with the beat; in other measures there are tones that are twice as long as the beat. In most of the measures the rhythm moves with two notes to the beat. Divide the class in two groups; one may tap the beat while the other taps the rhythm of the melody.

MELODY: Examine the melodic notation. The melody is in G. The I chord includes G, B, and D. Much of the melody moves by steps. Note the skip from A down to E in the third phrase. Listen to the recording and learn the French words. They tell the following story.

A friend asks Pierrot to lend him his pen to write a note by moonlight. The friend's candle has gone out and he has no more fire. Pierrot answers that he doesn't have a pen and that he is in bed. Pierrot tells his friend to go to the neighbor's. He thinks the neighbor is in because a fire is being made in the kitchen.

To help children learn the French words, this song is recorded with pauses, in the same manner as the Spanish song on page 43.

HARMONY: When children know the melody, help them improvise a harmonizing part. The first phrase may be harmonized a sixth below the melody. Encourage children to try harmonizing a satisfactory part for the third phrase, using their ears as they softly hum while other children sing the melody. When children have experimented, place the following part on the chalkboard.

Discover that there are only two tones in the harmonizing part, D and C sharp. Review the function of the sharp sign. Practice singing the harmonizing part. Sing the complete song in harmony.

Waltzing Matilda

Key: Eb   Starting Tone: G (3)
Autoharp Key: F   Starting Tone:
A (3)
Autoharp chords not in Pupil's Book
Meter: $\frac{4}{4}$ ($\frac{4}{\text{♩}}$)
Piano accompaniment on page 284

* EXPRESSION: Discuss the question in the pupil's book. Ask the children to offer their ideas about life in Australia. Compare it to life in this country when the West was being settled. The words mean: swagman—a tramp, billabong—waterhole, coolibah—a type of tree native to Australia, billy—a can to heat water for tea, waltzing Matilda—the swagman's blanket roll, jumbuck—sheep, tuckerbag—knapsack, squatter—rancher, trooper—sheriff.

* RHYTHM: LOOK AT THE NOTATION. WILL THE RHYTHM OF THIS SONG BE PRIMARILY EVEN OR UNEVEN? Help children conclude that because of the repeated dotted patterns, the rhythm will be primarily uneven. Practice tapping the dotted rhythm pattern (♪. ♪).

Remind children that the dotted eighth note must be three times as long as the sixteenth note. To be sure that they are clapping the pattern correctly, have them clap groups of four sixteenth notes: Then tap on the first and fourth note in each group: Ask one child to continue tapping sixteenth notes on sticks while the class chants the words.

To help children learn how to match the words of the remaining verses to the rhythm of the melody, listen to the recording.

FORM: Examine the song and determine the design. Write it in letters: A A′ (remember that the prime sign is added to indicate that the phrases are similar but not exact) B A′.

Waltzing Matilda

Music by Marie Cowan
Words by A. B. Patterson

This song is from Australia. You have discovered that the songs help you imagine how people live in other lands. How do you think people live in the land described in this song?

1. Once a jol - ly swag - man   camped_ by a bil - la - bong,
2. Down _ came a jum - buck to drink _ at the bil - la - bong,

Un - der the shade of a coo - li - bah tree,
Up jumped the swag - man, _ grabbed him with glee,

And he sang as he sat and wait - ed while his bil - ly boiled
And he sang as he shoved that jum - buck in his tuck - er - bag:

"You'll come a - waltz - ing, Ma - til - da, with me."

"Waltz - ing Ma - til - da, waltz - ing Ma - til - da,

You'll come a - waltz - ing, Ma - til - da, with me."

Record 7 Side A Band 5. VOICES: tenor, baritone, children's choir.
ACCOMPANIMENT: piano.
FORM: Introduction, 4 meas.; Vocal, vv. 1-4.

3. Down came the squatter mounted on his thorobred,
   Up came the troopers, one, two, three,
   "Who's that jolly jumbuck you've got in your tucker-bag?
   You'll come a-waltzing, Matilda, with me."
   "Waltzing Matilda, waltzing Matilda,
   You'll come a-waltzing, Matilda, with me."
   "Whose that jolly jumbuck you've got in your tucker-bag?
   You'll come a-waltzing, Matilda, with me."

4. Up jumped the swagman, sprang into the billabong,
   "You'll never catch me alive!" said he.
   And his ghost may be heard as you pass by that billabong:
   "You'll come a-waltzing, Matilda, with me."
   "Waltzing Matilda, waltzing Matilda,
   You'll come a-waltzing, Matilda, with me."
   And his ghost may be heard as you pass by that billabong:
   "You'll come a-waltzing, Matilda, with me."

A Spring Program

The traditional spring music program is usually made up of a number of carefully rehearsed compositions. Children sing songs, play accompaniments, or perform dances which have been prepared specifically for the occasion. It is often difficult for parents attending such a performance to discover what the subject content of the music class is, or what progress their child has made in developing musical understanding. Instead, plan a fourth-grade program around the major themes of their book. This will allow parents to see the kinds of activities children have been participating in throughout the year and the understandings which they have developed about music and other arts.

A program might be based on the theme "Musical Expression of People around the World." Ask children to review the songs which they have learned this year and to select examples for their program which express common topics: work, play, worship, nature, and so on. Precede each group of songs or dances with an explanation of the topic expressed and a brief discussion of the similarities and differences in the music of each composition. Encourage children to select songs which involve a variety of skills: playing or singing descants, playing percussion accompaniments, singing in harmony, planning a dance. The program might culminate with an original composition written by the class which is based on one of the common subjects.

Another program might center around the theme "Design in Music and Other Arts." Divide the class into small groups, assign each group a different art to present in the program. The groups who are working on architecture or painting and sculpture, for example, might prepare materials for a display (either original or collected from various sources) and prepare a brief presentation explaining the different ways the artist used his materials to create a design. The group assigned poetry might choose a poem and plan a choral reading in which all the class might take part. One child could then explain its expressive content and the design of the poem. The music group might explain the design of some compositions which have been studied during the year; the dance group could develop a dance presentation in which the class as a whole would participate. Present the dance as the finale for the program.

San Serení

Key: F   Starting Tone: C (5)
Autoharp chords in Pupil's Book
Meter: $\frac{2}{4}$ ($\frac{2}{\text{♩}}$)
Piano accompaniment on page 286

* HARMONY: Discover that this two-part song moves consistently in thirds. Ask the children if they can locate the two places where the parts are in unison. Observe also that the second phrase is similar to the first, only one step lower.

Sing up and down the scale in thirds to help children become accustomed to the sound of the harmony.

Divide the class into two groups and have them sing the first phrase of the song in parts on "loo." Discuss the problems encountered, then sing it again. Learn the complete song by this same process.

When children know the song, add an autoharp accompaniment. Help them recall that the I and V7 chords are the most common chords. Determine from the key signature that in this song, chord I will be F and V7 will be C7. Help the children determine the chord sequence needed for the accompaniment by ear, without looking at their books.

Plan a percussion accompaniment for this song as suggested in the pupil's book.

STYLE: After the study of "La Jesucita" on the next page, compare the sound of the two songs. Notice many of the characteristics mentioned under FOLK STYLE on page 179 can also be observed in "San Serení."

The Spanish words of this song mean: "This is the way (1) shoemakers do their work." Each verse uses a different worker. The other verses are: (2) carpenters, (3) bellringers, (4) women ironing, (5) women washing, (6) women sewing, (7) gardeners, (8) sailors.

San Serení

Spanish Folk Song

San Se - re - ní   de la bue - na, bue - na vi - da,

Ha - cen a - sí,   a - sí los
1. za - pa - te - ros.
2. car - pin - te - ros.
3. cam - pa - ñe - ros.

A - sí, a - sí, a - sí,   a - sí me gus - ta a - mi.

4. San Serení de la buena, buena vida, Hacen así, así las planchadoras.
5. San Serení de la buena, buena vida, Hacen así, así las lavanderas . . .
6. San Serení de la buena, buena vida, Hacen así, así las costureras . . .
7. San Serení de la buena, buena vida, Hacen así, así los jardineros . . .
8. San Serení de la buena, buena vida, Hacen así, así los barquilleros.

When you know the song, play an accompaniment. Use Latin-American instruments and rhythms.

Record 7   Side A   Band 6.   VOICES: soprano, tenor.
ACCOMPANIMENT: trumpet, guitar, marimba, double bass.
FORM: Instrumental; Vocal, *vv. 1-8.*

Learn to play this composition on bells, autoharp, and tambourine. Notice that the part for each instrument is written on a separate staff.

La Jesucita

Mexican Folk Melody

The autoharp part is written with chord names and with notes. You may strum the chords on the autoharp in the rhythm shown by the notes. The notes may also be played on the low keys of the piano.

Observe these signs as you play. "*D.S. al Fine*" means to return to the sign 𝄋 and play to the end marked "*Fine*."

𝄆 𝄇 means to repeat the music between the two signs.

Record 7 Side A Band 7.
ACCOMPANIMENT: autoharp, bells, tambourine, piano.
FORM: as written in the book.

HARMONY: Divide the class into three groups and give each group an opportunity to practice its part. Study the composition together in class. Notice that the autoharp plays only two chords: G, D7. Write the notes of these chords on the chalkboard. Examine the notation of the melody and discover that, in measures accompanied by the G chord, the melody is made up primarily of G, B, and D. In measures accompanied by the D7 chord, the melody uses the tone D, F♯, A, C.

MELODY: Study the melody of the bell part. Locate the different notes that are used in the melody and place the bells in this order: D E F♯ G A B C D.

If a piano is available, help the child who is assigned the autoharp part to locate also the two tones at the keyboard. Refer to the keyboard in the back of the book as a guide.

RHYTHM: Notice the repetition of rhythm patterns in the tambourine part. Review the relationship of a dotted quarter note to an eighth note. Be sure children understand the meaning of the rest signs. Notice places where the tambourine is to be shaken and where it is to be tapped.

FOLK STYLE: The melody, based on tones of the I and V7 chords, is very typical of Mexican folk songs. So is the syncopated rhythm and the use of the triplet. The tambourine is often used as an accompaniment in Mexican songs. The autoharp suggests the sound of the guitar, another typical Mexican instrument.

When children have learned to play the composition, the class may sing the following words while one group plays the accompaniment. The words do not appear in the pupil's book.

Come to the dance, hear the sweet music playing;
Come to the dance, see the colored lanterns swaying.
The music gay through the night air is ringing,
Come to the dance and your heart will soon be singing.

Oh, dance with me, Jesucita; ⎫
Oh, dance to the music gay. ⎭ sing two times

Weel May the Keel Row

Key: E   Starting Tone: A (4)
Autoharp Key: F   Starting Tone: B♭
Autoharp chords not in Pupil's Book
Meter: $\frac{2}{4}$ ($\frac{2}{\text{♩}}$)
Piano accompaniment on page 288

*FOLK STYLE: Listen to the recording of this song; discuss the instruments used. Compare the sound of the music to that of "La Jesucita." Talk about the differences. The dotted rhythm in the Scottish song is very typical of music from Scotland; the pattern ♫♩ is called the "Scottish Snap." Contrast it with the syncopated rhythms in "La Jesucita." "Weel May the Keel Row" may be accompanied by a single drone chord. Follow the direction in the pupil's book to create an open fifth. The sound of this chord is often heard in Scottish music. It is created by the sound of the bagpipe. In contrast, the Mexican song is entirely based on the I and V7 chords.

RHYTHM: Practice tapping the dotted rhythm. As children chant the words softly, help them observe that this is one of the few songs in their books in which the rhythm is entirely uneven.

*DESIGN: Study the notation; discover that the entire song is made up of only two melodies with slight variations. The design of the song would be A A′ B B′. HOW WILL THIS KNOWLEDGE HELP US LEARN THE SONG? Help children realize that, once they have learned two phrases, they have learned the entire song. Practice singing phrases one and three with numbers. Notice also that the last two measures of these phrases are exactly alike. When phrases one and three have been learned, sing the entire song with words.

HARMONY: When the drone accompaniment (suggested in the pupil's book) is played, the song must be sung in D major.

Weel May the Keel Row

Scottish Folk Song

Listen to the recording. Notice the accompaniment. The oboe, particularly, suggests the sound of the bagpipe.

1. As I cam' thro' Sand-gate, thro' Sand-gate, thro' Sand - gate,
2. "He wears a blue bon - net, blue bon - net, blue bon - net,

As I cam' thro' Sand - gate, I heard a las - sie sing:
He wears a blue bon - net, A dim - ple in his chin."

Refrain

"Oh, weel may the keel row, the keel row, the keel row,

Weel may the keel row that my lad - die's in."

Imitate the drone of the bagpipe on the autoharp. Press down the D major and D minor buttons at the same time. Stroke the strings on the accented beat of each measure.

Record 7   Side B   Band 1.   VOICE: soprano.
ACCOMPANIMENT: oboe, accordion.
FORM: Introduction, *8 meas.;* Vocal; Instrumental; Vocal; Instrumental (vocal on refrain).

The Roberts

Scottish Folk Dance

"The Roberts" is a favorite folk dance from Scotland. Listen to the dance music played on two accordions and a guitar.

This Scottish tune is divided into sections, each section 16 measures in length. You can dance the entire dance to each section of the music.

The dance is in the rhythm of the $\frac{6}{8}$ march with accents sounding two to a measure.

Form two circles for this dance, one inside the other. Each person faces a partner in the other circle. You will be doing the two-step, a foot pattern used in many dances. It is danced step-together-step. Practice the three foot patterns for "The Roberts":

> step-slide, walk-walk-walk-walk
> heel-toe, step-together-step
> 4 two-step patterns

Record 11 Side B Band 2.
Folkraft Americana Orchestra.
Folkraft Records, Newark, N. J.

Play the recording of the dance and assist the children to follow the instructions in their book. They should identify the three sections of the music (each section is 16 measures long; in section A and in section C, the first eight measures of the melody are repeated to make the 16-measure melody). They should clap the accents and be thoroughly familiar with the music before attempting the dance. It might be well to devote one lesson to the music and begin the dance work in the second lesson.

Children should practice the three dance patterns separately, first without music and then with the music. In starting formation, boys' backs are to the center of the circle, and partners join both hands.

The entire dance is 16 measures long. The first dance pattern (measures 1-4) consists of two side steps to boy's left, starting with boy's left foot, girl's right (step-slide, step-slide) and four walking steps in a circle away from partner, girl turning to right, boy to left. Partners finish facing each other, both hands joined. This is repeated (measures 5-8) but partners finish in counterclockwise position, inside hands joined.

The second dance pattern (measures 9-12) begins when the repetition of the first 8 measures of section A of the music begins. Partners start with outside foot:

> heel and toe and step-together-step
> heel and toe and step-together-step

The third dance pattern (measures 13-16) is a continuation as dancers continue to move around the circle in four two-steps (step-together-step), starting with outside foot, and finishing the pattern when the A section of the music is finished.

The entire dance is repeated with the B section of the music and again with the C section. When the class knows the dance, the third dance pattern can be changed so that the dancers have new partners for each repetition of the dance. The two-steps are danced in a circle away from original partner (girl turns to right, boy to left), and dancer finishes beside the next person in the circle.

Fugue and Three Old-Fashioned Dances

from Octet

BY PAUL HINDEMITH
BORN 1895   DIED 1963

Read the first paragraph in the pupil's book; discuss the word "fugue." WHAT IS AN OCTET? (A composition written for eight instruments.) Notice that the eight instruments include both winds and strings.

Before playing the fugue, read the second paragraph and write the names of the instruments on the chalkboard in the order in which they will be heard. The instrumental entrances follow one after another very quickly.

When children are familiar with the fugue, write the names of the instruments on cards which can be held up at the appropriate time.

Children will need to listen very carefully to hear the changes in meter which announce the different dances. As they listen to the waltz, invite children to tap 1 2 3 1 2 3 lightly. Help them to realize that when the polka begins, it moves 1 2 1 2. The beginning of the galop is easy to hear because all instruments join in a rapid dance which scampers about and prepares the way for the viola solo described in the pupil's book.

When children have listened to the music and discussed the different sections, answer the questions given in the last paragraph in their book. "Fugue" is a good name for the composition because "flight" describes the theme as it "flies" from instrument to instrument. These are old-fashioned dances because they were popular long ago.

The galop was popular during the middle 1800's; the polka, which comes from Bohemia, originated in the early 1800's. The waltz was first popular in Europe around 1800. Many nineteenth-century composers including Beethoven, Schubert, and others, wrote waltzes, polkas, or galops. However, the music of these composers did not sound like Hindemith's because he used unusual harmonies, quickly changing rhythms, and melodies which skipped about over a very wide range. The instrumental combination he chose for his dances would probably not have been used by the nineteenth-century composers.

Fugue and Three Old-Fashioned Dances

from Octet

by Paul Hindemith

This music, written in 1958 by a contemporary composer, is played by eight instruments. The octet is made up of clarinet, bassoon, French horn, violin, two violas, cello, and double bass. The word **fugue** means "flight."

You will first hear the main melody played by all the instruments in octaves. The melody then "flies about" as it is played first by the violin and one viola, then by the cello and double bass together. Soon you will hear it again as the other viola plays it, then the basoon, then the clarinet, and finally, the two violas in octaves. Whenever a new instrumental voice starts the main melody, the other instruments continue to play. Sometimes there is a countermelody, too. Try to hear the main melody each time it begins.

For a moment you will hear only the string instruments. Then the wind instruments enter. Together they build a loud climax.

The music does not stop, but you can hear the string instruments turn the melody into a waltz with the help of the bassoon and clarinet. Can you feel the 1-2-3, 1-2-3 of the waltz rhythm?

The French horn plays a little melody which leads to a polka in gay dance rhythm that people dance step-step-step-hop. The strings are sometimes plucked to help in the sound of the dance. Can you dance the polka step with the music?

The viola plays a bubbling melody in furious gallop. The movement ends as all the instruments say "Bravo!" in three loud chords.

Discuss the reasons the name "Fugue" is a good name for this music. Why does the composer call these dances "old-fashioned"? Why do they not sound old-fashioned here?

Record 11   Side B   Band 3.
Vienna Octet Members.

182

Review the way Mozart used variations in his *Quartet No. 10 in C Major*, page 108. Then compose a set of **variations** of your own. Use this familiar melody as your theme.

Create a variation by adding harmonizing tones to the melody.

Make another variation by changing the rhythm. Play the melody in a different meter. You might use changing meters.

Play the melody in a minor key.

Give your variation a new sound by playing some of the tones in a different **octave.**

Practice each variation until it pleases you and you know it by heart. Then start with the theme and play the variations as a complete composition.

Guide children to follow the instructions on this page. They may work individually or in small groups. The melody given in the pupil's book is "Go Tell Aunt Rhodie." It may be found with words in *Exploring Music 2.*

A variation with added tones might sound as follows:

When changing the rhythm, remind the children that the new patterns must include the proper number of beats per measure.

Here is an example of the melody in a new meter.

To play the melody in minor, change the E's to E flat.

Variations may also be created by adding a counter-melody.
The harmony for the song is as follows, by measures:

C	C	G7	C	C	C	G7	C

To add a counter-melody, choose tones from the appropriate chord for each measure.

Suggest to children that they choose another familiar melody and make another set of variations. Some children may wish to create their own theme which they may then vary.

America for Me

Key: B♭   Starting Tone: F (5)
Meter: $\frac{4}{4}$ ($\frac{4}{\downarrow}$)
Piano accompaniment on page 289

DESIGN: Study the design. There are four phrases, each four measures long. The design in letters would be A A' B C.

* RHYTHM: Determine the meter and the beat note. Notice that the rhythm alternates between even and uneven. Find measures where the rhythm sounds with the beat (3, 7, 9, 11). Notice the repetition of this pattern: $\frac{4}{4}$ ♩. ♪ ♪ ♩ ♩|. Practice clapping the even and uneven patterns. Divide the class into two groups; one group may tap the beat while the other taps the rhythm of the melody. Remind children to sustain the dotted half notes for three full beats.

* MELODY: Help the children discover that this song is in B flat major. Ask one child to build the B flat scale with bells, or play it at the piano. Ask children to find patterns in the song that move by steps (end of phrases one and two, phrase three, etc.). Draw attention to the fact that the first phrase is made up of three motives. The second is similar to the first, except that it is lower. Notice that phrase three includes a two-measure motive, which is then repeated. IS IT REPEATED EXACTLY? (No, the first skip is one step higher and the melody returns from the skip by skip, rather than by step as in the first presentation of the motive.) Draw attention to the accidental in the first measure of the fourth phrase. This tells us to sing B natural instead of B flat. Practice singing B flat, B natural, C.

Establish tonality by singing 1-3-5-8-5-3-1. Sing the song with "loo," then sing it with words.

America for Me

Words and Music by
William S. Haynie

1. A - mer - i - ca, A - mer - i - ca, A land of hopes and
2. A - mer - i - ca, A - mer - i - ca, U - nit - ed may she

dreams. I love her moun-tains, fields and plains, Her
stand, From snow - capped peaks far in the North, To

for - ests and her streams. A na - tion where all
shores of sun and sand. Oh, may we ev - er

men are free, Where strength is built on in - dus - try, A -
faith - ful be, And guard the torch of lib - er - ty, A -

mer - i - ca, A - mer - i - ca, We pledge our hearts to thee.
mer - i - ca, A - mer - i - ca, A - mer - i - ca for me!

Record 7 Side B Band 2. VOICES: children's choir.
ACCOMPANIMENT: 2 trumpets, French horn, trombone, timpani.
FORM: Introduction, *4 meas.;* Vocal, *v. 1;* Interlude, *4 meas.;*
Vocal, *v. 2;* Coda, *4 meas.*

Scored for instruments.
See "Exploring Music Instrumental Supplement."

CONSOLE

Organ in
The Riverside Church,
New York City

Courtesy of
The Riverside Church,
New York, N.Y.

The piano may be described as a string instrument and the pipe organ can be called a wind instrument. It was once described as a "chest of whistles" and this is actually a very good description. The sound in an organ is created in the same fashion that sound is created in a whistle by the vibration of air rushing through a pipe. In modern organs, air is pumped into the organ's pipes by an electric motor. When the performer touches a key, the pipe is opened, allowing the air to rush through the pipe. Knobs called stops control the choice of tone color. This makes it possible for the performer to produce a wide variety of tone qualities; the organ can be made to sound like almost any instrument in the orchestra from a flute to a tuba.

The organ is a very ancient instrument. It had its origin in the simple Pan's Pipes of ancient Greece. From these simple hollow reeds has grown the mighty instrument we hear today in concert halls, churches, and theaters. Modern organs may have as many as seven keyboards or manuals. Among these are the basic manual to all organs called the **great** and three other keyboards: the **swell,** the **choir,** and the **pedalboard** which is played by the feet. The pedalboard has the same arrangement of black and white keys as the manual keyboards. The pedals provide the same support for the organ which the double bass and the cello give to the orchestra. The organist is able to play a melody on one keyboard with one hand, the accompaniment on another keyboard with the other hand, at the same time playing the bass line on the pedals with his feet.

The organ is the solo instrument in "The Cuckoo and the Nightingale" (page 163), part of Handel's *Organ Concerto No. 13 in F Major.* It is also featured in the recordings for these songs: "All Beautiful the March of Days" (page 20), "O Savior Sweet" (page 78), "O Come, All Ye Faithful" (page 79), "Beautiful Savior" (page 139), and "A New Created World" (page 158).

PIPES

Organ in The Interchurch Center,
New York City

2. America

Music attributed to Henry Carey
Words by Samuel Francis Smith

1. My coun-try, 'tis of thee, Sweet land of lib - er -ty, Of thee I sing; Land where my
2. My na - tive coun-try, thee, Land of the no - ble free, Thy name I love; I love thy
3. Let mu - sic swell the breeze, And ring from all the trees Sweet free-dom's song; Let mor- tal
4. Our fa -thers' God, to thee, Au - thor of lib - er -ty, To thee we sing; Long may our

fa - thers died, Land of the pil - grims'pride, From ev - er y_ moun -tain-side Let_ free-dom ring.
rocks and rills, Thy woods and tem - pled hills; My heart with_ rap - ture thrills Like_that a - bove.
tongues a - wake; Let all that breathe par - take; Let rocks their si - lence break; The_sound pro - long.
land be bright With free-dom's ho - ly light; Pro - tect_ us_ by thy might, Great God, our King.

4. The Railroad Corral

Cowboy Song

1. We're up in the morn - ing ere break - ing of day, The chuck wag - on's busy, the flap - jack's in play. The herd is a - stir o - ver hill - side and vale, With the night rid - ers crowd - ing them in - to the trail.
2. Come take up your cin - ches, come shake out your reins, Come wake your old bron - co and break for the plains; Come roust out your steers from the long chap - ar - ral, For the out - fit is off to the rail - road cor - ral.
3. The af - ter - noon shad - ows are start - in' to lean When the chuck wag - on sticks in the marsh - y ra - vine; The herds scat - ter far - ther than vi - sion can look, You can bet all true punch - ers will help out the cook.
4. The long - est of days must reach eve - ning at last, The moun - tains all climbed and the creeks all are past; The herd is a - droop - ing and fast falls the night, Let them droop if they will, for the rail - road's in sight.

6. Hiking, Laughing, Singing

Old Swedish Hiking Song

1. Let us stride a - long to - geth - er In the sun-ny au-tumn weath- er, Tra-la-la-la-la-la-la - la-la-la-la-la- la, We are
hik -ing, laugh-ing, sing -ing To the tune with-in us ring -ing,

p (second time più f)

Tra-la - la -la - la-la-la - la - la-la-la-la-la-la - la. 2. We will throw a- way mis - giv - ing In the joy, the joy of

f

liv - ing, As we breeze a-long the high-ways And ex-plore for-got-ten by - ways. If the sun fails to keep shin - ing, We will

cook tho oil vor lin - ing. Tra-la-la-la - la-la-la-la - la -la-la-la-la - la. 3. In the new - born

au -tumn day we hike a - long the high -way. O'er the mead-ow and the lea we sing so mer-ri- ly.

Sing tra-la-la-la - la - la, tra-la, Sing tra-la-la-la- la - la, tra- la, Sing tra-la-la-la- la - la, Tra-la -la- la-la-la-la - la.

189

14. We Sing of Golden Mornings

Music from William Walker's *Southern Harmony*
Words Adapted by Vincent Silliman
from a poem by Ralph Waldo Emerson

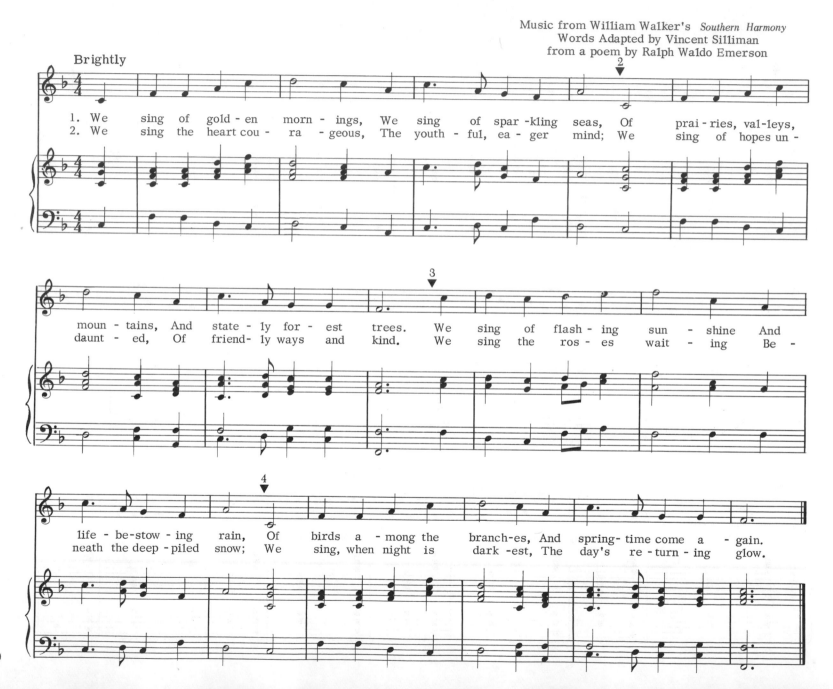

1. We sing of gold-en morn-ings, We sing of spar-kling seas, Of prai-ries, val-leys, moun-tains, And state-ly for-est trees. We sing of flash-ing sun-shine And life-be-stow-ing rain, Of birds a-mong the branch-es, And spring-time come a-gain.

2. We sing the heart cou-ra-geous, The youth-ful, ea-ger mind; We sing of hopes un-daunt-ed, Of friend-ly ways and kind. We sing the ros-es wait-ing Be-neath the deep-piled snow; We sing, when night is dark-est, The day's re-turn-ing glow.

15. The Cuckoo

Austrian Folk Song

Used by permission of the Cooperative Recreation Services, Inc., Delaware, Ohio.

16. A la nanita nana

Spanish Folk Melody
English Words by Beth Landis

Introduction not accounted for in Pupil's Book

A la na-ni-ta na - na, na-ni-ta e - a, na-ni-ta

e - a, An - gels your watch are keep - ing, will hush your weep- ing, bring peace-ful sleep - ing.

The night- in -gale is sing - ing, foun - tain is play - ing,

Your lit - tle cra - dle swing - ing in bran - ches sway - ing.

A la na - ni - ta na - na, na - ni - ta e - a.

A la na - ni - ta na - na, na - ni - ta e - a.

18. Blow the Wind Southerly

Northumberland Folk Song

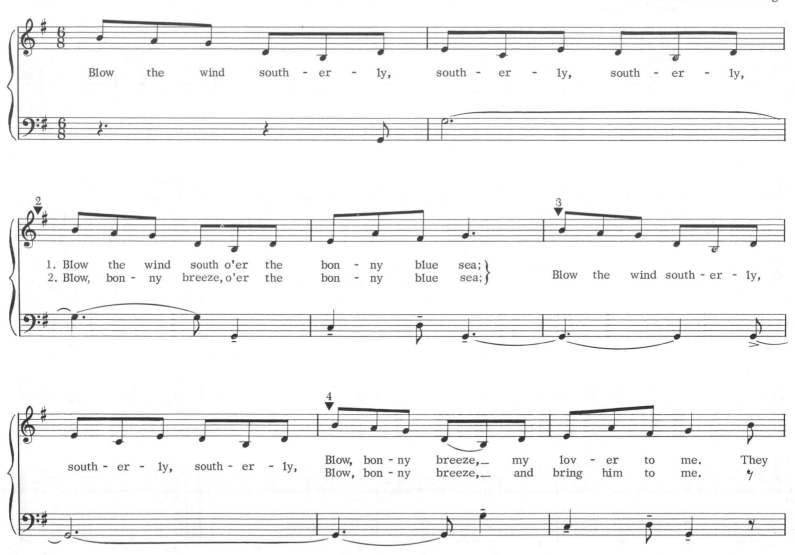

Blow the wind south - er - ly, south - er - ly, south - er - ly,

1. Blow the wind south o'er the bon - ny blue sea;
2. Blow, bon - ny breeze, o'er the bon - ny blue sea; } Blow the wind south - er - ly,

south - er - ly, south - er - ly, Blow, bon - ny breeze,__ my lov - er to me. They
Blow, bon - ny breeze,__ and bring him to me.

194

told me last night there were ships in the off - ing, And I hur - ried down to the
Is it not sweet_____ to hear the breeze sing - ing, As light - ly it comes o'er the

deep roll - ing sea. But my eye could not see it where -
deep roll - ing sea? But_____ sweet - er and dear - er by

ev - er might be it, The bark that is bear - ing my lov - er to me.
far when 'tis bring - ing The bark of my true love in safe - ty to me.

(sopra)

195

20. All Beautiful the March of Days

"Forest Green"
Traditional English Melody
Arranged by Ralph Vaughan Williams
Words by Frances W. Wile

1. All beau-ti-ful the march of days, As sea-sons come and go; The hand that shaped the rose hath wrought The crys-tal of the snow, Hath
2. O'er white ex-pan-ses spar-kling pure The ra-diant morns un-fold; The sol-emn splen-dors of the night Burn bright-er through the cold. Life
3. O thou from whose un-fath-omed law The year in beau-ty flows, Thy-self the vi-sion pass-ing by In crys-tal and in rose, Day

sent the hoar - y___ frost___ of___ heaven, The flow - ing wa - ters sealed, And
mounts in ev - ery___ throb - bing___ vein, Love deep - ens round the hearth, And
un - to day___ doth___ ut - ter___ speech, And night to night pro - claim, In

laid a si - lent love - li - ness On hill and___ wood and field.
clear - er sounds the an - gel___ hymn, "Good will to___ men on earth."
ev - er - chang - ing words___ of___ light, The won - der___ of thy name.

26. Lullaby

Johannes Brahms

Lul - la - by and good - night, With ros - es be - dight, With down o - ver - spread Is ba - by's wee

bed.   Lay thee down   now   and   rest,   May   thy   slum - bers   be

blest;   Lay thee down   now and   rest,   May   thy   slum - bers   be   blest.

27. The Blacksmith

Music by Johannes Brahms
Words by William S. Haynie

1. The black - smith is strong, his stur - dy arm
2. The sparks fill the air, his ham - mer is

swing - ing, His ham - mer of steel on the
pound - ing, And all through the vil - lage the

an - vil is ring - ing, With bang - ing and
rhy - thm is sound - ing. The black - smith has

clang - ing it sounds all the day
man - y good friends all through the

long.
town.

Coda not accounted for in Pupil's Book

32. The Happy Plowman

Swedish Folk Song
Translated by Mrs. Elbert Magnuson

1. Near a home in a wood, with a horse ver-y good, A poor young farm-er smiled as he stood; Look-ing
2. In the house near the wood, where the farm-er___ stood, There lived his help-mate love-ly and good. As she

down at his plow, In his heart was a glow, Then he sang as he plowed the row:
cooked and she stirred, She was glad that she heard, And she ech-oed___ ev-ery word:

Refrain
"Heigh - ho, my lit-tle but-ter-cup! We'll dance un - til the sun comes up!" Thus he
Thus she

sang as he plowed and he smiled as he sang, While the woods and the wel - kin rang.
sang as she stirred and she smiled as she sang, While the woods and the wel - kin rang.

202

36. Donkey Riding

Canadian Folk Song

1. Were you ev - er in Que - bec, Stow - ing tim - ber on a deck, Where there's a king with a
2. Were you ev - er in Car - diff Bay, Where the folks all shout, "Hoo ray. Here comes John with his

gold - en crown, Rid - ing on a don - key? Hey - ho! A - way we go!
three months' pay, Rid - ing on a don - key"?

Don - key rid - ing, don - key rid - ing, Hey - ho! A - way we go, Rid - ing on a don - key!

39. Sponge Fishing

Greek Folk Song

Lit - tle ship, we'll go a - fish - ing Out from the shore, Out from the shore.

When the eve - ning bell is ring - ing, Man - y spong-es we'll be bring - ing, And we'll sail for

home with sing - ing, O - lo lo lo, o - lo lo lo.

204

43. El burro de Villarino

Spanish Folk Song

1. Ya se mu-rió el bu-rro que a-ca- rre-a ba el vi - na- gre. Ya lo lle- vó
2. Es -ti- ró la pa- ta,___ ar- rru-gó el ho-ci - co, con el ra- bo
3. El e - ra va - lien - te,___ él e - ra mo-hi - no. Él e - ra el a-
4. To-das las ve-ci - nas___ fue-ron al en-tie - rro, la tí - a Ma-

Dios de es - ta vi-da mi-se - ra - ble.
tic so de - cí - a "A- dios Pe - ri - co." } Que tu - ru - ru - ru - rú, que
li - vió de to - do Vi - lla - ri - no.
rí - a to - can-do el cen - ce - rro.

tu - ru - ru - ru - rú. Que tu - ru - ru - ru - rú, que tu - ru- ru- ru- rú.

44. Pretty Little Pony

Music by Edvard Grieg
Words by William S. Haynie

1. Pret - ty lit - tle po - ny, Come in - to your lit - tle barn,
2. Pret - ty lit - tle po - ny, You shall have some oats and hay,

You shall have a blan - ket warm,— Pret - ty lit - tle po - ny.
You have had a long, hard day,— Pret - ty lit - tle po - ny.

You are ver - y tired now, You have climbed the hills so high,
I'll tell you a se - cret, Would you like to hear it now?

You have walked the moor so wide, My pret - ty lit - tle po - ny.
You can rest to - mor - row morn, My pret - ty lit - tle po - ny.

poco rit.

very calmly   slow down little by little to the end

3. Dream now of to - mor - row, Dream of all the oats and hay, You shall have a

very calmly

pleas - ant day, My pret - ty lit - tle po - ny.

46. Once

Israeli Folk Song

1. Once a lad went for a walk to the vil - lage square.
2. On the road guess whom he met? A young

maid - en fair. Hey! Yum - pa - pa, yum - tsa - tsa, yum - tsa - tsa,

yum - pa - pa. Won't you join me, pret - ty maid, Come let us dance.

47. Holla-Hi! Holla-Ho!

German Folk Song
Translated by Peter Kunkel

1. Who comes up the mead-ow way? } Hol-la-hi! Hol-la-ho! Sure-ly 'tis my sweet-heart gay; }
2. Peo-ple say with twin-kling eyes, } Love is blind but age makes wise; }

Hol-la-hi-a-ho! She goes by the___ o-pen door, } Hol-la-hi!
Lit-tle heed I___ when they tease, }

sostenuto

con Ped.

Hol-la-ho! Must not love me___ an-y-more, } Hol-la-hi-a-ho!
I may love just___ whom I please, }

48. Stodola Pumpa

Czechoslovakian Folk Melody
Words by A.D. Zanzig

1. Walk-ing at night   a - long the mead-ow way,   Home from the dance   be - side my maid-en gay.
2. Near-ing the wood,   we heard the night-in-gale,   Sweet-ly it helped   me tell my beg-ging tale.

Walk - ing at night   a - long the mead-ow way,   Home from the dance be   side my maid-en gay. *Hey!*
Near - ing the wood,   we heard the night-in - gale,   Sweet - ly it helped me   tell my beg-ging tale. *Hey!*

Refrain

Sto-do-la, sto-do-la, sto-do-la pum - pa, Sto-do-la pum-pa, sto-do-la pum - pa,   pum, pum, pum.

50. Swiss Roundelay

Swiss Folk Melody
Words by Beth Landis

1. When it's ear - ly Sun - day morn in   Swit - zer - land,   And the sun - light strikes the fields with
2. There a - gainst the sky she stands mid   moun-tains tall,   And the vil - lage chil - dren wak - en

gold - en bands, } All the val - ley ech-oes with the sound, As a maid-en sings her mer - ry
to her call.

round. Hol - la hi - a hi - a hi - a hol - la-ho, Hol - la hi - a hi - a hi - a

hol - la-ho, All the val-ley ech-oes with the sound, As a maid-en sings her mer - ry round.

211

52. Vreneli

Swiss Folk Song

1. "O Vren - e-li, my pret - ty one, Pray tell me where's your home?" "My home it is in Swit- zer-land, It's
2. "O Vren - e-li, my pret - ty one, Pray tell me where's your heart?" "O that " she said,"I gave a-way, Its
3. "O Vren - e-li, my pret - ty one, Pray tell me where's your head?" "O that I al - so gave a - way, 'Tis

Refrain

made of wood and stone." stone."
pain will de - part." part." Yo, ho, ho, tra-la - la - la; Yo, ho, ho, tra-la - la - la; Yo, ho,
with my heart," she said. said.

ho, tra-la- la- la; Yo, ho, ho, tra-la - la - la; ho, tra - la - la - la, Yo, ho, ho.

56. Mon merle

French Folk Song

1. Mon mer - le a per - du une plu - me, Mon mer - le a per - du une plu - me Elle n'chan - te plus, mon mer - le, Elle n'chan - te plus.

*) *Repeat the three notes in brackets for each "plume" in verses 2 and 3.*

213

58. Song of Itsuki

Japanese Folk Song

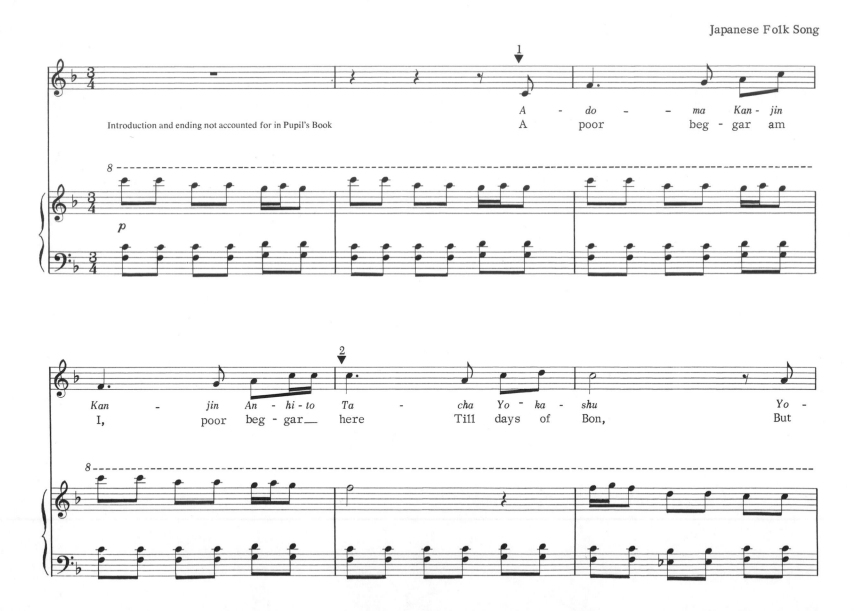

Introduction and ending not accounted for in Pupil's Book

A - do - ma Kan - jin
A poor beg - gar am

Kan - jin An - hi - to Ta - cha Yo - ka - shu Yo -
I, poor beg - gar__ here Till days of Bon, But

ka - sha   Yo -   ka   O -   - bi___ Yo - ka Ki -   - mo -
some like   you   have   O -   - bi fine and fin - est Ki -   - mo -

no.
no.

62. O Give Me a Cot

Welsh Folk Song
English Words by Florence Hoare

O give me a cot in the land of the moun-tains, Se - clud- ed Me - rion - eth whose
There let me a - bide a - mid tor - rents and foun -tains, That leap on the hill - side and

name I love well. }
spring in the dell. } O___ would I might ram - ble all day through the___

mead — ows, Charmed by the soft mur - murs of wan - der - ing bees; Or— lis - ten, while

eve - ning is cast - ing its shad - ows, To frol - ick - ing birds in the boughs of the trees.

64. Snug 'neath the Fir Trees

Finnish Folk Song

1. Snug 'neath the fir trees my cot - tage lies hid - den
2. Deep in the for - est the song of the cuck - oo

Deep in the qui - et of the Finn - ish wood.
Ten - der - ly prais - - es the charm of his mate.

High o'er the tree - tops the moun - tains are loom - ing
Tones of the wald - horn re - ced - ing, re - sound - ing,

Blue   in   the   light   of   the   glow   of   the   morn.
Come   to   my   ears   from   a - far _____ and   near.

Refrain

Hoi - la - ri, la - ri, la.   Hoi - la - ri, la - ri, la.

Ech - o   your   an - swer, my   Finn - ish   wood!   wood!

66. As the Sun Goes Down

Words and Music by Josef Marais

1. I think of my dar-ling as the sun goes down, The sun goes down, the sun goes down; I
2. I'll see my dear dar-ling as the sun comes up, The sun comes up, the sun comes up; I'll

think of my dar-ling as the sun goes down, Down, down be-low the moun-tain.
see my dear dar-ling as the sun comes up, Up, up a-bove the moun-tain.

Fine

I'll ride, I'll ride, I'll ride, I'll ride, I'll ride all night, When the moon is bright, When the moon is bright; I'll

ride, I'll ride, I'll ride, I'll ride, I'll ride all night, I'll get there in the morn - ing.

D. C. al Fine

74. Mister Urian

Music by Ludwig van Beethoven
Words Translated by Ronald Duncan

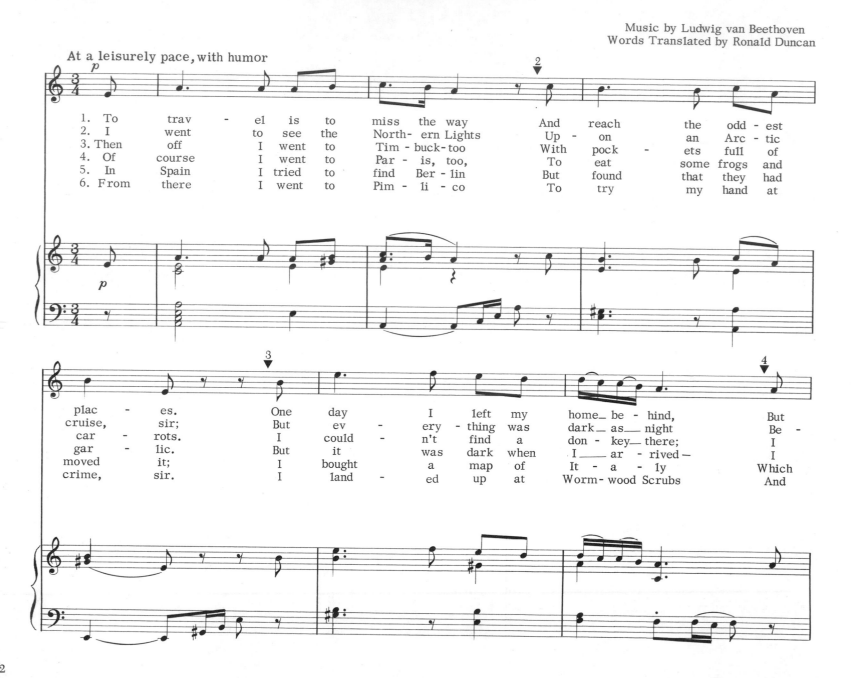

At a leisurely pace, with humor

1. To trav - el is to miss the way And reach the odd - est
2. I went to see the North- ern Lights Up - on an Arc - tic
3. Then off I went to Tim - buck-too With pock - ets full of
4. Of course I went to Par - is, too, To eat some frogs and
5. In Spain I tried to find Ber - lin But found that they had
6. From there I went to Pim - li - co To try my hand at

plac - es. One day I left my home__ be - hind, But
cruise, sir; But ev - ery - thing was dark__ as__ night Be -
car - rots. I could - n't find a don - key__ there; I
gar - lic. But it was dark when I__ ar - rived— I
moved it; I bought a map of It - a - ly Which
crime, sir. I land - ed up at Worm- wood Scrubs And

took   a - long   my   brac -   es.
cause   there'd been   a   fuse,_____ sir.
sold   them to   some par -   rots.
dined   on   dogs in   as -   pic.
on   - ly   went to   prove   it.
there   I learned to   rhyme,   sir.

5 Refrain *f*

It   seems you are a most ad -

6

ven - t'rous man,   So tell us some more, Mis-ter U - ri - an.

76. The Butterfly

Music by Franz Schubert
Words Translated by Iris Rogers

Etwas geschwind (Poco allegro)

dance__ in the sun - shine So free - ly and light - ly, And through wav - ing branch - es
joy__ to be danc - ing, As care - free I wan - der From morn - ing to eve - ning

Col - ors shimmer bright - ly. Bright - er, ev - er bright - er, See my wings are glow - ing;
O - ver hills and yon - der. When the sun is sink - ing, Breez - es mur - mur light - ly;

224

Sweet - er, ev - er__ sweet-er Scent- ed buds are blow-ing.
Woods and fields_ are__ green-er, Flow-ers glow more bright-ly.

I plun - der their

trea - sure, And feast_ at my plea - sure, I plun - der their trea - sure, And feast_ at my plea - sure.

Coda not accounted for in Pupil's Book

77. Come, Ye Thankful People, Come

Music by George J. Elvey
Words by Henry Alford

1. Come, ye thank - ful peo - ple, come, Raise the song of har - vest home;
2. All the world is God's own field, Fruit un - to his praise to yield;

All is safe - ly gath - ered in, Ere the win - ter storms be - gin;
Wheat and tares to - geth - er sown, Un - to joy or sor - row grown;

God, our Mak - er, doth pro - vide For our wants to be sup - plied;
First the blade, and then the ear, Then the full corn shall ap - pear;

Come to God's own tem - ple, come, Raise the song of har - vest home.
Lord of har - vest, grant that we Whole- some grain and pure may be.

78. O Savior Sweet

German Folk Melody
Arranged by Johann Sebastian Bach
Words by Beth Landis

1. O Sav - ior sweet, O Sav - ior dear, On this glad day we feel___ thee near. We cel - e - brate thy

2. O Sav - ior sweet, O Sav - ior dear, Thy chil - dren would we to thee___ be near. We serve thee best with

ho - ly   birth   With   thank - ful   hearts   and   joy   and
deeds   of   love   And   ask   thy   bless - ing   from   a -

mirth,   O   Sav - ior   sweet,   O   Sav - ior   dear.
bove,   O   Sav - ior   sweet,   O   Sav - ior   dear.

79. O Come, All Ye Faithful

Music from John F. Wade's "Cantus Diversi"
Translated by Frederick Oakeley

1. O come, all ye faith - ful, joy - ful and tri - um - phant, O
2. Sing, choirs of an - gels, sing in ex - ul - ta - tion,

come ye, O come ____ ye to Beth - - le - hem;
Sing, all ye cit - i - zens of heav'n _____ a - bove!

Come and be - hold him, born the King of an - gels;
Glo - ry to God, all glo - ry in the high - est;

Refrain
O come, let us a - dore him, O come, let us a - dore him, O

come, let us a - dore him,___ Christ,_____ the Lord.

231

80. The Yodlers' Carol

Austrian Folk Melody
Arranged by Mary E. Caldwell
Words by Mary E. Caldwell

(Descant)

3. We have found   lit - tle Je - sus, and we kneel by his

1. From the snow - crowned moun - tain mead - ows, from the green wood - ed
2. Lit - tle stars shall be our can - dles as we jour - ney this
3. We have found him, lit - tle Je - sus, and we kneel by his

bed   The star   o'er his cra - dle, how it crowns his

heights,   We shall seek for the ___ man - ger on this calm, ho - ly
night —   Ti - ny dia - monds in the heav - ens — we'll not want for a
bed.   See the bright star o'er his cra - dle; ra - diant light crowns his

232

head! We'll sing "Hol - di - ri - o" for a soft lul - la -

night. Let's sing "Hol - di - ri - o" for a car - ol sweet and clear, "Hol - di - ri - o" as
light. We sing "Hol - di - ri - o" for a car - ol sweet and clear, "Hol - di - ri - o" as
head! We'll sing "Hol - di - ri - o" for a lit - tle lul - la - by, "Hol - di - ri - o" so

by. Ah, ___ not a sound, ___ home a-cross the snow. ___

on we go; Then comes "Hol-di-ri-o" for an ech - o soft and clear, far a - cross the snow. ___
on we go; Then comes "Hol-di-ri-o" for an ech - o soft and clear, far a - cross the snow. ___
soft and low. Now on tip-toe go, do not make a sin- gle sound; then home a-cross the snow. ___

82. Jesus the Christ Is Born

Words and Music by John Jacob Niles

1. Je - sus the Christ is born, Give thanks now, ev - ery
2. Ye might-y kings of earth, Be - fore the man - ger
3. For in this low - ly guise The Son of God doth
4. Two an - gels at His head, Two an - gels at His
5. Je - sus the Christ is born, Give thanks now, ev - ery

one.   Re - joice ye great ones and ye small, God's will, it hath been done.
bed,   Cast down, cast down your gold - en crown From off your roy - al head.
sleep; And see the Queen of Heav - en kneel, Her faith - ful vig - il keep.
feet;   Be - side His bed the flow - er red, Per - fum - ing there so sweet.
one.   Re - joice ye great ones and ye small, God's will it hath been done.

83. Joseph Dearest, Joseph Mild

Old German Carol
Accompaniment Adapted from Johannes Brahms
Words Adapted

Mary: "Jo - seph dear - est, Jo - seph mild, Help me rock my
Joseph: "I will glad - ly, la - dy mine, Help thee rock the

lit - tle child. God will give you your re - ward in
child di - vine, God's pure light on thee will shine from

heav'n a - bove," So prays the moth - er Mar - - y.
heav'n a - bove, As we both rock the ba - - by.

84. Sing a Merry Noel

French Folk Carol
Words by Beth Landis

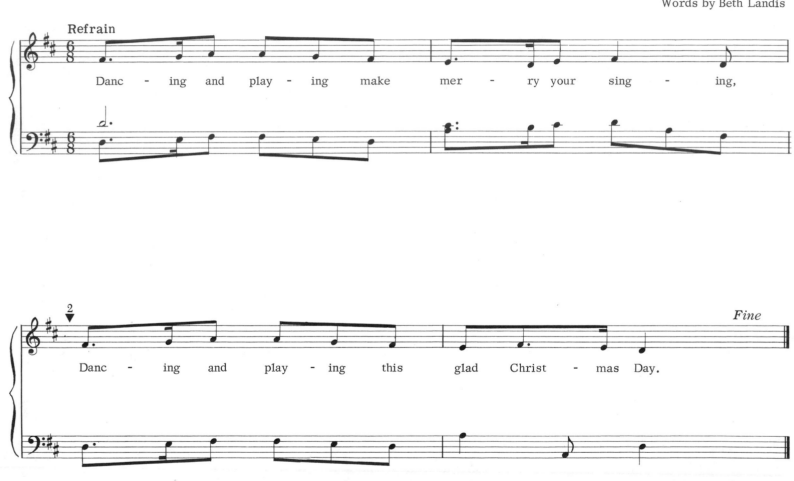

Refrain

Danc — ing and play — ing make mer — ry your sing — ing,

Danc — ing and play — ing this glad Christ — mas Day.

Fine

236

Sing a mer-ry no - el, Sing a mer-ry no - el!

4 Verse

1. Sing to the Child as he
2. Play on your drum as you

D.C. al Fine

peace - ful - ly slum - bers, Sing a sweet song to the moth - er and child.
dance for the moth - er, Play on your flute as the lit - tle one smiles.

85. We Wish You a Merry Christmas

English Folk Song

We wish you a mer - ry Christ - mas, we wish you a mer - ry Christ - mas, We

wish you a mer - ry Christ - mas and a hap - py New Year.

Good tid - ings we bring for you and your kin: Good

tid - ings of Christ - mas and a hap - py New Year.

5

1. Now bring us some fig-gy pud - ding, now bring us some fig-gy pud - ding, Now
2. We won't go un -til we get some, we won't go un -til we get some, We

6

7

(after verse 2, D.C. al Fine)

bring us some fig-gy pud - ding, and bring some right here.
won't go un -til we get some, so bring some right right here.

86. Cuckoo Carol

Czechoslovakian Carol

1. Walk - ing a - long the road, I bear a hap - py load;
2. Wise men who came from far, Guid - ed by one bright star,

One cuck - oo do I to the Christ Child take, This will a pret - ty
Bring on their cam - els won-d'rous gifts for you: Myrrh, frank - in - cense, and

pres - ent for him make, This bring I for his sake.
gold of shin - ing hue; Glad shep - herds came____ too.

90. Sir Eglamore

Old English Ballad

as   he   rode   o'er   hill   and   dale,   All   arm - èd   with   a   coat   of   mail,
when he   saw   Sir   Eg - la - more,   If   you'd   but   heard how   the   drag-on   did   roar!
as   the   drag -   on   yawn-ing   did   fall,   He   thrust   his   sword   down   hilt   and   all,
sword it   was   a   right   good   blade,   As   ev - er   Turk   or   Span - iard   made,

Refrain

Fa   lank - y down,   la   lank - y down,   Fa   la   lank-y down   dil - ly.

92. The Wraggle-Taggle Gypsies

Old English Ballad

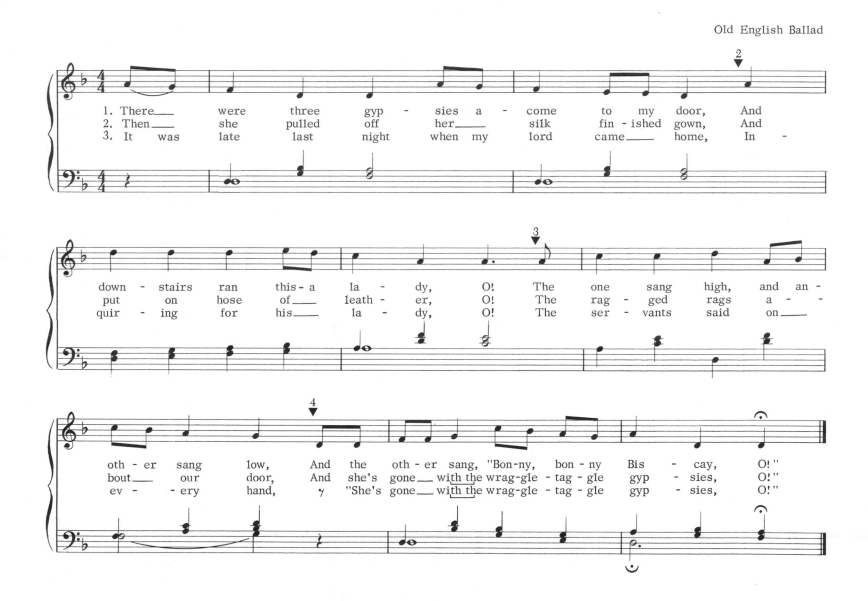

98. The Riddle Song

American Folk Song

99. Bound for the Rio Grande

Sea Chantey

Introduction not accounted for in Pupil's Book

1. Oh, say were you ev - er in Ri - o Grande? It's
2. And good-bye, fare ye well, all you la-dies of town, Oh, _____ Ri-o. ____ We'll
3. So it's pack up your don-key and get un-der way, We'll

Refrain

there that the riv - er flows down gold - en sand.
see you a -gain when our trip is full round. And we're bound for the Ri - o Grande. Then a - way, love,—a - way.
head for the South where they'll give us more pay.

Way___ down Ri-o,___ So fare___ ye well, my pret-ty young gel, For we're bound for the Ri - o Grande.___

100. The Young Voyageur

Canadian Folk Melody
Words by John Andrews

1. Oh, the voy - a - geur bold from the north - land so cold, See the wild game he
2. Oh, this voy - a - geur dreams of the for - est and streams; Rough the por - tage and

takes from the riv - ers and lakes.
long, but he still sings his song.

Refrain

Hap - py and free, dar - ing is
he. Hear the ech - o - ing call of the young voy - a - geur.

103. Sweet and Low

Music by Joseph Barnby
Words by Alfred Tennyson

Sweet and low, sweet and low, Wind of the west - ern sea,___ Low, low, breathe and blow,

Wind of the west - ern sea,___ O - ver the roll - ing wa - ters go, Come from the dy - ing moon__ and blow,

Blow him a - gain to me,___ While my lit - tle one, While my pret -ty one sleeps.___

104. Old Folks at Home

Stephen Foster

1. Way down up-on the Swa-nee Riv-er, Far, far a-way, There's where my heart is
2. All up and down the whole cre-a-tion, Sad-ly I roam, Still long-ing for the

turn-ing ev-er, There's where the old folks stay.
old plan-ta-tion, And for the old folks at home.

All the world is sad and drea-ry

Ev-ery-where I roam; O loved ones, how my heart grows wea-ry, Far from the old folks at home.

106. Polly Wolly Doodle

American Folk Song

1. Oh, I went down South to see my Sal,
2. Oh, my Sal - ly is a maid- en fair,
3. Be -hind the barn, down on my knees,
4. He— sneezed so hard with whoop- ing cough,

Sing Pol-ly wol-ly doo-dle all the day;

My__ Sal - ly is a
With_ curl - y eyes and
I___thought I heard a
He__sneezed his head and

spunk- y gal,
laugh- ing hair,
chick- en sneeze,
tail right off,

Sing Pol-ly wol-ly doo-dle all the day.

Fare thee well, fare thee well, Fare thee well, my fair-y

fay, For I'm going to Loui-si-an-a, for to see my Su-sy-an-na, Sing Pol-ly wol-ly doo-dle all the day.

112. The Galway Piper

Irish Folk Song

1. Ev - ery per - son in the na - tion, Or of great or hum - ble sta - tion,
2. When the wed - ding bells are ring - ing, His the breath to lead the sing - ing,
3. When he walks the high - way peal - ing, Round his head the birds are wheel - ing,

Holds in high - est es - ti - ma - tion, Pip - ing Tim of Gal - way. Loud - ly he can play or low;
Then in jigs the folks to swing - ing, What a splen - did pip - er. He will blow from eve to morn,
Tim has car - ols worth the steal - ing, Pip - ing Tim of Gal - way. Trush and lin - net, finch and lark,

He can move you fast or slow, Touch your heart or stir your toe, Pip - ing Tim of Gal - way.
Count - ing sleep a thing of scorn, Old he is but not worn out. Know you such a pip - er?
To each oth - er twit - ter, "Hark." Soon they sing from light to dark, Pip - ings learned in Gal - way.

251

118. Little Fox

English Folk Song

1. Lit-tle fox went out on a chil - ly night; He prayed to the moon to
2. So the fox he ran till he came to the pen; The ducks and the geese were
3. Well he grabbed a grey goose— by the neck; He flung it___ up a -
4. Now___ old Mis-sus Flip-per-flop-per jumped out of bed; And up to the win-dow she
5. Lit-tle fox he ran till he came to his den; And there were his lit - tle ones,

give him light. He'd man-y a mile to go that night Be -
put there - in. "A cou-ple of you will grease my chin Be -
cross his back. He did - n't mind the quack, quack, quack, And the
cocked her head. She cried, "John,— o John, the grey goose is gone, And the
eight, nine, ten. They said, "Dad-dy, you'd bet-ter go back a - gain, It

122. It's Quiet on the Moon

Words and Music by Ruth De Cesare

It's qui - et on the shin - ing moon to - night;____ We've seen its pic - ture
Per - haps we'll reach the shin - ing moon to - night;____ from our sat - el - lite.____ Now all the stars are wink - ing, bright-en - ing the sky; Lone - ly plan - ets blink - ing show it's time to try.

254

123. A Timely Rhyme

Music by Jean Moe
Words Anonymous

Introduction and ending not accounted for in Pupil's Book

The time of day I do not tell as some do by the clock, Or by the dis-tant chim-ing bell set on some steepled rock; But by the pro-gress that I see in what I have to do, It's ei-ther "done o'-clock" for me or on-ly "half-past through."

255

128. Psalm 100

Music by Jane M. Marshall

256

giv - ing,_____ and his courts, his courts with praise:_____

Make a joy - ful noise un - to__ the Lord,_____ all

ye lands._____

130. Banana Boat Loader's Song

Jamaican Folk Song

Day oh! Day oh! Day is break - ing, — I wan' go home. —

1. Come, Mis -ter Tal- ly - man, come tal - ly my ba - nan - as.
2. Came here for work I did - n't come here for to i - dle.

Day is break - ing, — I

wan' go home. — 3. Three han', four han', five han', Bunch!

258

Six han', seven han', eight han', Bunch! Day is break - ing, ___ I

wan' go home. ___
4. So check them, and check them, but check with cau - tion.
5. My back is a - break - ing with bare ex - haus - tion.
6. Don't give me all the bunch-es, I'm no horse with bri - dle.

Day is break - ing, I wan' go home. ___   wan' go home. ___

4.-5.   6.

132. Old Texas

Cowboy Song

I'm goin' to leave___ old___ Tex - as now,___ ___ They've got no use___ for the long-horn cow.___

132. Doney Gal

Cowboy Song

We're a - lone, Do-ney Gal, in the wind and hail;___ Got to drive those___ do - gies___

260

Collected, adapted, and arranged by John A. Lomax and Alan Lomax.

down the trail.____

1. We'll ride the range from sun to sun, For a
2. A cow - boy's life is a wea - ry thing, For it's

cow - boy's work is___ nev - er done; He's up and gone, at the
rope___ and brand and___ ride and sing; Yes, up day or night, in the

break of day, Driv - in' the do - gies on their wea - ry way.
rain or hail, He'll stay with his do - gies out___ on the trail.

134. Brethren in Peace Together

Jewish Folk Song
Paraphrase of Psalm 133:1

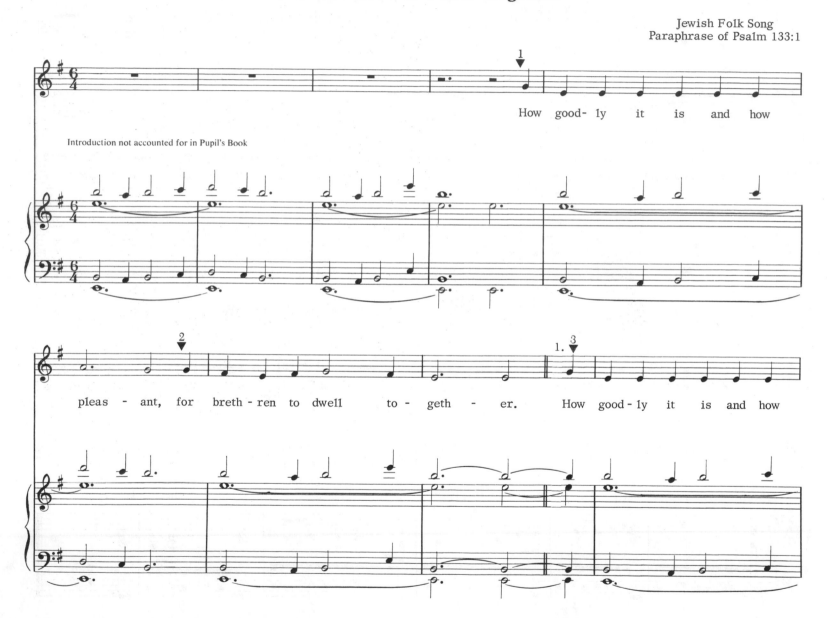

Introduction not accounted for in Pupil's Book

How good- ly it is and how pleas - ant, for breth - ren to dwell to - geth - er. How good- ly it is and how

262

135. This Train

American Folk Song

Introduction and ending not accounted for in Pupil's Book

1. This train is bound for glo - ry,
2. This train don't pull no ex - tras,

This train,— This train is bound for glo - ry, This train,—
This train,— This train don't pull no ex - tras, This train,—

This train   is   bound for glo - ry,   Don't ride noth-in' but the good and   ho - ly,
This train   don't pull no ex - tras,   Don't pull noth-in' but the mid - night spe - cial,

This train   is   bound for glo - ry,   This train!__
This train   don't pull no ex - tras,   This train!__

136. My Lord, What a Morning

Spiritual

My Lord, what a morn-ing, My Lord, what a morn-ing, My Lord, what a

morn-ing, When the stars be-gin to fall.

1. You'll hear the trum-pet sound
2. You'll hear the sin-ners mourn To wake the
3. You'll hear the Christians shout

na - tions un-der - ground, Look-ing to my God's right hand, When the stars be-gin to fall.

138. Windy Nights

Music by William S. Haynie
Words by Robert Louis Stevenson

1. When ev-er the moon and stars are set, When -ev-er the wind is high,___ All night long in the
2. When ev-er the trees are cry-ing a -loud, And ships___ are tossed at sea,___ By on the high way,

dark and wet, A man goes rid - ing by.___ Late in the night when the fires are out,
low and loud, By at the gal-lop goes he: By at the gal - lop he goes, and then,

1. Why does he gal - lop and gal - lop a - bout?
2. By he comes back at the gal - lop a - gain.

139. Beautiful Savior

Silesian Melody
Translated by Joseph A. Seiss

Stately

1. Beau - ti - ful Sav - ior, Lord of the na - tions, Son____ of
2. Fair are the mead - ows, Fair - er the wood - lands, Robed____ in
3. Fair is the sun - shine, Fair - er the moon - light, And____ the

God and____ son of man; Glo - ry and hon - or,
flow'rs of____ bloom - ing spring; Je - sus is fair - er,
twin - kling____ star - ry host; Je - sus shines bright - er,

Praise, ad - o - ra - tion, Now and for - ev - er - more be thine.
Je - sus is pur - er; He makes our sor - row - ing spir - it sing.
Je - sus shines pur - er Than all the an - gels heav'n can boast.

144. How Does My Lady's Garden Grow?

Music by Arthur Frackenpohl
Words from Mother Goose

How does my la - dy's gar - den grow? How does my la - dy's gar - den grow? With

How does my la - dy's gar - den grow? How does my la - dy's

sil - ver bells and cock - le shells, And pret - ty maids all in a row.

gar - den grow? With sil - ver bells and cock - le shells, And pret - ty maids all in a row.

145. Jasmine Blossoms

Chinese Folk Melody
Words by Beth Landis

1. White stars on the hill - side there, Sweet a -
2. White stars with the light of morn, Like bright

The first two measures may be played twice, as an introduction.

Hold pedal throughout

ro - ma, jas - mine fair, I will wear you
gems of dew - drops born. I will wear you

Fine

in my___ hair,   All   may___   then   your___   fra - grance___ share.
in my___ hair,   All   will___   see   my___   jew - els___ rare.

Bells:

D. C. al Fine

146. Sing for the Wide, Wide Fields

Music by Rena M. Parish
Words by Fannie R. Buchanan

Sing for the wide, wide fields,_____ Sing for the

wide, wide sky;_____ Sing for the good, glad earth,_____

_____ For the sun on hill-tops high._____ And let us

sing for the com - rade true,_____ Sing for the

friend - ship sweet;_____ Sing as to - geth - er we

swing a - long With the turf be - neath our feet._____

273

148. Marching to Pretoria

South African Folk Melody
Words by Josef Marais

I'm with you and you're with me, And so we are all to-geth-er, So we are all to-geth-er, So we are all to-geth-er. Sing with me, I'll sing with you, And so we will sing to-geth-er As we march a-long.

275

154. Weggis Dance

Swiss Folk Dance

1. From Lu - cerne to____ Weg - gis fair,
2. When we row a - cross the bay,
3. Weg - gis leads to a moun - tain high,
Hol -di-ri-di - a, hol - di-ri- a,

Shoes and stock - ings we need not wear,
There we see pret - ty maid-ens gay,
Gai - ly sing as____ we go by,
Hol - di - ri - di - a, hol - di - a.

Refrain

Hol -di - ri - di - a, Hol-di-ri-di-a, hol-di-ri-a; Hol - di - ri - di - a, Hol-di-ri-di-a, hol-di- a.

158. A New Created World

Joseph Haydn

A new cre - at - ed world, a___ new cre - at - ed world, Springs

up, springs up at___ God's com - mand.

158. Lo, the Winter Is Past

Music by Walter Ihrke
Words from the "Song of Solomon"

For, lo, the win - ter is past;

the rain is___ o - ver and gone; The flow - ers ap-pear on the earth; the

time of the sing-ing of birds is come.___

160. May Day Carol

English Folk Song

1. The moon shines bright, the stars give a light, A lit-tle be - fore 'tis day; Our heav-en-ly Fa - ther, he called to us, And bade us a-wake and pray. A - wake, a - wake, oh, pret-ty, pret-ty maid, Out of your drow-sy dream! And step in - to your dair-y be - low, And fetch me a bowl of cream.

2. If not a bowl of thy sweet cream, A cup to bring me cheer; For the Lord knows when we shall meet a - gain, To go May - ing an - oth - er year. I have been wan -d'ring all this night, And some time of this day; And now, re - turn - ing home a - gain, I've brought you a branch of May.

3. A branch of May I've brought you here, And at your door I stand; 'Tis noth-ing but a sprout, but well bud-ded out By the work of our Lord's hand. My song is done and I must be gone, No long - er can I stay; So it's God bless you all, both great and small, And send you a joy - ful May.

161. Nightingale's Song

Somerset Folk Melody
Words by Beth Landis

1. How brief is the night, O how ear - ly the light, When the tones of the night-in-gale flow!___
2. O tell me how soon Will the light of the moon The___ sun-light re - place with her glow?___

O could we pro - long The night-in-gale's song, As she sings in the mead-ow be -

low, _____ As she sings in the mead-ow be - low. _____

164. The Wielewaal

Dutch Folk Song

Introduction not accounted for in Pupil's Book

Come to the coun - try, join us all, And let us find the
wie - le - waal. When we can hear his hap - py strain, Then_ sum - mer's come a - gain. "Du - del -
do"_ so he sings, "Du - del - do,"_ so he sings, "Du - del - do!"_ thro' the mead - ow rings.

From Folk Songs and Games from Holland, collected and arranged by Ann E. Roeder, copyright, 1956 by G. Schirmer, Inc. Used by permission.

165. The Upward Trail

Words and Music Traditional

We're on the up-ward trail, we're on the up-ward trail, Sing-ing, sing-ing, ev-ery-bod-y sing-ing, as we go. We're on the up-ward trail, we're on the up-ward trail, Sing-ing, sing-ing, ev-ery-bod-y sing-ing, home-ward bound.

175. Au clair de la lune

French Folk Song

1. Au clair de la lu - ne, Mon a - mi Pier - rot, Prê - te - moi ta
2. Au clair de la lu - ne, Pier - rot ré - pon - dit: Je n'ai pas de

plu - me, Pour é - crire un mot; Ma chan - delle est mor - te,
plu - me. Je suis dans mon lit. Va chez la voi - si - ne,

Je n'ai plus de feu; Ou - vre - moi ta por - te, Pour l'a - mour de Dieu.
Je crois qu'elle y est, Car dans la cui - si - ne On bat le bri - quet.

283

176. Waltzing Matilda

Music by Marie Cowan
Words by A. B. Patterson

1. Once a jol - ly swag - man camped— by a bil - la bong, Un - der the shade of a
2. Down— came a jum - buck to drink— at the bil - la-bong, Up jumped the swag - man,—
3. Down— came the squat - ter mount-ed on his thor - ough-bred, Up came the troop - ers,—
4. Up — jumped the swag - man, sprang in -to the bil - la-bong, "You'll nev - er catch me a -

coo - li - bah tree, And he sang as he sat and wait - ed while his bil - ly boiled:
grabbed him with glee, And he sang as he shoved that jum - buck in his tuck - er bag:
one,— two, three, "Who's that jol - ly jum - buck you've got in your tuck - er bag?
live!"— said he. And his ghost may be heard as you pass by that bil - la-bong:

"You'll come a-waltz - ing, Ma-til - da, with me." "Waltz - ing Ma-til - da,

waltz - ing Ma-til - da, You'll come a-waltz - ing, Ma - til - da, with me."

178. San Serení

Spanish Folk Song

San Se - re - ní de la bue - na, bue - na vi - da,

Ha - cen a - sí, a - sí

1. los za - pa - te - ros.
2. los car - pin - te - ros.
3. los cam - pa - ñe - ros.
4. las plan - cha - do - ras.
5. las la - van - de - ras.
6. las cos - tu - re - ras.
7. los jar - di - ne - ros.
8. los bar - qui - lle - ros.

A -

sí, a - sí, a - sí, a - sí me gus - ta a mí.

180. Weel May the Keel Row

Scottish Folk Song

1. As I___ cam' thro' Sand - gate, thro' Sand - gate, thro' Sand - gate, As I___ cam' thro'
2. "He wears a blue bon - net, blue bon - net, blue bon - net, He wears a blue

Sand - gate, I heard a las - sic sing: Oh, weel___ may the keel row, the
bon - net, A dim - ple in his chin."

keel row, the keel___ row, Weel___ may the keel row that my___ lad - die's in."

184. America for Me

Words and Music by William S. Haynie

1. A - mer - i - ca, A - mer - i - ca, A land of hopes and dreams. I love her moun- tains,
2. A - mer - i - ca, A - mer - i - ca, U - nit - ed may she stand, From snow-capped peaks far

fields and plains, Her for - ests and her streams. A na - tion where all men are free, Where
in the North, To shores of sun and sand. Oh, may we ev - er faith - ful be, And

strength is built on in - dus-try, A - mer - i - ca, A - mer—i - ca, We pledge our hearts to thee.
guard the torch of lib - er- ty, A - mer - i - ca, A - mer - i - ca, A - mer - i - ca for me!

GLOSSARY OF MUSICAL TERMS USED IN THIS BOOK

Accent   The stress of one tone over others.

Accidental   Chromatic alteration of single tones within a measure.

Andante grazioso   Moderately slow and graceful.

Art song   An accompanied solo song in which the words and music combine to create a musical mood.

Ballad   A narrative song in which all verses are sung to the same melody.

Calypso   Rhythmic music of the West Indies usually performed extemporaneously.

Canon   A composition in which one part is imitated strictly in another part at any pitch or time interval.

Chamber music   Music for small combinations of instruments, usually one instrument to a part.

Chant   A repetitive pattern sung as a vocal accompaniment below the main melody.

Chord   The simultaneous sounding of three or more tones.

Climax   The point within a musical line or composition which serves as the highest point of intensity

Coda   A section added to the end of a composition as a conclusion.

Dal segno (D.S.)   From the sign.

Dynamics   The expressive markings used to indicate the degree of force or intensity of sound. The most common are *pianissimo (pp):* very soft; *piano (p):* soft; *mezzo piano (mp):* moderately soft; *mezzo forte (mf):* moderately loud; *forte (f):* loud; *fortissimo (ff):* very loud; *crescendo:* increase in loudness; *descrescendo* or *diminuendo:* decrease in loudness.

Fermata   Hold; pause.

Fine   End; close.

Fugue   A contrapuntal style of composition based on the development of a short melody, or theme, which is stated at the beginning by a single voice and imitated in each of the other voices in close succession.

Harmony   The combination of tones sounded simultaneously.

Home tone   The first step of a scale on which a song or composition is based; the tone for which the scale is named.

Interlude   A short passage between two larger sections of a composition.

Interval   The distance in pitch between two tones.

Introduction   An opening section of a composition.

Legato   A smooth, almost imperceptible connection between successive tones.

Mode   A scalewise arrangement of the tones that may form the basic tonal material of a composition; specifically refers to the medieval church modes.

Motive   The shortest recognizable unit of notes of a musical theme or subject.

Octave   The interval between two tones having the same name and located eight notes apart.

Ornamentation   The embellishment of a main melody by the addition of decorative melodic figures such as trills, tremolos, appoggiaturas, etc.

Pattern   A succession of notes which form a recognizable unit.

Period   A term used to describe two phrases which together form a natural division of the melody.

Phrase   A natural division of the melodic line, comparable to a sentence in speech.

Ritard   Gradually slower.

Rondo   A musical form resulting from the alternating of a main theme with contrasting themes (A B A C A etc.).

Sequence   Immediate repetition of a tonal pattern at a higher or lower pitch level.

Slur   A curved line placed above or below two or more notes to indicate that they are to be sung or played without a break in sound.

Staccato   An indication that the music should be performed in a short, detached manner.

Symphony   A sonata for orchestra.

Syncopation   A temporary displacement of the regular rhythmic pulse.

Tempo   The rate of speed of a composition or section thereof.

Theme   A complete musical idea which serves as a subject in a musical composition.

Tie   A curved line between two or more successive tones of the same pitch. The tones so connected are sounded as one, equal in length to their combined durations.

Trill   A rapid alternation between two adjacent tones.

Troubadours   Poet-musicians who flourished from the eleventh to the thirteenth centuries in southern France and northern Italy.

Variation   The modification of a theme melodically, rhythmically, and harmonically.

CLASSIFIED INDEX OF MUSIC AND POETRY

291

CLASSIFIED INDEX OF MUSICAL SKILLS

ALPHABETICAL INDEX OF MUSIC AND POETRY